IN SEARCH OF PLENTY

In Search of Plenty

A History of Jewish Food

Oded Schwartz

With line drawings by Jane Human

KYLE CATHIE LTD

To Saul.
And to all Jewish mothers
and a special ex Moslem.

First published 1992 in Great Britain by
Kyle Cathie Limited
3 Vincent Square London SW1P 2LX

ISBN 1 85626 025 9

Oded Schwartz is hereby identified as the author of this
work in accordance with Section 77 of the Copyright, Designs
and Patents Act 1988.

A Cataloguing in Publication record for this title is
available from the British Library

Designed by Beverley Waldron
Typeset by DP Photosetting, Aylesbury, Bucks
Printed by Butler & Tanner, Frome, Somerset

CONTENTS

ACKNOWLEDGEMENTS

To all those who tasted, tested, accommodated and encouraged. Special thanks:

North America.
Ruthie Goodelman, Barbara Kirschenblatt-Gimbeltt, Thelma Barer-Stein, Esther Schwartz, Sandra Ruben Temes, Peter Graben and especially to Ron Soskolne and Howard Cohen and families.

Israel.
Yakove Lishansky, Hagit Matras, Ester Shalev, Dr. Eli Zigler, Rachel Ben-Chaim, Chef Uri Gutman, Chef Chaim Cohen, Aliza Livny, Gadi Triger, Tova Aran, Yakira Dori, Ofra and Yaeir Zalamonovitz, Yadin Saker, Eitana and Yehuda Padan, Pascal Perez-Rubin, Chaki Barak.

Britain.
Sally Mercer, Jean Collingwod, Suzan Lopert, Sara from the bread shop, Jenny Gallaway, Jill Jago, Lina of the Finchley Ort Shop and special thanks to Ron Berglas and Jill Furmanovsky.

South Africa.
Toby Kay and Thelma Weinstein.

PREFACE

JEWISH FOOD and Jewish cooking do not simply feed the body; ingredients and the way they are prepared, cooked and served provide rich clues to the history of the Jewish people and to their religious beliefs. Their history is as old as civilisation itself. In this book I have tried to explain how Jewish food and eating habits have developed and to explore the cultural background which has made Jewish cooking more than just a 'cuisine'.

Being an Israeli Jewish man, cooking did not come to me by right. Males, especially after the age of three, the traditional time for a child to start his studies, are not encouraged to spend time in the kitchen. I was lucky because there were no girls in the family and therefore I was tolerated. When it was discovered that I was interested in cooking, I was allowed to observe and absorb, although not actually permitted to cook. When, much later, I started to cook professionally these unconscious influences asserted themselves in my work.

I suppose it is the natural tendency of every 'Western' chef to work in the French style. I find this cuisine delicious, sophisticated and exciting, yet enigmatic. It belongs to the luscious pastures of northern Europe rather than to the parched landscape of my Middle Eastern origins. It has been essential for me to find a personal way of cooking which would echo this semi-conscious culinary heritage. This search made me face a fundamental problem encountered by every Jew: how does one identify what is Jewish? Being a second generation Israeli made the matter even more confusing. Is my food heritage from my maternal grandmother's kitchen (her origins were in Besarabia on the Romanian–Russian border, though she spent some of her formative years in Odessa) or does it come from the kitchen of my Israeli-born mother who creatively prepared dishes from a wide range of cultures? This book is the result of my search for the identity of the food which I cook, and also for the identity of my culture.

In spite of its diversity Jewish food has few uniting forces. The first and most important is the adherence to the kosher laws. These laws were, until a century ago, observed with few variations by all Jews. They affected not only the choice of ingredients but also cooking methods, and even the material of which cooking utensils were made.

The second major influence stems from the fact that certain ingredients are written into the culture. Both the Bible and the Talmud use food as part of their symbolic language. Those images are especially potent in the description of the land which God has promised the Jews: the land of milk and honey, of almonds and olive groves, dates, figs and raisins. These ingredients are still used, in one form or other, in the celebration of most festivals.

There is one further common experience which cannot be ignored. Constant hunger and expulsion throughout history, and the devastating effect of the Holocaust have left their mark, and continued to influence the Jewish attitude to the table.

As an Israeli one more aspect must be taken into consideration: the influence of the indigenous Middle Eastern Palestinian population on the everyday life of all Israelis. The Middle Eastern kitchen has had a profound effect on Israeli and global Jewish kitchens. Hummus and falafel appear on Jewish tables all around the world.

Researching and writing the book has been an emotional and personal exploration for me. As a Jewish Israeli, to deal critically with Jewish culture has been a sensitive exercise, carrying with it the full burden of what is known as 'Jewish guilt'. Isolation of the Jews, imposed or otherwise, has resulted in an obsessive suspicion of everything which is not Jewish. Yet the Jewish kitchen, especially as it is developing in Israel, is a wonderful mixture of East and West, Jewish and Arab. One day, hopefully, the harmony which exists in the kitchen will spread and create a harmonious society in which various ethnic minorities will maintain their own identities while creating together a culture which is contemporary and truly Middle Eastern.

Laurence van der Post's *First Catch Your Eland* is one of the most important books written on the development of a national cuisine. His South African experience has some parallels with the Israeli situation.

With the change of just two words, the following can be said for both sides of the Arab–Israeli conflict.

> If only the heart in South Africa could be governed for a year or two by the national palate, there would be no apartheid or racial prejudice left in the land, because our cooking is the best advertisement the world could possibly have for a multi-racial society, free of religious, racial and other forms of discrimination, if not even for immediate and unbridled miscegenation.

A HISTORY OF
JEWISH FOOD

INTRODUCTION

THE DEFINITION of who is entitled to be called a Jew is an ancient dispute which still rages amongst the Jews themselves. With the creation of the State of Israel, the Israeli Bill of Rights stated that repatriation to Israel is the birthright of every Jew. The question then to be asked is: 'Who is a Jew?' Does being a Jew mean having a common cultural heritage or a common religious affiliation? Which of the many sects is the true Jewish sect? Which is the 'official' or dominating culture? Is it the Ashkenazi, European-based culture or the Sephardi, Eastern-based culture? The same questions could be asked about Jewish food.

When you ask Western non-Jews to describe Jewish food you are most likely to hear a description of Ashkenazi food, typified by classic dishes such as beigel and lox, *gefilte fish*, *latkes*, salt beef (corned beef in North America) and pastrami. The same answer would have been given by most English-speaking Jews until the early 1950s when Israeli food was introduced into the diaspora* communities.

Before going any further it is necessary to explain the terms Sephardi and Ashkenazi. Sephardi means 'of Spain' and originally applied to Jews from Spain. *Sfarad* is an ancient Hebrew name for Spain where, until the expulsion in 1492 by Ferdinand and Isabella, there existed a prosperous and influential Jewish community. This community dispersed and settled all over the world, establishing and revitalising existing communities in

---

* The word diaspora means dispersion (of Jews). It became a general term meaning exile, anywhere which is not Israel.

Europe, all around the Mediterranean and in most of the established communities of the Islamic countries. In common use, the word means a Jew who comes from any Eastern (Islamic) country, including the North African coast. The word Ashkenazi, strictly speaking, means a Jew whose origins are German since *Ashkenaz* is the old Hebrew name for Germany. In common use, the name applies to any Jew who comes from Christian European countries, although in Balkan countries and southern Russia the definition becomes less clear.

The two most important elements of Jewish culture linking the Sephardi and Ashkenazi are the fundamental belief in the same religion which dictates every aspect of daily life, and the inborn habit of travel. From the moment that the Hebrew identity was conceived by the Patriarch Abraham, the forefather of the nation, travel was written into the Jewish culture: 'and God said to Abraham, get out of thy country, and from thy kindred, and from thy father's house, unto a land that I will show you' (Genesis 12:1). In the Jewish mythology, travelling started even earlier than Abraham. Both the epic stories of the fight between good and evil related in the accounts of Adam and Eve and of Cain and Abel were connected with travel and expulsion. Travel which was essential for the bonding of the Jewish identity was also conceived as a punishment for not obeying the Lord's word.

Before one starts to untangle the complex web of the development of a Jewish cuisine one must be aware of the outline of Jewish history. For practical reasons I have divided the whole of Jewish history into three periods. First, the Hebrew period: from its conception around 2000BC to the settlement in the Promised Land (c. 1230BC). Second, the Israeli period: from the establishment of a defined Jewish, self-determined nation until the destruction of the First Temple and the First Exile (586BC). Third, the Jewish period: from the establishment of a Jewish identity in the Babylonian diaspora and the dedication of the Second Temple (516BC) until today.

In the ancient world the Jewish people were known as the Hebrews. The name derives from the Egyptian word *habiru* or *ibri*, describing an inferior social class or a foreigner. The Bible cites the roots of the Hebrews as being in Ur of the Chaldees. The site of this city is thought to be in Iraq in the northern area of the Fertile Crescent, a band of land which stretches from the valley of the Tigris and Euphrates rivers through the coastline of what is now Israel to the Nile delta.

The land of Israel, which the Hebrews first travelled through and then settled in, lies in the middle of the Crescent on one of the ancient world's most important commercial routes. Two roads bisected the country: the

Via Maris or 'sea road' led from Egypt along the coastal plain to the Phoenician coast (now Lebanon) with branches leading to the Beka'a valley, Damascus and Mesopotamia, and the 'King's way', which ran right through the Sinai desert to Kadesh-Barneah near the Israeli town of Beersheba to the Trans-Jordan plateau and then on to Damascus and Mesopotamia.

Since the beginning of civilisation, control over those roads meant exposure to new ideas and people. Caravans, exotically described in the Bible, crossed the country carrying strange and wonderful ingredients — herbs, spices, dates, figs and oils — on their way from the southern power base of Egypt towards Mesopotamia in the north, the gateway to India and the Far East.

Historical evidence suggests that the wandering Hebrew tribes began to leave Ur at around 2000BC, probably as the result of being pushed out by the approach of the warring Hyksos. This was probably the period during which the Bible started to be collated. By the 13th century BC there are indications of a Hebrew presence in Egypt. Although there is no firm historical evidence for the Exodus from Egypt, tradition sets it around 1280BC, and in this period the first drafts of the laws were collated.

The Israelite period began around 1230BC, the traditional date for the Israeli conquest of the Holy Land. The following 200 years were turbulent, and were marked by constant wars under the leadership of tribal chieftains and religious prophets; leaders who are known by the collective name of Judges. This system was replaced at around 1020BC by an hereditary monarchy. The royal house was supported by a large religious administration based in the Temple in Jerusalem which was constructed during the reign of King Solomon (965–922BC).

The Babylonian exile (586–536 BC) and the destruction of the Temple which marked the beginning of the Jewish period forced the Jews to take a retrospective look at their religion and holy writing. This was the period when official versions of old texts were established and oral traditions were written down. The writing of the Mishnah, which is the basic collection of the laws, and the Talmud — the interpretation of those laws — was probably started in this period.*

As a result of changes in world power the Jews were permitted by the conquering Persians to establish a new Temple in Jerusalem (516AD). Not

---

* In the following pages I will refer to the Old Testament as the Bible. The Bible in the Jewish tradition, unlike the Christian tradition, does not include the New Testament. It consists of twenty-four books, divided into three parts. These are the Torah (the law which includes the first five books, known also as Pentateuch), the Prophets and the Hagiograph (writings).

all the community left Babylon; the ones who stayed established a strong and influential community which played an important role in the future development of the Jewish dogma. In the following period, until the destruction of the Second Temple (586BC–70AD), the Jews enjoyed a certain amount of self-determination, though their land changed hands four times. By the time the Second Temple was destroyed in 70AD there were numerous Jewish colonies all over the civilised world. As the historian Cecil Roth observes: 'Just as today a Jewish community exists in every city of the United States of America which has a population of 50,000 souls, a railway station, and a public theatre, so one was to be found in all probability in every Municipium of the Roman Empire, sufficiently important to have its forum and its Hippodrome.'[1]

As always, exile strengthened the Jewish identity, once more forcing the Jews to examine their religion in order to adjust to a new set of circumstances. Exile also brought about the rise of a new and powerful administration, the Rabbis or scholars. Rabbinical schools were established at the old and powerful Jewish colonies in Mesopotamia and in relatively new settlements on the Mediterranean coast of Africa. Influential Jewish centres were established in Spain at Cordoba, Granada, Toledo and Seville.

It is safe to assume that the Sephardi kitchen is the true torchbearer of the original Jewish food tradition. Together with the financial and spiritual advances, food developed too. It grew in a sympathetic culture which shared the same origins as the culture of the Jewish forefathers. Basic Muslim concepts of dietary purities and impurities stem from the same roots as the Jewish ones. The Muslims, like the Jews, share the same abomination of pork and blood. Their cuisines also use similar raw ingredients and share a liking for certain types of flavouring and common staples.

A Sephardi kitchen was almost indistinguishable from the kitchen of their neighbours. The situation was different in the Ashkenazi Jewish communities which sprang up in Central Europe from about 1000AD. The Jews shared with their Christian neighbours neither basic ingredients, dietary prohibitions or food symbolism, nor did they have common attitudes to food or hospitality. The Ashkenazi kitchen was thus forced to find solutions to the problems of cooking amongst Christians. Because of constant mixing of the communities as a result of anti-Jewish laws and expulsions, a defined European Jewish 'stock' was created. This distinctive line of Jewishness, which is referred to by the Ashkenazi Jews as *Yiddishkite*, runs throughout Jewish European culture. A European Jew will argue about the best way of making *gefilte fish* (stuffed fish), but all will agree that *gefilte fish* is served at every holiday table. The Sephardi Jew from Iraq might recognise the general spiciness of Jewish Moroccan food, but probably would not identify any of the dishes served.

From the onset of my research I was fully aware of the different forces which are at play in the shaping of the general Jewish culture. At the beginning I thought that Sephardi and Ashkenazi cultures could be described side by side. As my research progressed I discovered that Sephardi food differs fundamentally from country to country. Therefore the development of such food must be understood against the particular historical backdrop of the country of origin. To do full justice to such a vast subject merits a different book. Yet the following pages will emphasise the fundamental influence Sephardi food and the common Middle Eastern ancestral backgrounds have had to play in the shaping of European Jewish food. Sephardi food also had a profound effect on the merging style of Israeli food, in particular, and on global Jewish food in general. Nevertheless I have included a short chapter on Sephardi cooking which will outline the main historical and cultural influences which shaped the Sephardi kitchen.

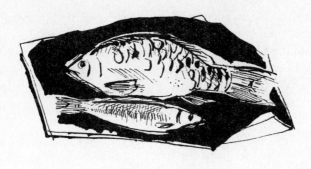

1

FOOD IN THE BIBLE

WHEN DEALING with a book as complex and forbidding as the Bible it is important to separate legends from historical accounts and from practical advice about everday life. The Bible contains instructions on matters as diverse as agricultural management, medicine, education, personal hygiene, general customs, manners, eating habits and cooking. There may have been an ancient book dealing exclusively with food and cooking, but it did not survive.[1] Nevertheless, there are enough clues to enable us to deduce how Jews lived and cooked in ancient times.

It is notoriously difficult to determine the chronological order of the Bible. The book Jews refer to as the Bible is a collection of documents written by different authors at different points of the nation's history. The content is based on oral tradition, historical fact and contemporary theological and philosophical understanding of the world. Food plays a vital part in the symbolic language of the Bible. Hunger is one of the first stimuli of every baby. Food is something which we face — if we are lucky — every day of our lives. Therefore food metaphors and symbolism are globally understood. They are used both in God's vocabulary and that of his Prophets who found food a convenient way to illustrate their moral teachings. Their traditional preaching place was the market, where they had to use narrating techniques which could compete with the noise and bustle of the market, using symbols which would be recognised by all.

When Ezekiel prophesies the fate of sinful Jerusalem he drives his message home by describing the methods of making a soup: 'Thus said the Lord God; Set on a pot, set it on, and also pour water into it; Gather the pieces thereof into it, even every good piece, the thigh, and the shoulder; fill it with choice bones' (Ezekiel 25:3–6). This technique of cooking soup was familiar to his audience; the soup is made not only with the usual soup meat — the cheap parts and the bones — but also with the best parts — the leg and shoulder — which are normally reserved for roasting. 'Best parts' are as a symbol for the best of Israeli society: the Levites and the aristocracy.

The first sin mentioned in the Bible involves food: 'And the woman saw that the tree was good for food . . . pleasant to the eye . . . a tree to be desired to make one wise' (Genesis 3:6). Food from the beginning was seen as something more than just for eating. It could also make one wise. The shape or flavour of the tempting fruit in Genesis is anybody's guess, though Biblical scholars tend to agree that the tempting fruit was an apricot.

Food also appears in legends which, to be effective and real, had to include recognisable contemporary details of life. The legend of the creation of two nations, Edom and Israel, is described in the story of the struggle between Jacob and Esau over Isaac's inheritance, which was won over a pot of pottage or stew: 'And Jacob sod pottage . . . And Esau said to Jacob, feed me, I pray thee, with that same red pottage; for I am faint: therefore was his name Edom [*adom* is red in Hebrew]. And Jacob said, sell me this day thy birthright . . . Then Jacob gave Esau bread and pottage of lentils' (Genesis 25:29–34). The attempt to identify Jacob's lentil pottage fired the imagination of cooks and food researchers for centuries. Various lentil dishes which claim to be that stew are served all over the Middle East and India and contain various kinds of pulses and grains cooked to a thick porridge with onion, spices, vegetables and sometimes meat. Madhur Jaffrey's *Indian Cookery* mentions a red split lentils dish, *masoor dal*, which might fit the Biblical dish — red lentils, ghee, turmeric, cumin and coriander. However, the most likely contender is *megadarra*. Claudia Roden's *A Book of Middle Eastern Food* mentions that *megadarra*, which she dates to medieval times, is also known as Esau's favourite. The dish contains brown lentils, rice and onions. It is more than likely that burgul was used in the original because rice was a relative latecomer to the area. The Bible stresses that the colour of the dish was red, indeed, the word red is mentioned twice: the dish was redder than red. The choice of the colour is symbolic of blood, for the story tells of an epic fight of primogeniture.

Food and sex are associated closely in the Bible. The Song of Songs deals with the love of a man, possibly King Solomon, for his God but reads clearly as a love duet between a man and a woman. In highly erotic language the book records not only the sexually related symbolism of food but also food which was eaten either before (aphrodisiac) or after (restorative) the sexual act by the Jewish ruling classes. The Hebrew word used in the Song of Songs for beloved (*dod*), shares the same origin as the word used for the fruit of the mandrake (*duda*). The roots of the mandrake contain poisonous drugs, but the fruit is edible and considered to have aphrodisiac properties.

Food is used to describe the beloved: 'Thy belly is like a heap of wheat ... breasts like bunches of grapes ... mouth sweeter than wine ... temples [are red] like a piece of pomegranate within thy locks.' Sexual satisfaction is described with tender, erotic food images: 'I have come into my garden, my sister, my bride, I gathered my myrrh with my spice, I have eaten my honey with my honey-comb; I have drunk my wine with my milk. Eat lovers and drink until you are drunk with love' (Song of Songs 5:1–2). The beloved, exhausted from love-making, cries: 'Restore me with raisin cakes, refresh me with apples, for I am love-sick.'

In Biblical writing the fig is closely connected with fertility; barrenness is described as a fruitless fig tree (Habakuk 3:17, Judges 9:10). The word used to describe an unripe fig (*paga*) is the same word used for a premature infant (*pag*) or a prepubescent girl while sexual maturity (spring) is described as the time when the figs begin to ripen (Song of Songs 2:13). The word which the Bible uses to describe a female on heat probably comes from the same root as the word for fig (Jeremiah 4:24). In folk tradition the fig is always associated with the vagina. To ward off the evil eye, a gesture called *A'fieg* (Yiddish for fig which also means nothing or very little) was employed. The thumb is inserted between the first two fingers and covered with the other hand, the shape created looks like a vagina with the clitoris jutting out. In modern Jewish literature the image of sex and food comes to its ultimate conclusion in the masturbation scene in Philip Roth's *Portnoy's Complaint*. Liver intended for the family dinner is used for masturbation, thus including all the most poignant taboos of the Jewish religion, blood, food and sex.

2

*KASHRUTH**

IN AN attempt to understand the evolution of the kosher laws one should explore the roots of the Jewish dogma. From its conception the central theme of the Jewish religion was purity. The first thing God did after creating the world was to separate light from darkness: 'Then God made the firmament, and separated the waters which were under — from the waters which were above' (Genesis 1:1–8). Separation, and therefore classification, are present in all aspects of Jewish life. There is a strong separation between holy and mundane, and a special blessing is recited to separate the Sabbath from the rest of the week. In the diaspora and among the very Orthodox, even now in Israel, there is a separation of langue; Hebrew is used only in connection with religious ceremonies and studies while everyday life is conducted either in Yiddish or in the local language.

There are laws which forbid the sowing of two different seeds in one field and ploughing with two different animals. It is forbidden to wear a garment woven from two different fibres (Leviticus 19:19) and Deuteronomy 22:9–10). There is a defined separation between the roles of man and woman and mixed marriages are strictly forbidden.

The first clue to the dietary habits of our forefathers appears in the first chapter of Genesis:

> And God said, Behold, I have given you every herb bearing seed, which is upon the face of all the earth, and every tree, in the which is the fruit of a tree yielding seed; to you it shall be for meat. (Genesis 1:29)

* The word kashruth comes from the Hebrew root *kasher* (kosher) and literally means ritual lawfulness, especially of food.

Paradise until the original sin was a vegetarian heaven. The association of a vegetarian diet with innocence is emphasised by the poet in Proverbs who quotes the moral attitude of his day: 'Better is dinner of herbs where love is, than fatted ox and hate therewith' (15:17). It is curious that the same image, 'dinner of herbs', is also associated with poverty.

Tradition suggests that Adam started eating meat as a punishment for his sin after the expulsion from Eden when he was introduced to the mortality of flesh.[1] The permission to consume flesh had to wait until after the flood. It was to Noah that God granted permission to eat meat. 'Every moving thing that liveth shall be meat for you; even as the green herb have I given you all things' (Genesis 9:3). Tradition explains that the granting of this permission was inevitable. The ground was covered with water with no vegetation surviving and it would take a long time to grow a new crop. Thus man was dependent for his immediate survival on meat. Tradition also quotes the episode of Cain and Abel to prove that man could not live on vegetables alone. Such explanations reflect an economic truth. Meat was seldom eaten amongst nomadic people as sheep, goats and cattle were much too important for their milk production and monetary value to be killed for everyday use. They were slaughtered only in religious celebration or for entertaining important guests.[2]

The story of the Flood also lays down one of the fundamentals of the dietary laws: 'but the flesh with the life, which is the blood, You shall not eat' (Genesis 9:4). Blood lies in the centre of the Jewish dietary prohibition. Blood is the essence of being, it is the property of God; it is both holy and sinful, therefore out of bounds to humans. The rejection of blood in the Jewish tradition comes from a basic cultural abhorrence of paganism which was associated with blood-drinking rituals. Only by dedicating blood to God, by spilling it on the ground and covering it, can man come to terms with the killing of another of God's creatures. This concept of the sacredness of all God's creation was probably as important as the belief in a single God in setting the Jews apart from all their pagan neighbours.

RITUAL SLAUGHTER
'Eat not the blood: for the blood is the life'

Ritual slaughter is mentioned briefly in laws permitting the eating of flesh outside the Temple. Slaughter for domestic use was left to the individual (Deuteronomy 12:20–24), the only stipulation being that the animal should be bled and the blood should be poured on the ground and covered

13

with earth. The verse also permits, with the same stipulations, the eating of hunted meat. Slaughter laws as practised now are a Talmudic addition although tradition claims that the laws were given to Moses and transmitted orally until transcribed in the Talmud in great detail.

In addition to the basic rules against blood consumption, there are laws concerned with other parts of the animal, such as fat and sinews, which are forbidden for human consumption. All these laws seem to stem from the particular ritual of sacrifice practised in the Temple though it is difficult to ascertain the origins of the laws. The prohibition of fats is mentioned in Leviticus (7:25), which emphasises that it is forbidden to eat only the fat of a sacrificial animal because it is the property of God and should be consumed by fire. The Bible defines very clearly the fats which are forbidden for consumption: those which cover the stomach, the liver, the kidneys and the loin (Leviticus 3:3–5, 17). This law might be related to the ancient method of telling fortunes by examining the distribution of fat on the intestines of sacrificial animals which was practised by pagan priests. Fat seems to have had magical properties in many cultures.[3]

The law concerning the removal of the sinew of the femoral vein is more obscure. It stems from a verse in Genesis (32:32) describing the fight between Jacob and the Angel during which the Angel damaged Jacob's femoral vein. It concludes that this is the reason why the Israelites do not eat the sinew. The verse mentioning the custom appears at the end of the chapter and seems to be an afterthought, giving credence to some obscure ritualistic practice. It is not mentioned elsewhere in the Bible.

The removal of those forbidden parts is called *nikur — trabor* or *prog*[4] and was probably the speciality of the Levites in the temple. It required great skill, and was economically wasteful as the best parts of the animal — the hindquarters — have to be dissected, thus spoiling the shape so that it cannot be sold as prime meat. The method of proging is controversial as the Ashkenazi and Sephardi Jews differ on the finer details of the practice. For these reasons hindquarters are usually not sold by kosher butchers outside Israel. In the diaspora the hindquarters are usually sold to the general public in *Halal* (Muslim) shops since the Muslims stipulate that a proper slaughterer must be of the sons of Abraham.[5] This kind of convenient religious interchange has been recorded in Jerusalem since the arrival of the first Sephardi Jews in 1492.[6] Sadly it has now stopped in Israel.

After the meat has been ritually slaughtered it is left for the cook to complete the koshering process by soaking and salting the meat. Both these practices are mentioned in the orders of sacrifice (Leviticus 1:13 and 2:13). Salt and water, both of which have a purifying effect, have a long association with Jewish ritual. The covenant man had with God is called the covenant of salt. Margaret Visser relates the salt covenant to the tradition by which a Bedouin will never fight a man with whom he has once eaten salt. The salt bond is fundamental and everlasting. She also mentions another reason for the salt covenant: meat eaters need very little salt as animal flesh is naturally salty. The salt covenant shows the commitment of the nomadic Hebrews to settle down and eat the fruit of their harvest, especially grain which is tasteless without salt.[7]

To kosher meat, it should be first immersed for 30 minutes in clean cold water using a vessel kept exclusively for that purpose. This is done to remove all traces of blood from the surface and to open the meat's pores to help salt penetration. The meat is then salted with medium-grained salt and left for one hour on a slanted, grooved or perforated board which allows the blood to drain. Medium-grained salt should be used, as fine salt melts too quickly while coarse salt does not adhere readily and may fall off. The salt should be sprinkled on the meat, covering its surface entirely. After salting, the meat must be completely rinsed either by washing three times under running tap water or by soaking each time in clean water. Only then is the meat ready for cooking. Liver and other offal which contain a large amount of blood are koshered by roasting on an open fire or under a grill. The liver must be slashed to expose as much of the surface as possible and grilled until it changes colour or a crust is formed.

The process of koshering meat must be done no later than 72 hours after slaughter. Meat, especially beef, is sold very fresh by kosher butchers; the law does not permit ageing. That may be one reason behind the Jewish preference for slow-cooked meat dishes as it is necessary to soften meat which is not allowed to age and tenderise. According to non-Jewish culinary practice, meat needs to be matured for between ten days and 3 weeks to tenderise and develop its full flavour.

KOSHERING
'Thou shalt not eat any abominable thing'

Ritual slaughter and koshering are not enough to make the animal kosher. The animal itself must belong to the list of kosher animals mentioned in the Bible. The first indication of a distinction between fit and unfit (*kasher* and *tame*) animals comes in the story of the Flood when Noah was instructed to take into the Ark both clean and unclean animals. The distinction seems to be between animals which are fit and those which are not fit for sacrifice and possibly relates to a much earlier set of purity laws understood and observed by the ancients.

The literal meaning of the word kosher is fit or proper. The word is mentioned three times in the Bible yet none of the references has anything to do with food (Esther 8:5, Ecclesiastes 11:6, 10). The basic rules of kashruth are mentioned in Leviticus 11 and repeated in Deuteronomy 14:3–21. The fit beasts must have split hooves and chew their cud. The list includes ox, lamb, kid, deer, gazelle, fallow deer, ibex (wild goat), antelope, buffalo and chamois, a wild mountain antelope. Curiously enough all the animals mentioned in this list played an important part in the Hebrew economy. The unfit list includes two categories: firstly, animals who chew the cud but do not have cloven hooves, such as the camel, rabbit and cony or hyrax;[8] and secondly, an animal which has cloven hooves but does not ruminate — the pig. Unfit animals defile even by touch, alive or dead.

The Bible does not give a ruling on unfit birds, but lists prohibited birds — birds of prey, with two exceptions, the ostrich, which probably because of its size and general strangeness could not be classified, and the dochiphat (*hoopoe*) which, perhaps because of its feathered crown, was considered to have a special significance. The Talmud concludes that fit birds should have a crop, a gizzard which can easily be peeled off and an extra talon. Today only birds considered traditionally fit are eaten.

The fit fish should have 'gills and scales and swim in rivers and seas'. The Talmud specifies that the scales should be visible to the naked eye and will overlap in a regular fashion. Therefore crustacea, bivalves and other sea creatures are forbidden. The attitude to fish is more difficult to understand. Although there is a general reluctance among nomadic tribes to eat fish[9] the Hebrews encountered fish in Egypt, and according to Biblical accounts became very fond of it.[10] There is a theory which associates the forbidden fish with bottom feeders, which does not hold up as there are many bottom feeders which are kosher, such as most flat fish. The more convincing explanation is that fish is an important symbol in Jewish culture. When God gives his blessing at the end of every day of the creation he singles out fish as exceptionally fertile (Genesis 1:22). Muslim legend has it that at the birthplace of Abraham there is a holy spring containing fish sacred to the Hebrew. Fish have a special place in Jewish symbolism; therefore any water creature which does not conform to the acceptable shape of a fish is banned. Eels and cat fish, which were known to the Hebrews, do not have scales — the eel does not have fins either — and do not look like the accepted shape of fish; neither do shellfish or bivalves, therefore they are unfit and taboo.

The Bible also forbids the consumption of any animals which crawl on the earth. These include rats, mice, lizards, snakes and all insects which have four legs but 'do not have an extra two legs to hop with'. It permits the eating of four kinds of locusts. This makes sound ecological sense, since it allows man to utilise one of his biggest enemies which is also rich in proteins and oils. The head and feet of the locust are first removed and the body is either roasted or dried in the sun and fried in honey. Locust can also be dried, milled and added to gruels.

MEAT AND MILK
'Kid in its mother's milk'

At the end of the repetition of the kosher laws (Deuteronomy 14:21) there is a reference to the most curious law of all: 'Do not cook kid in its mother's milk.' This law is mentioned twice before in Exodus 23:19 and 34:26 and always in connection with the celebration of the harvest festival.

Milk and meat were served together at Abraham's feast (Genesis 18:8) and appear in the description of a meal served to King David (Samuel 2, 17: 28–9). A general prohibition on mixing milk and meat together would have been impractical for a society which used milk and milk products as its main intake of animal protein. Maimonides,[11] an important medieval Jewish physician and scholar, discusses the milk/meat prohibition thus: 'Meat boiled with milk is undoubtedly gross food and makes a person feel overfull . . . I think that most probably it is also prohibited because it is somehow connected with idolatry. Perhaps it was part of the ritual of certain pagan festivals.' A young kid or lamb cooked in its mother's milk is believed to have been a Canaanite celebration of the harvest.

The blanket prohibition on meat with milk was imposed much later when all the laws were written down, canonised (200–420AD) and expanded to create 'fences around the law' to prevent even accidental breaches. It orders a total separation between milk and meat. Two separate sets of implements are used for cooking, serving, washing and drying milk and meat dishes. In some households a third set of utensils is kept for ingredients which are neither milk nor meat (parve). A special pot is kept for cooking udders which, like all other offal, are extensively eaten. The milk contained in the tissue would contaminate a meat utensil while the meat itself would contaminate a milk-cooking vessel. Great care must be taken when cooking in case accidental splattering from one pot should contaminate another.

Meat can be eaten immediately after a milk dish if the mouth is cleansed with clean water and a piece of bread is eaten. Milk or milk products cannot be consumed after meat unless some time has passed. The time varies from one community to another and can be as long as six hours, though most Western Europeans wait for three hours and Dutch Jews wait for as little as one hour.

One of the accepted 'health' explanations of the milk and meat prohibition is based on an adverse enzyme action which occurs when raw milk is drunk with meat. It is claimed that this process hinders efficient digestion of protein from both, especially in people with a low tolerance to milk. This explanation ignores the fact that our forefathers drank very little raw milk. Milk was consumed as curds and yoghurts, the proteins of which are already broken, making them as digestible as those of meat. In any case the association between enzymes and digestion was only made in the 20th century.

Parve or neutral food can be eaten with both. This group includes bread (if not baked with milk), fruit, vegetables and oils. Fish can be eaten with milk products, but traditionally is never mixed with meat either in preparation or as a part of the same course.

PORK
'Eating swine flesh and abomination . . .'

The pig, although it has cloven hooves, does not ruminate and therefore is not kosher. Its avoidance is entrenched deeply in the Jewish psyche. Health and aesthetic aspects are the most popular explanations for this taboo. In the 12th century Maimonides, trying to rationalise the law, says: 'The principal reason why the law forbids swine's flesh is to be found in the circumstances that its habits and its food are very dirty and loathsome.' Yet the eating habits and habitat of the free-ranging, wild Middle Eastern pig were no more loathsome than those of the scavenging chicken or the mud-wallowing *jamus* (water buffalo). It is true that pigs can infect humans with trichinosis, yet most of the permitted animals, for example, goats, sheep and cattle, transmit diseases such as brucellosis and anthrax which cause human death at about the same rate as trichinosis. The trichina is transmitted only if the flesh of the pig is not well cooked. With their obsession about raw meat and blood it is unlikely that the ancient Jews would have consumed raw or partially cooked meat. Also, there is strong evidence that trichina infestation is rare in free-ranging, foraging pigs. Another reason attributes the prohibition against pork to the speed in which fatty meat putrefies in a hot climate. However, wild pig is no fatter than mutton, and the same speed of putrefaction could also be attributed to fish. It could be that with the agricultural development of the Fertile Crescent the pig lost its place. As the forest was destroyed to make land available the pig was seen as a threat, vying for the same food resources as goats. To my mind the most acceptable explanation is simply that the pig did not fit the nomadic way of life. It cannot travel long distances, unlike sheep, goats and cattle, nor can it supply milk or wool nor be harnessed as a ploughing or carrying animal. For Jews the ban on pork took on additional symbolic importance. The pig represented everything oppressive and foreign. The enemy from the south, the Egyptians, deified the pig while the Greeks, in an attempt to Hellenise the Jews, marched pigs into the Temple and forced the Jews to eat pork. Later in the diaspora the pig came to symbolise the oppressive and unjust rule of the Christian church.

The dietary laws, although written down, are open to interpretation by the individual rabbi, especially if the rabbi has a reputation for being a gifted scholar. In Judaism there is no supreme authority which can exercise power over the whole population. Decisions are taken locally and are usually biased by the attitude of the rabbi, the sect he belongs to and the internal politics within his court. Therefore the law sometimes differs in more than just nuances from one community to another.

The implementation and policing of the kosher laws necessitates a vast army of *mashgichim* (observers) whose only purpose in life is to watch that the laws are observed properly. These people are paid out of the community pocket, making kosher food notably more expensive than any other food.

The division between different sections of the orthodox community started an ugly war of kashruth, particularly recently. In Britain alone there are at least three kosher authorities: Bait Din, Kadasia and Sephardi Bait Din, each maintaining its piety over the others. In Israel the situation is much more complicated. The most extreme example of this situation is the relatively new popularity of *glat* kosher. *Glat* means smooth in Yiddish and refers to the smoothness of the lungs of the slaughtered animal. For an animal to be declared kosher its lungs have to be free of lesions and hold air when inflated. Under normal proceedings, healed scabs which do not let out air are considered acceptable. In *glat* the lung has to be completely free of any sign of injury. The term should only be used to describe the condition of meat of large animals. Fraudulently *glat* now means 'more kosher than kosher' and is applied to any kind of food, adding confusion to an already confused market.

3

FOOD OF THE PATRIARCHS
'And he fetched a calf tender and good'

THERE ARE few food details in the story of the Patriarchs, even though we know that food was an important part of all celebrations. Special meals were made for each important occasion, be it the signing of a contract (Genesis 31:47 and 54), a wedding (Genesis 29:22), hospitality (Genesis 18:1–8) or circumcision which was celebrated with a 'great Feast' (Genesis 21:8).

The first meal to be described fully in the Bible is the impromptu feast Abraham gave the Angels:

> And Abraham hastened into the tent unto Sarah, and said, make ready quickly three measures of fine meal, knead it, and make cakes . . . And Abraham ran unto the herd, and fetched a calf tender and good, and gave it unto a young man; and he hasted to dress it. And he took butter, and milk, and the calf which he had dressed, and set it before them; and he stood by them under the tree, and they did eat. (Genesis 18:6–8)

This descriptive picture gives us a detailed account of food and encapsulates the essence of the lifestyle of an important, rich feudal family. The haste and elaboration of the meal indicate that hospitality was an important part of these people's life. The host used to go beyond his boundary to meet his guests and escort them to his tent. He first offers them water to wash their feet. Water, the most essential element for survival in the desert, was the first thing to be offered to a guest, not only for drinking but also to clean his face, hands and feet, in other words, to purify himself. Only then was food offered. Although wine was not mentioned on this occasion, we know that it was served, probably diluted, at important dinners (Genesis 20:19).

The order in which Abraham arranges the meal indicates that bread, which was ordered first, was the most important item on the menu and was the responsibility of the women of the household. The bread mentioned was probably unleavened, and similar to the Indian chapatti or unleavened pitta bread. The reference to fine meal and the use of the word cake indicates that it was different from an everyday bread.

The meat, which comes next, was treated with great reverence as it was eaten rarely. Although not as important as the bread, the choice of meat, a tender young calf, indicted the social standing of the host. Cattle on the whole were less economical to rear than goats or sheep. Cattle were also too large to be eaten in one sitting and therefore were slaughtered only for large or very important gatherings. Slaughtering a calf was a sign of great wealth.

Abraham probably did the slaughtering himself as it involved a certain religious ceremony. His boy (servant) would have skinned and cleaned the animal. The meat was roasted, probably whole, on an open fire under Abraham's active supervision and was served accompanied by butter and milk. No vegetables are mentioned.

In the above context the words milk and butter should be examined further as their meaning is probably different to what they imply today. In the Bible milk is sometimes used as a generic term for milk products. Butter describes the wholeness of the milk, the best. When Sisera asks Yael for water to drink she gives him milk 'butter (she served) in a lordly dish' (Judges 5:25).

Although it is possible that raw milk was drunk, serving it was a tricky business because milk goes sour quickly in the hot climate of the Middle East. Milking was done into vessels made mainly from skin or wood, both of which were absorbent and carried spores of souring bacteria which were impossible to eradicate. Therefore curdling was unavoidable. The resulting curds or yoghurt probably helped the Patriarchs maintain their health as souring destroyed some of the harmful bacteria present in raw milk (especially tuberculosis). The word yoghurt is not mentioned in the Bible, but one can safely assume that most of the milk drunk was curdled — yoghurt.

Some form of butter[1] was definitely made at the time of the Patriarchs, but it was not the butter we know now. Archaeological sites from the Chalcolithic period (4500–3150BC) in Israel revealed clay vessels with holes in the handles at both ends. The purpose of these strange utensils was not clear until a close examination and comparison with similar implements used today by desert Bedouin revealed that they were butter churns. The raw material for butter was *leben* or yoghurt. The whole milk soured and was put with water into the churn. Churning was done by swinging the suspended churn which separated the *zivda* (cream) from the yoghurt. The resulting mass of small coagulated cream lumps, soft curds and liquid was filtered by pouring over burgul, which soaked up the curd and serum, leaving the cream globules on top ready to be collected. The burgul, soaked with curds, was then drained of all liquid and preserved for further use. The remaining liquid is called by the Arabs *shnina*. It is slightly sour and is used as a refreshing drink during summer. Salt was not enough to preserve the butter in the hot climate so the cream collected was heated over a slow fire to melt, thus separating the fat from any remaining milk solids and liquid. *Samna* (ghee) or clarified butter keeps longer and enriched the plain grain gruel which was the staple diet.

The Patriarchs were also partial to game, as indicated in the continuation of the story about the primogeniture fight between Esau and Jacob:

> Isaac called Esau his eldest and said . . . I am old, I know not the day of my death: now therefore take thy weapons, thy quiver and thy bow, and go out to the field, and take me some venison. And make me savoury meat, such as I like, that I may eat; that my soul may bless thee before I die . . . and Rebekah said to Jacob: go now to the flock, and fetch me two good kids and I will make them savoury meat for thy father, such as he loves. (Genesis 27:2–9)

Although the English translation mentions venison, the word used in the original means game in general and probably referred to one of the numerous species of gazelle which roam the desert. The identity of the dish is harder to guess. The Bible just mentions that it was savoury meat, or as the Hebrew word suggests, delicacies.

We are told that the Patriarchs attached great value to honey, pistachio and almonds, as they are mentioned in the list of gifts Jacob sends to Pharaoh (Genesis 43:11). The honey mentioned was not however for eating, but a special mixture of honey and spices which was used for mummification. We are also told that the Hebrews had a different manner of eating which was abhorrent to the Egyptians:

> and they set the table for him, by himself [Joseph, as a sign of rank], and for them [his brothers] by themselves, and for the Egyptians . . . by themselves: because the Egyptian might not eat bread with the Hebrews; for it is an abomination unto the Egyptians. (Genesis 43:32)

EGYPTIAN FOOD
'When we sat by the flesh pot'

The move to Egypt exposed the Hebrews to a new way of life: a settled, well-organised society with a developed religion, a monarchy and a sophisticated culinary tradition. Joseph's account of the Egyptian court details a hierarchy of food providers, each responsible for a different branch of the royal kitchen, with a special steward or officer responsible for drink, baking and cooking. The Egyptians were the first to discover fermentation and baked leavened bread. The Egyptians had a developed agricultural system which produced a variety of vegetables and fruit; they also bred, specially for meat, cattle, pigs, ducks and geese. They used a wide variety of fish, mostly caught in the Nile but also farmed in special ponds.[2] Food distribution was highly organised and stores of grain were kept for times of need.

It seems that the Hebrews liked the food which was available in Egypt and adapted to it with relish. It is not surprising that when in the desert they complained bitterly: 'We remember the fish, which we did eat in Egypt freely; the cucumbers, and the melons, and the leeks, and the onions, and the garlics' (Numbers 11:5). Onions and garlic were either used in stews or eaten raw with bread. So were the cucumbers and melons (water melon or gourds). Leeks are mentioned in a strange translation of the Hebrew word *hazir* which means grass or hay. Biblical scholars mostly associate *hazir* with *hilbeh* or fenugreek, which in Latin (*Fenum graecum*) means 'Greek hay'.[3] *Hilbeh* was an important crop in Egypt; it was believed to have health-giving properties, especially for lactating mothers and as a general tonic.[4] A relish made of *hilbeh* is used now by Yemenite Jews for breakfast, accompanied by bread or raw vegetables.

MANNA FROM HEAVEN
'It was as the taste of fresh oil'

Throughout the forty years' wandering in the desert, the Hebrews reverted to their original way of eating. Cooking on the move, in the desert, depended entirely on the availability of fuel, which was scarce and cumbersome to carry. Nor was there time for building ovens to bake bread. For raw ingredients they relied heavily on wild plants, game and the flocks they took out from Egypt. Food was in short supply as their constant complaining reveals. The Bible tells us that when God heard the complaints he supplied the Hebrews with manna from heaven instead of bread and quails to satisfy their craving for meat. The attempt to identify the manna has inspired many Biblical scholars. Manna is described in the Bible: 'like coriander seed, white, and the taste of it was like wafer made with honey (Exodus 17:31)' and as: 'like a coriander seed (white), as the colour of bdellium.* And the people gathered it, ground it in mills, or beat it in a mortar, baked it in pans, and made cakes out of it: the taste of which was as the taste of fresh oil' (Numbers 11:7–8). Opinions differ about the identity of manna. A multitude of natural phenomena have been suggested, from the secretion of aphids and ants to an edible lichen.[5] Most scholars now agree that it was probably sap which is produced by the tamarisk tree or by a small insect which lives on the tamarisk; it is still collected today by the desert Bedouin.

There is no dispute about the identity of the quail that God provided. Travellers' accounts tell of flocks of quail which appear in the Sinai desert at the end of winter. They arrive after a long journey so exhausted that the Bedouins collect them by hand and with nets. The quail is eaten either fresh or salted for further use.

LAND OF WHEAT AND BARLEY

When at last the Hebrews arrived in the Promised Land, their lifestyle changed again. They developed a settled agricultural economy based mainly on cereal growing. Grain cultivation and fruit growing became essential for survival in the new land. Wheat and barley are indigenous to the Middle East. Aharon Aronson,[6] the first Jewish agronomist/botanist to work in Palestine, identified a wild species which he called 'mother wheat'. Later a species of wild barley was also found growing on Mt Tabor. Both these species exist only in the Middle East and especially in the Fertile Crescent.

Grain has a deep symbolic meaning to do with fertility and continuation. Strange stone objects have been found from the Neolithic period showing what is supposed to be an abstract presentation of a fertility goddess. These stones, oval in shape, have a carved groove going through the centre, which can look either like a grain of wheat or a vagina. Grain is also associated with rebirth or reincarnation. Mummified effigies

* *Bdellium* is a crystal-like resin used as a perfume.

of the Goddess Osiris, made from pitch-impregnated papyrus, were found to contain barley. The Egyptians associated the ability of grain to sprout when introduced to water with reincarnation and thus with Osiris, the sun goddess, who is reincarnated every day.

Barley was probably the first grain to be grown domestically. It grows well in poor soil and thrives even in very dry conditions. Barley was eaten in early summer as it ripens before wheat. It was the most important staple until the introduction of the new easily husked wheat at around 4000BC. Gradually barley assumed an image of poverty and affliction. Barley flour is believed to be the original flour used for the ceremonial Pesach *matzah* or 'bread of affliction'. When Ezekiel describes the horrors of siege he refers to the poor quality of the bread which will be eaten as 'barley cake' (Ezekiel 4:12).

Wheat became more popular when a new variety was developed. The old, near-wild species scattered off the ear immediately after ripening and buried itself in the ground. It was therefore only possible to gather part of the crop during a very short season. The new varieties were easily harvested, but it was difficult to separate the chaff from the berry. The only way was by heating or parching the chaff; then the hard inedible chaff could be removed and the berry broken or pounded into rough groats. The groats, already roasted, needed no further cooking. They were mixed with water and eaten as a thick grain paste.[7]

The Bible mentions four ways of using grain.[8] The first stage of maturation was called *aviv* (spring), a word of Aramaic origin which means to grow or to bear fruit. In this stage the wheat is still green, soft to the bite and deliciously sweet. The soft berry was eaten either raw or slightly roasted. Its main disadvantage was that it could not be kept for further use but had to be consumed immediately. This way of eating grain is probably the most ancient. The second stage of maturation is *carmel* and describes a stage where the ears change their colour but have not yet reached optimal weight or maturity. The berries are delicious when eaten raw, but the most popular way was to roast them which imparted an interesting flavour. Roasted dry berries were coarsely broken and used to make gruel or added to other ingredients. They could also be made edible by soaking in liquid. *Carmel* was considered a great delicacy. The third way of using grain was to roast the fully mature berry. This technique is known as *kali* (roasted). Roasting fully matured wheat on the ear makes the hard berry softer and delicious when warm. This method was practised mostly by harvesters as roasting in the field saved bringing food from home. The method is described charmingly in the story of Ruth: 'And he reached her parched corn, and she did eat, and was sufficed, and left' (Ruth 2:14). The English translation fails to capture the romance and detailed observation which the original Hebrew portrays. More importantly, grain was roasted for convenience and preservation. Roasted grain is more absorbent and the process converts some of the starch into sugars, which means that the grain does not need much cooking. Flour made out of roasted grain keeps longer as some of the essential oils, which deteriorate quickly, are removed. The roasted flour, being easily digestible, could be mixed with honey or dry fruit pulp, made into cakes and eaten without further baking, therefore making it suitable for travelling. The fourth way of using grain was by making *riffot* or burgul, the most popular, convenient and nourishing staple porridge of the Middle East. It is used in the same way as rice to accompany meat and as a basic ingredient for other dishes. It is known as burgul or burghul, *tzavar* (Armenian), *burgur* (Turkish), *burguri* (Greek), *gurgur* (Kurdistan) and *lapsi* (Indian). The dry wheat berries are boiled until they are swollen and tender but still maintain their shape. The cooked wheat is then flattened on a cloth and allowed to dry in the sun.[9] It is then milled or pounded in a mortar to coarse grains — for gruel — or fine grains — for making a kind of dough for plain or stuffed dumplings. Nowadays burgul salad, or tabouleh, is popular all over the world.

BREAD
'With the sweat of thy brow shalt thou eat bread'

Grain was used not only for cooking but also to make the most popular and convenient staple, bread. In God's curse on Adam for disobeying his orders (Genesis 3:19), bread is used as a metaphor for food and life. The verse in this context defined from the beginning the attitude of Jewish people towards their food: life, therefore bread, carries with it the guilt of the original rebellion against the rule of God.

The origin of bread baking is unclear. The most logical chain of events[10] is that man discovered that a paste made from a mixture of roughly broken grain and water is more palatable if the paste is left for a while for the grain to absorb water and become more moist. The next step was the discovery that the paste could be dried in the sun, which preserves it, then that toasting the grain paste on a hot stone gave a quicker, better result and produced a smell which is one of the most appetising known. The bread the Patriarchs baked was probably made from an unleavened mixture of pounded grain, water and, probably, although there is no concrete evidence, salt. The resulting dough was kneaded, probably left to rest for a while, and then shaped. Shaping was done by nimbly stretching and flattening the dough with circular, clapping hand motions. The dough was then baked and usually eaten hot. The thin, chapatti-like breads were probably baked on flat heated stones. The stones were later replaced by concave clay utensils with holes in them. The bread was thrown onto the heated surface which was suspended above burning embers. It was baked quickly on one side, turned over, and baked on the other. A metal version of this utensil is still used in India (*tava*) to bake chapatti.

As a rule nomadic people do not ferment their bread as it is difficult to maintain a stable 'sour dough' on the move. Yeast becomes unstable and over-active and eventually dies in the heat of the desert. To the nomad leavened bread was the symbol of permanency, which threatened the essence of the nomadic way of life. In the desert the Hebrews reverted to the food of their origin, the nomadic unleavened bread. When they finally settled, they readopted the skill they learned in Egypt of making fermented bread. This act is still performed each year in the celebration of Pesach (Passover).

Bread was of enormous importance to the Egyptians. They were referred to in Greek writings as 'bread eaters'; bread effigies were used by the poor as sacrifices and bread also had sexual overtones. The Egyptians made it in the shape of a phallus, an association which was suggested by the swelling, rising motion of the dough.[11] These pagan and sexual associations might be the reason for the ambiguity of the Bible about yeast. This is reflected in the Hebrew idiom 'leaven in the dough' which has a dual meaning. On one hand, the idiom means positive, active and lively, and on the other it can mean an evil nature and the cause of decay. Leavened bread was forbidden for sacrifice as atonement (Leviticus 2:11), but it was allowed for thanksgiving (Leviticus 7:13, 23:17).

No meal was considered complete without bread. Shaped to a round, flat pitta, it was the means by which food was scooped and brought to the mouth. Breakfast consisted mainly of bread served with raw vegetables, *samna*, cheese, olives, oil or vinegar (Ruth 2:24). There is a special word in Hebrew which describes foods to be eaten with bread — *lefet*. Translated, the word means to clasp or wind around. It probably suggests the habit of wrapping a piece of thin bread around food. The word now means turnip but is also used as a generic name for root vegetables, indicating that they were mainly served with bread.

The Bible gives breads descriptive names which represent their shape, ingredients or methods of making. The simple, everyday bread was called *matzah* (Samuel 128:24), which probably means that the bread was not leavened. The Bible distinguishes between four types of matzah: *hallah matzah* (Leviticus 8:26), which was made from a special quality of flour; *matzah blula*, which was probably the same mixture combined with oil (Leviticus 2:4); *rakik matzah* (Exodus 29:23), which describes the bread as being very thin (there was another kind of *rakik* which was brushed with oil (Exodus 29:2)); and *ugah matzah* (Exodus 12:39) or round bread. The most popular shapes of leavened breads included *kikar*, a loaf of round, flattish bread; the word means also a town square, a centre. The most frequently mentioned shape is *hallah*, which will be discussed later as it occupies an important niche in Jewish symbolism after the destruction of the Temple.

Baking in an oven is not the only way leavened bread was made. *Tz'lil* (Judges 7:13) indicates a technique of roasting leavened bread directly on burning ashes like ash cakes. With *ugat retzaphim* (Kings 1:6), round bread was baked on a *rezef* or *re'aff* (tile) which had decorative grooves or holes which stamped the bottom of the bread with a characteristic pattern.

Oil was probably the most frequently used additive to bread, enriching it and keeping it moist longer. The importance of oil is indicated in a story about the meeting between the Prophet Elijah and the widow in Zarephath (Kings 17:10–15). The widow attributes her inability to make bread to the fact she does not have enough oil and flour, coining the phrase: 'The bowl will not run out of flour or the jar — run out of oil.'

Bread still plays an important part in Jewish life and is treated with great reverence. It should not be defiled by blood, raw meat or spilled wine. Bread should never be thrown out. When found lying on the ground it should be lifted and placed on an elevated surface. Providing bread for the poor is a great religious duty with origins in Biblical writing (Isaiah 58:7, Proverbs 22:9). Folk belief ascribes magical protective powers to bread, especially in combination with salt. Bread and salt are blessed at every meal. They are given to newlyweds and are a part of welcoming ceremonies. The association of bread and salt is fundamental. In Hebrew the words bread, salt and war (*lechm*, *melach* and *milchama*) come from the same three letter root L-ch-m. The Biblical accounts attribute at least one war to a power struggle over salt mining.

SEDER
'And you shall eat it in haste'

The best example of the changing way of eating is recorded in the celebration of the most important Jewish holiday, the Passover or Pesach. The Biblical origins of the holiday are in the dramatic recounting of the events that led the Hebrews to leave Egypt. In the process of trying to persuade the Pharaoh to release the Hebrews from bondage, Moses cursed the Egyptians with ten plagues. The last and most awesome was the death of all the first-born males. To protect the Hebrews from the plague Moses instructed that a sign of blood from the Pascal sacrifice be put on all doorposts:[12]

> and the whole congregation shall kill [the Pascal lamb], in the evening. And they shall take the blood, and strike it on the two side posts and on the upper door post of the houses . . . and they shall eat the flesh in that night, roast with fire, and unleavened bread; and bitter herbs . . . Eat not of it raw nor sodden [boiled] at all with water but roast with fire; [whole, with] his [the lamb's] head with his legs, and with the purtenance [entrails] thereof. And you shall let nothing of it remain until the morning; and that which remains, you shall burn with fire.
>
> And thus shall you eat it; with your loin girded, your shoes on your feet, and your staff in your hand, and you shall eat it in haste; it is the Lord's passover (Exodus 12:6–12).

The origin of the Pascal lamb tradition predates the exile in Egypt and stems from the pagan habits of a nomadic past. Holiday ritual plays an important part in both tribal and national life. Past ceremonies are resuscitated every few generations and given a more contemporary meaning which answers the demands of a new understanding. Pesach was a spring thanksgiving festival when nomadic people settled down for a few months to enable the ewes to give birth and suckle their young. It was the only time of the year when they had the opportunity to gather in fertile green enclaves, to tend their flocks, to meet friends and relatives, arrange marriages and conduct business. These gatherings were celebrated with joy and involved mysterious ancient blood rituals to ensure a prosperous year ahead.

The original meaning of the word Pesach is 'to leap, skip or gambol', describing the movement of young lambs and kids, especially those used for sacrifice. The word 'skipper' was used to describe a young lamb and goat in general. Another theory is that the word refers to a special ritualistic dance around the Pascal lamb.[13] The other meaning of the word Pesach is to 'pass over, to exclude'. The Pascal holiday was celebrated with the sacrifice, just before nightfall, of a young sheep or goat. The blood of the sacrificial animal was daubed on the tent posts with swabs made out of *azov* (a species of marjoram, probably *marjorana syriaca*). The meat of the sacrificial animal was roasted whole and eaten at midnight; no meat was allowed to be left over until the morning. The meal was eaten with unleavened bread.

The prohibition against eating leaven is connected with a different holiday altogether. The holiday of the unleavened bread has its origins in the *fallahim* (settled cropgrowers') celebration of the beginning of the barley harvest when it was the custom to destroy all old leaven stocks. We do not know if grain was also destroyed, but the symbolic sale before Pesach of all Jewish grain stores, still practised now, indicates that symbolic destruction was practised in the past. This kind of practice is related to a global folk tradition of symbolically sacrificing leftovers of the previous year to guarantee a prosperous new year; a tradition which in modern times is probably echoed in 'spring cleaning'.

After the exodus from Egypt the Pesach included a new meaning. The deliverance from Egypt was depicted by reverting to the old customs, both in food and in dress. The Hebrews celebrated the Pesach dressed in their old travelling costumes and rejected the leavened bread which symbolised for them a despised (Egyptian) settled way of life.[14] When finally settled, and after the pastoral nomad economy had changed to crop growing, the holiday of the Pascal sacrifice was enlarged to incorporate the holiday of the unleavened bread, which fitted perfectly with the new concept: celebration commemorating national liberation and freedom.

With the establishment of the First Temple in Jerusalem, Pesach, which used to be a domestic holiday celebrated within the clan, became a public holiday. The Pascal sacrifice was done at the Temple, making the Pesach the most important pilgrimage of the year. When the Second Temple was destroyed, and during the exile which followed, Pesach regained its domestic character. It is still the most domestic of the Jewish holidays, celebrated mainly at home (as opposed to the synagogue) with the active involvement of the whole family. Living as a minority in exile introduced yet another element to the national holiday; the expectancy of the arrival of a new Messiah who will deliver the Jews from their constant misery. This element still remains in the tradition of leaving a door open and pouring a symbolic glass of wine for the prophet Elijah, who according to tradition is the forerunner of the Messiah.

In the Middle Ages a new and sinister element was added to the celebration of Pesach. Deeply rooted anti-semitism, and a deliberate misinterpretation of Jewish blood taboos, led to blood libel, a groundless ignorant belief that the Jews used blood, especially that of innocent Christian children, in the celebration of the Pesach. The first blood libel occurred in Norwich (Britain) in 1147 and the last one as late as 1911 in Kiev (Russia). The blood libels brought in their wake indiscriminate destruction, property confiscation and expulsions, giving poignancy to Messianic expectations and the liberation elements of the holiday.

The Pesach ceremony is called Seder (order in Hebrew) by the Ashkenazi Jews and Haggadah (narration) by Sephardi Jews.[15] The Haggadah is also the name of the book which contains the procedure of the celebration and a collection of fragments of very ancient text mixed with later additions, including homilies, witticisms and collections of folk songs and parables. The book also specifies the order of the meal and contains a list of compulsory foodstuffs, each of which signifies an event in the Exodus from Egypt. Some of the ingredients and especially the order of the meal were acquired at a later date, probably during the Greco-Roman period. There are seven essential ingredients on the Pesach table: *matzah*, two, sometimes three, different kinds of herbs, two dips and two roasted dishes which are not eaten.

Three *matzoth* are displayed on the Seder table; two represent the usual two *halloth* (plural of *hallah*) and are not eaten, the third is used as a part of the ceremony and shared between all present. The three *matzoth* also represent the three sections of ancient Israeli society: Cohen, Levi (the priesthood) and Israel. The *matzah* used at the Seder are usually special; *shmura* (meaning kept or guarded) is made by hand from flour gathered before the first rain and guarded carefully from any moisture. The water used is kept covered overnight. This curious custom was due to an ancient belief that the sun, setting at night, went underground and heated the water of the well. Therefore water was kept overnight to cool in case the heat should encourage fermentation. *Matzah shmura* is usually made and baked by a man. There are strict rules about the time the dough can rest without suspicion of fermentation, usually eighteen minutes from the moment water is mixed in. Work surfaces are constantly cleaned to prevent the presence of old particles of dough which might ferment. There are even special rolling pins made of stone or glass which are not absorbent and therefore cannot be suspected of contamination. *Matzah shmura* is usually round with little perforations on the *matzah* which are there to prevent the dough from rising during the short baking time. Everyday *matzah*, which is not compulsory,[16] used to be kneaded and shaped by women although the men were responsible for the baking. Today *matzah* is mass-produced and made by machines, though *matzah shmura* is still made by hand.

The ceremonial third *matzah* used during the Seder is divided into two, the first part of which is shared between the eaters and is eaten ceremonially at the beginning. The second part, called *afikoman*, is kept to be eaten at the end of the meal. This word comes from a Greek word describing joyous revelry and entertainment after a banquet. The eating of the *afikoman* heralds the end of the meal. As it is impossible to end the meal without the *afikoman*, a charming tradition evolved whereby the children are supposed to steal the *afikoman* and not relinquish it unless promised a gift. Some say the tradition evolved as a ploy for keeping the children's attention until the end of the meal. The *afikoman* also has the reputation of being a good talisman for protecting travellers.

The herbs on the Seder table are *karpas* (celery) and *maror* (bitter). Bitter herbs are mentioned in the Biblical instructions, indicating an old tradition of starting a meal with a refresher of herbs, usually bitter. This, with a help of a tart sauce, clears the palate and tingles the tastebuds, very much like a bitter herbal aperitif today. The bitter herbs symbolise the bitterness of the Hebrews' life under the Egyptian yoke. The reason why two herbs are used is obscure. The most acceptable reason is that in the Bible the word is mentioned in the plural. The herbs most commonly used today are celery, romaine lettuce, parsley, chicory and horseradish root.

The herbs are dipped into salt water or lemon juice (sometimes vinegar) and *haroset*. The salt water represents the salty tears the Hebrews shed in Egypt. The name *haroset* comes from the Hebrew word for clay (*chres*) and symbolises the clay the Hebrews used in Egypt. The *haroset* is a thickish sauce made from various kinds of fruit, mashed with the addition of honey and sometimes wine. Spices used are mainly cinnamon and cloves, but also cardamom, allspice and black pepper in some communities. There is no set rule about which fruit should be used, but the tradition is to use fruit which is associated with the Land of Israel: dates, figs, raisins and pomegranates. When well made the *haroset* is extremely delicious. Most recipes include lemon juice which makes it a delightful, fragrant, sweet-sour sauce. Sauces very much like *haroset* were used by the Greeks and Romans as a pre-meal appetiser and were probably adopted in Israel under the Greek and Roman occupation.

The ceremonial roast dishes on the Seder plate representing the abolished Pascal sacrifice are a shank bone of lamb (sometimes chicken wing is used) and a roasted egg. The shank bone symbolises the strong hand of God, who delivered the Hebrews from Egypt. The egg is usually boiled and then roasted on a naked flame and is supposed to represent the extra sacrifice that was offered in the Temple on a holiday, thus symbolising mourning for the destruction of the Temple. Although the ceremonial roasted egg is not eaten there is a tradition of serving hard-boiled eggs with salted water at the beginning of the Seder meal. The presence of eggs at the Seder table might stem from a much earlier association with fertility and rebirth, which is basically at the heart of the Pesach tradition, as it is also at the heart of the Christian Easter, celebrated at almost the same time.

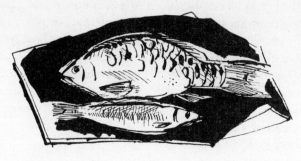

4

FOOD OF THE KINGDOM
'And seethe his flesh in the holy place'

THE ESTABLISHMENT of the Temple and the monarchy which marked the transition from Hebrews to Israelites brought also a new dimension to the Jewish way of cooking and eating. Sacrifice at the Temple was done according to an elaborate and meticulous set of rules. What was sacrificed and the technique used depended on whether the sacrifice was for atonement, expiation or thanksgiving. Most sacrifices, except the ones for reparation of major sins and very solemn oaths, were not burnt; food was too precious. The meat of the sacrifice was eaten either by the priests as part of the ceremony (Leviticus 6:18–23), or shared amongst the administration (Leviticus 7:10, 34), or sold to bring revenue to the Temple. We know that food was sold as there are, especially in the Talmud, numerous references as to which of the Temple foods could be eaten by the common people. There were also prohibitions against selling these foods to non-Jews. Food for the priests (*cohanim*) and the Levites was also supplied by law by the nation. There are complicated rules about the share each citizen had to give and which parts of the harvest were exempt.

It is reasonable to assume that all preparation techniques produced food which was edible. It is also reasonable to assume that only the best was given to God. Considering the social and political power of the religious hierarchy, it is likely that those ceremonial cooking techniques influenced the cuisine of the aristocracy and therefore of the whole nation.

The ceremonial food preparations needed an army of qualified butchers, bakers, cooks and store men. The slaughtered animals had to be butchered, proged of all the forbidden parts and cooked in different ways. The Bible mentions a large number of implements to deal with this. There were ovens (Leviticus 2:4), *machvatot* or frying pans (Leviticus 2:5) and *marcheshet* or deep frying pans as well as both clay and copper cooking pots (Leviticus 7:21). There were also different kinds of basins, plates, troughs (Chronicles 2 35:13), *mazlegot* (forks) (Samuel 1 2:14) and other miscellanea. In a remarkably detailed description of the Second Temple the Prophet Ezekiel (46:23) mentions the Temple kitchens which were in the outer court of the Temple, the only court that was open to all. The kitchens were built in the four corners of the court, each kitchen surrounded by a colonnade, probably with a roof and chimney. The kitchens were furnished with ovens and stoves, probably made out of metal.[1] There were also houses for the food collected (Nehemiah 10:39).

Two techniques were used for cooking meat: boiling and roasting. We may assume that boiling was the most common as it was pointed out that the Pascal lamb should be roasted and not boiled as usual (Exodus 12:9). There is a vivid description of the way the *cohanim* got their share of the meat from a boiling pot of meat (Samuel 1 2:14–15). The priests used to send their servants, armed with special three-pronged forks which they plunged into the cooking pots, to extract their share. Although the episode described is pre-Temple, it is safe to assume that the procedure at the Temple was similar. In another passage in Samuel (1 22–5), there is a detailed description of a public meal (sacrifice). Samuel, to indicate the importance of his young ward, seats the future King Saul at the head of the table. The table was probably placed in sacred ground, on an elevated stage. He instructs the cook to give young Saul the best portions, the leg and tail fat, which were usually given to the priests in the temple.

Among numerous ways of making sacrificial bread at the Temple one was especially fascinating — *tuphin* (Leviticus 6:14). The word, usually ignored in English translations, stood for a special sacrifice which the High Priest offered on the day of his anointment and as such had to be burned completely. The name might be an indication of the way it was made as *tafan*, to hide or seal, describes a dough envelope which is stuffed with a filling. In modern Hebrew the word is used to describe a turnover which can be either sweet or savoury.

THE ROYAL KITCHEN
'Fallow deer and fatted fowl'

The introduction of a central monarchy was probably the most important influence on the Israelite way of cooking. The Queen of Sheba is reported to have fainted when she saw the magnificence of King Solomon's Temple, his wisdom, the sumptuousness of his table and the splendour of his servants' attire.

The list of King Solomon's food for one day is impressive: a large selection of varied raw materials, 1200 kg of fine wheat (semolina), 2400 kg ordinary flour, 10 'healthy' (fatted) beef, probably calf, 20 beef, which were grazed in an enclosed meadow, and 100 sheep. In addition there was game, which included several kinds of venison, and fatted geese or swans. Even if some allowance is made for Biblical bragging, the list is indeed impressive. Estimating that one lamb could provide around fifteen large portions, the lambs alone would serve 1500 people. It is curious that fruit and vegetables are not mentioned. This might indicate that vegetables were considered a poor man's food.

The best description of courtly entertainment is given in the book of Samuel (2, 17:28–9), where three chieftains meet to honour King David and his court. The meal was sumptuous and was served with great elegance. There were beds and soft sofas on which to recline and good clay tableware to eat from. The menu included breads, both wheaten and barley, other goods made of flour, roasted green wheat (probably made into a gruel), fresh and roasted young *ful* (brown beans) and fresh and roasted young lentils. There was also honey and butter, and two different meats were served, lamb — probably roasted — and boiled beef.

The demands of the aristocracy and the Temple for quality meat encouraged the farmers to produce specially fatted animals. Those animals were kept in confined pens and were fed on a rich diet of carob pods, sycamore figs and probably pulp left over from the oil and honey industries. The Prophet Amos, who gives his occupation as a herdsman and gatherer of sycamore figs (Amos 7:14), has some strong words of warning to the idle women of Samaria whom he calls Bashan cows (Bashan was an area which was famous for its fat cattle). He also points a warning finger at the idle people who lie on ivory beds and stuff themselves with calf and lamb fatted on specially tender grass.

POOR MAN'S FOOD
'Land of milk and honey'

Little is known of the poor man's diet, but from accounts of foods which were sent to battlefields one can build a fairly accurate picture of the common foods of the Israelites. The list of food sent to King David included: bread, wine, roasted grain, five dressed sheep, raisins and dry figs. The reference for sheep is unclear. It is possible that cold roasted meat was sent, but it makes more sense if the dressed sheep is interpreted as dressed (brined) sheep's milk cheese (Samuel 1, 25:18). Cheese was also sent by the future King David's father to his sons who fought the battle against Goliath (Samuel 1, 17:18), an action which decided the fortune of the battle because the messenger, young King David, slew the giant with a well-aimed single stone.

Cheese is mentioned only once more in the Bible, but probably, like all over the Middle East, goat and sheep cheeses were the main supply of animal protein to the diet of the poor man. We do not know anything about the shape of the cheese or at what stage of maturity it was eaten. Curds and young cheese were probably eaten in the milking season, but mostly the cheese was preserved for future use. Preserving in liquid is one probability. There are Roman recipes, admittedly of a much later period, for preserving food in honey.[2] Oil and vinegar were probably used also. The Palestinian Arabs still preserve their fresh yoghurt cheese (*labaneh*) in fragrant olive oil. Cheese was also mixed with burgul and shaped into balls which were placed in dry gourds, covered with a lid and made airtight with either pitch or resin. These were eaten in hard times.[3]

The most popular way of preserving cheese was salting and drying. The cheese was first pickled in salt brine for a varied length of time and then dried almost rock hard in the sun. Those cheeses had a very high flavour. Some of them probably required certain preparations before being eaten. Cheese was probably grated into dishes as there is a dispensation for carrying cheese graters on the Sabbath, though carrying tools on the Sabbath is forbidden.[4] A hard sheep's milk salted dry cheese is still made today in the ancient city of Zfad. Sheep or goat milk curds are salted and pressed into baskets made of reeds from the Sea of Galilee. These give the cheese its characteristic shape. The cheese is then brined and dried. There is no record of when those cheeses were first made, but I would suspect that their history goes far back. Although now, with their renewed popularity, they are made from cow's milk and sold in little plastic containers, their glory can be still seen in a few shops in Israel where the original version is sold, beautifully pungent, ready to be grated, mixed with fresh curd cheese and stuffed into a variety of savoury pastries.

As sugar production was probably unknown at the time, honey was the only sweetening agent used. Honey is mentioned profusely in the Bible. It symbolises all which is sweet and good, from the taste of the beloved mouth (Song of Songs 4:11) to the word of God (Ezekiel 3:3). The Bible recommends eating honey, but warns against eating honey excessively (Proverbs 25:27). Yet there is no mention of bee-keeping. The only record of collecting honey describes how it was gathered in the wild from a lion's corpse (Judges 14:8). This led Biblical scholars to suspect that most of the honey references did not refer to bee's honey, but to the concentrated juice of sugary fruit such as dates, carob, grapes and figs.[5] Those 'honeys' are still made today by boiling down the juice of grapes, dates and carob. The leftover pulp was used for animal fodder.

Dates, figs, grapes and to a lesser extent carobs were the most important fruit crops grown by the Israelites. Date eating is not mentioned in the Bible, but the date palm is used as a metaphor for grace (Song of Songs 7:7) and a symbol of fertility (Psalms 92:12) which says that the righteous shall flourish like the palm tree. The erect unopened young shoot of the palm tree, the *lulav*, was and still is used as a symbol for maleness in the celebration of Sukkoth (Leviticus 23:40). Date palms also appeared on Maccabeean coins symbolising the victory over the Greek oppressors.

The date palm is a native of the Fertile Crescent. It was probably the first fruit tree to be cultivated and its fruit was one of the most important energy-giving foods of the Middle East. As well as supplying energy, the date palm is very versatile. Although not a shade-giver, its wide palms were used to top roofs and to make floor coverings and baskets. The fibrous casing of the trunk was used for making ropes. The trunk itself, which is exceptionally straight, was used for poles. The sap of the palm tree was made into an alcoholic drink. The fruit, when dried, was pressed into a round cake (sometimes the stones were removed first — they were used as fuel), and covered with palm leaf mats. In this way they could be kept for a long time. Dried dates were one of the main foods to be taken on long journeys. It is said that Muhammad's soldiers survived on three dates a day.

The town of Jericho was world famous for its dates and was referred to as the 'city of palm trees' (Leviticus 23:40). The Roman chef and gourmet Apicius mentions Jericho dates in a large number of recipes, usually as an addition to stuffing or as a sweetener in sauces for meat, game and fish. One of the Apician recipes for stuffed dates is remarkably similar to a Sephardi Pesach specialty of dates stuffed with nuts or marzipan.

The first mention of the fig in the Bible is in Genesis 3:7: 'And the eyes of them both were opened, and they knew that they were naked; and they sewed fig leaves together and made themselves aprons.' This magnificent tree dominated large parts of the Middle Eastern landscape with its widespread crown of luscious large dark green leaves. In the mythology of the area the fig always symbolises the feminine and motherly. Like the mother, the tree supplied not only food but also protection from the harsh sun. Fig trees also symbolised peace and content (Kings 1, 5:5): 'And Judah and Israel dwelt safely, every man under his vine and under his fig tree.' Like dates, figs are an important carbohydrate source, and were taken on expeditions and to war. The fig was dried and pressed into round cakes which were wrapped in fig leaves to aid preservation.

5

BY THE RIVERS OF BABYLON

As the Prophet Amos predicted, overeating of all those fatted calves brought about the moral deterioration of the nation. Power squabbles and moral laxity among the monarchy and the religious administration exposed the Israelites to their old adversary from the north. The Babylonian occupation and the destruction of the First Temple was followed by a massive expulsion of the Israelites to Babylon:

> [Nebuchadnezzer King of Babylon] carried away all Jerusalem, and all the princes, and all the mighty men of valour, even ten thousand captives, and all the craftsmen and smiths: none remained, save the poorest sort of people of the land. (Kings 2, 24:14)

Strangely enough, the expulsion did not bring about the destruction of the culture. On the contrary, being stateless forced the Jews to look at their past history, codify their holy writing and start recording and explaining their oral traditions. Religious and civil laws were collected in a group of six books known as Mishnah which were concluded at around 200AD. Mishnah then became the basis of Talmudic and Rabbinical literature, and one of the main sources of all later legislative (*halachic*) writings.[1] An important part of the Mishnahic narration is concerned with food, not only the dietary laws, but also the boundaries by which general and religious rules could be understood. In order to set these parameters a detailed analysis of each dish was needed. For example, when the Mishnah discusses taking an oath not to eat meat, it is necessary just to clarify what exactly constitutes meat, to consider which way it was cooked and whether the juice and vegetables flavouring the stew are regarded as meat, whether the eggs, cooked with the meat and absorbing some of the meat's flavour are permitted.[2] This gives a vivid description of a sophisticated and technically advanced cuisine where food terms were also used to denote quantities, the smallest measure being a grain, then an olive and an egg.

The exile also created a new social order which, although still ruled by the priests and the old royal house, gave an opportunity for a new class of successful merchants to establish themselves. Thus the Jewish community in Babylon flourished.

At the time of their arrival, Babylon was one of the wonders of the ancient world, with a highly developed culture and an agricultural tradition which specialised in gardening and vegetable growing. Fish, meat and fowl were also in abundance. It is difficult to assess the extent of the influence of Babylonian food on the Jewish kitchen as both stem from the same origins. Yet the documentation which started at this period emphasises different raw ingredients and mentions new agricultural techniques which are not present in the Bible. The Jews were probably introduced to new spices such as ginger, and also to rice; fish became important. They learnt advanced methods of market gardening and fruit growing, became expert croppers and were involved in bee-keeping and beer brewing.

The success of the community in Babylon can be measured, if one can trust Biblical statistics, in the number of exiles returning to Israel after Babylon fell to the Persians in 536BC. When Cyrus the Great granted the Jews permission to return to Israel and rebuild the Temple, 42,000 went, leaving behind a prosperous community who chose to stay. Those who stayed were the core of the Babylonian community and later played a vital role in shaping Jewish culture.

TOWN AND COUNTRY

After their return from exile, the Jews settled to a relatively peaceful and prosperous way of life. The colonising Persians did not have any interest in changing the culture of the Jews and were quite satisfied just to collect taxes. By the time the Greeks led by Alexander the Great entered Jerusalem in 332BC Israel had become a semi-urban nation with the Jewish population concentrated in the centre and northern parts while the coast was primarily occupied by non-Jews, mainly Greeks.[3] Mishnahic sources show a clear division between rich and poor with specific rules about who is considered poor and what is considered to be the minimum requirement for existence. Charity plays an important role in Jewish religious observance. The Mishnah tells us that the minimal weekly alimony a divorcee could expect consisted of about 4.4 litres of wheat. In areas where barley was eaten the quantity doubled to about 8.8 litres. She could also expect 1.25 litres of beans, 0.25 litres of oil, 2.2 litres of dried figs or a coin's worth of fig cake. If there were no dried figs available she could be given some fruit instead.[4] This kind of diet was probably the diet of the poor. It was supplemented by collecting wild leaves and vegetables, and the very poor had the right to glean what was left over in the fields.

A further national division related to geographic origin. Those who lived in Jerusalem (Judaea) considered the northerners (Galileans) uncouth and ill-educated. There were different preferences in flavourings and some different foodstuffs were used. For example, we are told in a discussion about donations to the temple that coriander, sumac (fruit used for its acidity) and malt vinegar were considered untaxable in Judaea where they were rarely used although they were taxed in the north where they were preferred.[5]

THE HOME

The middle and upper classes living in towns and cities fared much better. Life in the towns was organised around courts which constituted the most common lodging unit in Palestine. The court was a collection of buildings enclosing a common area or yard. Rich families owned their own court and all the units around it, but commonly the court was shared by a few families. Buildings around the court also provided storage space and stables, and in the centre of the court there were pigeon-cotes and henhouses. Often fruit and vegetables were grown, and commonly a well or water-hole collected rain water.

The courts were grouped together into 'alleys' or *mevo'ote*. This way of living solved some practical problems. A protected outside area to work and sit in was a necessity in the long, hot summers. The street was unacceptable as it did not conform with the religious requirement of modesty; women were not allowed to be seen outside. Also eating in the street was considered very bad form and done only by animals. This semi-communal living also solved a problem which is inherently Jewish: carrying objects is forbidden on the Sabbath unless it is done within one household. This way on the Sabbath the whole court and sometimes the whole alley would declare themselves a single household by sharing a dish, thus extending the allowed range of carrying throughout the court and the other households.

Roofs were used as an extension of the court. They were the safest and cleanest place for drying fruit, vegetables, grains and seeds. It was the duty of the children of the household to keep watch over the food, so it would not be eaten by birds. Roofs were also used to grow culinary herbs.

Cooking was usually done outside in the court. In winter the portable stoves and cooking range were moved to the main room of the house. The range, *kira*, was usually rectangular, made of clay, with facilities to accommodate one pot or *kiraym* (plural) which could hold two pots or more. By the range or attached to it there was a little tray which had three containers for spice, oil, and a candle for light.[6] Although there were craftsmen who specialised in building ranges, most of the ranges were homemade and most were portable.

The portable ovens were in the form of a beehive-shaped clay pot with an opening in the top. The pitta was baked by sticking the thinly rolled dough onto the walls. One or two could be baked at the same time. The ovens were heated by first burning wood, letting the flame die and then baking while the embers were glowing. As fuel became scarcer, a new type of oven was introduced which could be heated with lower quality fuel such as straw, dried animal dung or dry thorns. This extremely successful and ecologically sound oven, the *tabun*, is still used by peasants all over the Middle East.

A few houses had an inside kitchen, a room called *magirion* with a stove and a range. The stove was a permanent structure made of clay and constructed in two parts. A bottom cavity was used for burning wood and a concave upper part had a small opening which could be sealed off with plaster for baking and roasting. The ovens were sited next to a wall by a window to allow the building of an 'eye' (chimney). Ovens were also made out of metal but these were imported, therefore very expensive and were presumably used only in the Temple. Some ovens had a stone shelf which was a part of the structure and was used for keeping dishes warm or fermenting dough.[7] In Jerusalem, where fuel was scarce and expensive and living conditions were cramped, central ovens were used either by specialised bakers or by the community.

The houses were sparsely furnished, though a table was essential as etiquette demanded that food should not be eaten from the ground. The table was not a permanent structure, but a counter which rested on a tripod; floors were uneven and a tripod is more stable. The table was erected and dismantled when needed. There was also a small table which was used as a sideboard. Purity laws demanded that pots were placed on the sideboard or on a defined and separate part of the table as a precaution against cross-contamination.[8]

Cooking and eating utensils were numerous and varied. Although clay was the cheapest and most popular, there was a preference for utensils which were made from uncontaminable materials such as stone and metal. Rich families used gold, silver and metal utensils as they were a sign of social status and were practical for use. Glass was relatively cheap as Israel was near the glass-making centre, Phoenicia, in the north. Clear 'white' Phoenician glass was more expensive than the coloured glass made locally, probably in Hebron, which was widely used for drinking vessels.

The most widely used material for domestic utensils was clay. Archaeological digs have revealed numerous shapes and sizes of clay dishes, pots and storage vessels. Although clay absorbs impurities and must be broken if defiled, it was probably cheap enough to be replaced easily. Special pots were kept for water heating and water, wine, oil, grain and flour were stored in clay containers. To avoid any chance of contamination full vessels had to be sealed tightly. The Mishnah recommends the use of lime, plaster, pitch, wax, mud, dung, clay, and red clay. It forbids the use of dried fig paste and dough which was made with fruit juice as they might absorb defilement. Stoppers were made out of papyrus, pieces of skin and paper soaked in tar.

It is curious that most of the clay utensils found on ancient Jewish sites are plain, or simply decorated and usually unglazed. Glazed dishes were found mostly in coastal sites where the majority of the population was not Jewish. The lack of decoration might indicate the attitude of the Jews to clay utensils; since clay was disposable, it was a waste of time to decorate it.

We know that wooden utensils were used, though probably not very much as it was wasteful to use a material which was scarce, expensive and more important as fuel.

Baskets were found in every household. They were used for storage of bread and dried fruit and as containers for carrying foodstuffs. Baskets were made mostly from palm leaves though reed and willow baskets were also in use. There were special baskets or oven trays with handles which held a collection of bottles, pourers and pots containing liquids such as oil and vinegar and spices. These were very convenient as the accoutrements could be carried with ease. Some of these divided spice boxes were made from clay (*bait tvalim*) and some of wood (*kalmar*).[9]

Most houses had a stone flour mill, which stood near the cooking area and flour was usually milled every day. A pestle and mortar was important to grind spices, grains such as burgul and beans and chickpeas. Sieves and sifters sorted out grains and flours. Of the specialised implements there were a three-part pepper mill and two kinds of fork-spoon combinations. The first, a *koligraphon*,[10] had a container for removing ashes on one end and a fork to turn roast meat in the other. The second, *zumalestrah*,[11] had a spoon in one end and a fork in the other, probably for using with meat stews. A special sieve or sifter for mustard is mentioned in a few places,[12] and there was also a special roasting pan with a handle for roasting grain, seeds and nuts, an *abov shel kalayim*.[13]

BEANS AND LENTILS

The market gardening techniques learned in Babylon had a profound effect on the Jewish diet. Market gardening is rarely mentioned in the Bible,[14] nevertheless by the numerous references to vegetables, fruit and vegetarian cooking the Mishnah suggests that they became an important part of the diet. Wild leaves and roots were also extensively gathered. The Mishnah mentions a long list of cultivated vegetables, the most popular of which are a large variety of beans and lentils. These were eaten raw, roasted green or cooked, both fresh and dry. Dry beans were also broken into rough groats and cooked in porridge-like dishes, similar to Indian dals, and probably flavoured with onions, garlic, coriander and cumin. It is difficult to identify the specific variety of beans mentioned as the Mishnah gives local and contemporary names which have lost their original meaning. Amongst the ones which were identified are *pole* (*ful*, brown bean or Egyptian beans), white bean, lentils and *turmos* (lupin).

Strangely, although the lupin was classified as food for the poor, it is mentioned a lot in the Mishnah, being used as an example for boundary setting for a variety of laws. Lupin 'beans' are bitter when raw and need lengthy preparation to sweeten them; indeed the Mishnah goes so far as to suggest that they should be parboiled seven times. An easier method was to boil them twice or three times or to 'sweeten' them by soaking in salt or plain water, changing the water every day. It took three to four days to get rid of the excess bitterness.[15] The beans were then boiled and usually peeled to remove the tough outer skin. They were eaten, probably with oil, as a nutritious main dish, for the beans contain up to 40% protein and 15% oils. Lupin beans were sold in public places, and one can still buy the golden lupin in season in all Middle Eastern markets. Stored in slightly salted water, they are sold in paper cones as street snacks and although sometimes slightly bitter have a delicious earthy flavour. Amongst Sephardic Jews, lupins and chickpeas together with roasted nuts and seeds constitute a favourite appetiser for all kinds of gatherings or are eaten just as a snack to keep the hands and mouth busy. To prepare beans for snacks they are first soaked overnight in water. Once drained, they are either fried crisp in deep oil or roasted in the oven, just salted, or salted and peppered, and served warm. Lupins, like lentils and hard-boiled eggs, are served to mourners because they are 'round, don't have a mouth, therefore are struck dumb as a mourner'. Lupins, for an unknown reason, were also used to mark bread, as a way of identifying loaves in communal ovens.

The second in importance were vegetables which were grown in *miksha*. The word comes from the Hebrew *kishu* which means either courgette or cucumber and refers to a patch for growing all kinds of vegetables, especially those which grow spreading on the ground, such as melons, water melons, gourds and marrows. These vegetables were convenient for cooking, being suitable for a variety of techniques such as boiling or roasting whole. Gourds and pumpkins are especially versatile. Their flesh and seeds were eaten either raw or cooked and their tough outer skin could be dried to seal a variety of cooking and eating implements.

Bitter wild leaves were commonly eaten as an appetiser with bread. The list of bitter herbs used for Pesach includes: horseradish, chicory or dandelion, *tmkah* (chervil), *harhavina* (*Eryngium*) and *maror* (probably a kind of bitter coriander). As most of the leaves were bitter, a special cooking technique was developed as illustrated in the use of *luff* (*Arum palesetinum*): the leaves were first blanched and then chopped, probably mixed with flour or breadcrumbs, shaped into patties and fried.[16] A special clay strainer (*lapas*) with a long handle was kept to strain greens after blanching.

Young shoots, sprouts and buds of both wild and cultivated plants were used extensively. This allowed the farmer to utilise the crop from the moment it was useful; by clever husbanding one can stretch the productivity of a plant to its limit. Selective budding also encourages the growth of the plant. Strong-tasting sprouts like fenugreek, mustard, beans, *gargir* (watercress) and pepper wart (*Lepidum piper*) were used,[17] though it is not clear how. Some had harmful alkalis or acids which had to be removed before the sprout was ready for use. This was done by either blanching or pickling.

The word which the Mishnah uses for pickle is *kavush* which literally means 'pressed under weights'. Heavy stones were put on top of the vegetables to stop them from floating and being exposed to air. The technique refers to steeping ingredients in liquid, not necessarily to add flavour or to preserve them, but rather to remove bitterness and make them softer, thus reducing their bulk and making them easier to process. It is reasonable to assume that the steeping water contained some salt.

Pickling and preserving were an important part of the housewife's duty. The Mishnah indicates that all kinds of foods were preserved, from luxury items like *kur* (pickled palm shoots or heart)[18] to mundane salted green beans. It is likely that gourds, cucumbers, courgettes and melons were also pickled (fermented) in salt brine. Pickled capers were used widely. The caper bush, *tzalaf* (*Capparis spinosa*), grows profusely all over the Mediterranean and the Middle East where it is also employed as a protective fence because of its thorns and its ability to recuperate quickly when damaged. Young shoots, which have an attractive purple colour, are eaten fresh when their flavour resembles spicy cabbage. The leaves, fruit (*evyonoth*) and especially the flower buds are pickled, to be eaten on their own as an appetiser with drinks (as is still done in Greece) or added to cooked dishes.

The Mishnah describes many other kinds of vegetables, some of which are not precisely identified. Mushrooms and truffles (*shmarkaym*)[16] are mentioned, but probably refer to a truffle-like tuber which is found in desert areas. Artichoke (*kurnas* or *kirnas*) was used widely, both the unopened flowering globe and the stem and the leaves were eaten. Asparagus is mentioned,[17] but might be either a kind of cabbage or young shoots of *acoovit* (*Gundelia tournefortii*) which is a kind of thistle tasting vaguely like modern asparagus.[18]

FRUIT

As well as the Biblical dates, figs and grapes, of which a staggering variety was named, the Mishnah mentions apples, apricots, melons, watermelons, pears, peaches and pomegranates. Numerous varieties of wild fruits and berries are also mentioned.

The Mishnah also refers for the first time to *etrog* (citron) by name.[19] The Jews use citron in the religious celebration of Sukkoth, the Feast of the Tabernacle. It is thought to be the fruit of the 'Goodly' tree mentioned in the Bible. The cultivation of the citron in the holy land is thought to date back to the reign of King Solomon. Its seed, like that of the carob,*

* The carat, the measure of weight for precious stones, is based on carob seed.

was proposed as a standard measure. The citron is a large fruit growing on a lush, evergreen tree. The fruit is very sour but has a superb fragrance of citrus. It is still grown for its fragrant oil, its ornamental quality and for making a wonderful candied peel which is an important ingredient in rich fruit cakes and marmalade. Apicius[20] mentions two recipes for preserving citron. Grafting techniques produced larger, more perfect fruit and Jewish traders introduced it to Northern European countries throughout the 2000 years of diaspora. Records show that in the 15th century it was almost exclusively Jewish merchants who were granted permission to import citrus fruit to Germany, Prague and Austria.[21] Jews were also the main importers of citruses to Victorian England.[22] As a result, surnames which have a connection with citrus fruit such as Limon (lemon), Pomerance (orange), Citron, Zitrin or Citrine are still common amongst German and English Jews.

HERBS, SPICES AND SAUCES

Judging by the frequent mention of herbs, spices and strong-tasting sauces, one can assume that the food was very flavoursome. The Mishnah gives a long list of flavouring ingredients though many are difficult to identify. Among the most used herbs were coriander, dill, cumin, fennel (*Foeniculum vulgare*), anise seeds (*Pimpinella anisum*), caraway (*Carum carvi*) and celery (*Apium graveolens*). This group of fresh, spicy flavours together with a large variety of herbs of the *Labitatae* family (various thymes, marjorams, hyssops, sages and mints) represent the flavour of the Middle East and are used in both sweet and savoury dishes.

Spices were extensively used to give flavour and colour and for their preservative and anti-bacterial properties. The most commonly used were *kusht* (nutmeg or mace), *hems* or *hamam* (probably ginger or cinnamon), *rashy besamim* (cloves), black pepper and *chalath haria* (the dried leaves of safflower).* Asafoetida, a strong-smelling spice still used in Indian cooking, was usually mixed with water, wine or vinegar.

The Mishnah refers to a large number of sauces and flavourings, some of which were pre-mixed and preserved. Mustard was used frequently, probably mixed with egg yolk and flour. A mixture of water, oil and salt

---

* Okatzim 3:5. The herb is known in French as bastard saffron (*safran bâtard*) and all over the Middle East as 'poor man's saffron'. It is used instead of the expensive plant to give a yellow colour and a hay-like flavour. It is even cheaper and not as pungent as turmeric which is used for the same purpose.

and a sauce made from pounded garlic and young milky grain was used for dressing or dipping bread and vegetables. *Charoset*, the fruit dip eaten now only in Pesach, was probably eaten throughout the year as the Mishnah specifies that flour is not allowed just in a Pesach *charoset*. The list of foodstuffs forbidden during the Pesach reveals a fascinating variety of drinks, sauces and vinegars which were either imported or named after the country of their origin. The list includes: *kutach bavli* (Babylonian sauce, probably made from liquid left over from salted cheese, and possibly mixed with starch), *shechar maday* (Persian beer), vinegar from Edom (probably wine vinegar brewed with the addition of barley), *zitum mizri* (Egyptian beer with turmeric and salt). The most curious ingredient in the list is *amilan shel tabachim* or cook's starch, its origin and usage is unclear.

Both wine and vinegar were used in cooking. They were used as dips for bread, to flavour raw vegetables and as an addition to various stews. The Jews have a long history of wine and beer drinking, but cooking with wine was probably introduced by the Romans. The Romans developed a range of flavoured wines which were probably used exclusively for cooking. Although must (partially fermented grape juice) is not mentioned in the Mishnah, there is a reference to a vinegar made from unripe grapes (*stavaniyot*) and which was probably used unfermented. Barbara Flower in her translation of Apicius,[23] suggests that wines used for cooking were first reduced and then added to the dish just before serving. A large quantity of wine was probably reduced at one time and then kept for later use. The boiling down preserved the unripe grape juice and may have been used for cooking wine generally. Cooked and smoked wine are mentioned in the list of wines which were not allowed to be offered as a gift in the Temple.[24]

Sweet wines were made for drinking and probably used to add sweetness to dishes. *Eelyaston* (from *helios*, sun in Greek) wine was made from grapes which were harvested late and then left in the sun to sweeten. Wine was also sweetened by steeping carob and dried figs in it.[25] Generally wine was drunk before the meal with appetisers. It was also served after the meal. Wine for drinking was usually mixed with water, although mixing wine with honey, oil and pepper (*anomlin*)[26] is also mentioned. Old wine was considered to be of medical benefit.[27]

MEAT

As in Biblical times meat was still eaten rarely. The rich probably had meat every day or at least two to three times a week, but the majority of the population ate meat only on special occasions. If available it was eaten on the Sabbath, though this was not compulsory. Three main techniques were used for cooking meat: boiling, roasting and stewing. Boiling was used to cook old and tough parts. Instructions for cooking the Pascal lamb detail a variety of ways in which meat was roasted. Pomegranate wood skewers were used to suspend the Pascal lamb over the fire as pomegranate was considered the driest of woods. Not even a suspicion of moisture could be allowed to affect the roasting as boiling the lamb is strictly forbidden.[28] Roasting was also done on an *eskala*,[29] a grill or griddle which was probably made of clay and was used for cuts of the meat which are not easily skewered. The Mishnah indicates that meat was basted while cooking with wine, oil and fruit juice (sauce). Basting was not allowed on the Pascal lamb, but the same sauces were served as a dip to be eaten with the roasted meat.[30]

In stews, meat was used to give flavour to the dish and to produce enough juice to be eaten with bread. The sauce (*kiffah*) of the stew was as important as the meat itself. A basic mixture of onions, garlic and other strong flavourings, like leeks and shallots,[31] was used, probably first fried in oil to achieve the favourite caramelised brown sauce. The meat was then added and simmered slowly for a long time. Garlic was used extensively as it was believed to have health-giving properties. It was especially recommended to be eaten on the Friday (the customary day for copulation) as it was supposed to have a beneficial affect on the quality of semen.[32]

Meat stews were also flavoured with wine and cooked with different kinds of beans and grain. There was also a special meat stew with onions and eggs[33] which was cooked for the Sabbath. The Mishnah stipulates that for the dish to be allowed on the Sabbath it has to be fully cooked on Friday, but may be 'buried' in a cooling oven or covered (like hay cooking) and kept hot until it is needed at Saturday lunch. The Mishnah refers to the dish as *hamin* (hot or warm).[34] The Mishnah recommends a list of materials which are allowed for covering the *hamin*, including skins, wool, old cloth, feathers, dry grass, flax, pillows and featherbeds.[35] The problem of keeping food hot for Saturday, when fire lighting is not allowed, was ingeniously solved by the citizens of Tiberias. They constructed a network of ducts to bring hot water from the local hot springs to their homes. The Mishnah permits this arrangement for heating but forbids it for cooking.[36]

The exact origin of the *hamin*, which Heine calls divine,[37] is unknown, though some say that its history goes as far back as ancient Egypt, which is very likely. The same kind of technique is used all over the world for it is based on a sound peasant logic which stems from knowledge of how to use food and energy resources properly. A short burst of high heat brings the dish to the boil, after which the cooking is done by the energy which remains in the oven after the fire has been extinguished. Alternatively the dish is insulated so that the initial energy is captured and keeps the dish at a certain temperature until needed. The *hamin* belongs to a vast family of dishes which also includes the American Boston baked beans, French *cassoulet*, and the Spanish *cocido*.

Basically the *hamin* is a dish of beans and grains which is flavoured with meat and cooked gently for a long time. Because of the length of cooking, the meat used can be cheap, gelatinous and tough. The quantity of meat can vary without affecting the flavour of the dish. *Hamin* is still cooked and has remained practically unchanged for the last 2000 years and probably longer. Until recently it was, for most Jews, the taste of Sabbath. It is served by all classes and crosses all barriers of ethnic origin, being eaten by Sephardi and Ashkenazi alike. The name may differ but the basic technique remains the same. The Ashkenazi call it *chulent, cholnt* or *shalet*. The Sephardic Jews call it *hamin, haminado* (Mediterranean), *matphonia* (Kurdistan), *shahina* and *deffina* (North Africa), *haris* (Yemenite) or *tabit* (Iraqi). Some of the names indicate a technique — *deffina* and *matphonia* probably come from the Hebrew *dafan* which means 'to press to the wall'. This alludes to the technique of sealing or plastering the opening of the oven with wet clay. Most of the names originate from the Hebrew word for hot (*ham*). The words *chulent* or *shalet* are probably derivations from the old French word *chald* — in modern French *chaud*, warm. There is a charming if unlikely theory that the word *cholent* comes from the Yiddish *shul* (synagogue) *ende* — indicating the time the dish was served, at the end of the synagogue service or Saturday lunch.

Pascal Perez-Rubin in her book *Israeli Flavour*[38] observes that the main difference between Sephardi and Ashkenazi *hamins* is that in Europe the pulses used are mainly beans (*bebalach*) such as lima, navy or haricot beans while in the Sephardi *hamin* chickpeas are used.[39] There are two more differences. The Sephardi kitchen uses mostly wholewheat grain while in the Ashkenazi pearl and pot barley are customary. The Ashkenazi use beef, duck, goose and *schmaltz* (fat); the Sephardi use beef, mutton, chicken and oil.

Fruit and vegetables are usually included in the *hamin*. In the Ashkenazi *hamin* this means prunes and potatoes. In the Sephardi *hamin* the variety is greater. *Hamins* are made wonderfully fragrant with quince and dried apricots and sweetened with sweet potatoes and pumpkin. In addition to adding flavour and sweetness, fruit and vegetables are also used to stretch the dish and replace expensive meat. Yet the most favoured 'extensions', both in the East and the West, are the numerous dumplings, stuffings and savoury croquettes which are added. Kurdistani Jews prepare a special cracked wheat and semolina dumpling stuffed with beef (*zbeybye*). The Moroccan Jews serve a wonderfully fragrant large dumpling made with a mixture of ground nuts, minced lamb or beef and breadcrumbs flavoured with sugar, black pepper, mace, ginger, cinnamon and nutmeg.

There is no doubt that the most popular addition is a pudding stuffed into a beef casing. *Derma* or intestine is the Jewish haggis. In the East it is usually filled with minced meat and rice and flavoured with spices such as turmeric, pepper, cinnamon and nutmeg. In Central and Eastern Europe the pudding is known as *kishke* and is traditionally stuffed with a mixture of flour, breadcrumbs (*matzah* meal in Pesach), boiled potatoes and raw chopped chicken, goose or duck fat. It is usually flavoured only with salt and pepper, although parsley and dill are sometimes added. The same pudding is made using the neck skin of chickens, duck or geese as casing, in which case it is known as *helzel* (neck in Yiddish)).

Wholewheat berries and rice are used in many of the Eastern *hamins* which make them lighter and less stodgy than their European cousins. It is interesting to note that when the *hamin* contains both pulses and grain, the latter are usually cooked separately either in a cloth or a pudding basin, a habit which might stem from the cultural reluctance to mix different kind of ingredients.

The inclusion of eggs, which is also mentioned in the Mishnah, is essential in Eastern and especially in Mediterranean *hamins*. The eggs are supposed to symbolise the continuous mourning for the destruction of the Temple. Symbols apart, they were included to stretch the stew when meat was scarce. The eggs are added raw and cooked slowly, absorbing the flavour of the stew and becoming brown and fragrant with a soft melting texture.

Especially in large communities the *hamin* was cooked in the communal oven. This was sealed on Friday afternoon, to be opened by a non-Jew on Saturday after the end of the morning synagogue service. The gathering took place around the communal oven and the young carried the *hamin* pot home. Carrying is considered work and therefore was forbidden on the Sabbath. This gave rise to one of those ingenious Jewish solutions. The town, district or village was surrounded by a string or tape thus making it a unit, like one household. Carrying within the borders of a household is permitted on the Sabbath and therefore the *hamin* could be carried home.

FISH

Although fish is mentioned in the Bible there is no reference to the eating of fish except in the lament of the Israelites in the desert about the fish they consumed in Egypt. It is possible that although fish was eaten it was not considered an important food. There is no mention, for example, of fish in the list of foods eaten in King Solomon's court. It is also possible that the Jews, until the exile, had the same reluctance to eat fish as most nomadic people.[40] It seems that fish didn't become an important part of the Jewish diet until the settlement in Babylon when it became almost a must at the Sabbath table.[41]

The Talmud describes several ways of fishing in the Lake of Galilee (Lake Kinereth). Fish were caught with a wooden fishing rod, in several types of nets, in trap-like fish ponds and in specially woven fish traps which were suspended behind a boat. The Talmud warns against the use of long traps as they disrupted lake traffic when boats got entangled in the long ropes.[42] Fish was also caught at the Hulla, a swampy lake north of the Sea of Galilee, and along the mostly gentile Mediterranean shore. Supplying fresh fish to the inland Jewish areas, especially Jerusalem, was impossible as it took up to three days to make the difficult journey from the coastal plains to Jerusalem. Nevertheless there are references to fresh fish arriving in Jerusalem from the Jordan river packed in leaves and straw. The inland population relied mainly on preserved and salted fish, and processing became an important industry in Jewish Galilee. This is reflected in place names such as Bethsaida (the fishing place) and Tarichaea (fish).

Salt fish is mentioned in a discussion dealing with the kashruth of dishes cooked by non-Jews. The rabbis decreed that salt fish was kosher even if it had been made by gentiles. This is because salt fish is not cooked and therefore is not considered as *bishuley acum* (gentile cooking). This decree had an important effect on the eating habits of the Jewish Ashkenazi diaspora as it allowed the Jews to eat salt and brined herrings even if these were not made by Jews or under Jewish supervision.

The Mishnah mentions a few kinds of salt fish: new salt, salt fish which had been salted for more than a year (*yashan*, old), small fish (probably sardines, called *kulyas ha'ispanin*, which some translators refer to as Spanish trout and some as Spanish tuna) and an Egyptian speciality which was pieces of salted fish which were imported in wooded boxes.[43] To cook the salt fish it was first soaked in water to remove excess saltiness and then either eaten uncooked or poached in warm water.[44] Another method was to grill the salt fish wrapped in a piece of paper (*en papillote*) which was previously soaked in water to prevent the fish burning and sticking to the grill.[45]

Among the pickled fish specialities the Mishnah mentions several fish sauces, although the way they were used is unclear. It is probable that these sauces were a variety of the Roman *liquamen*, a fermented fish sauce which was used to flavour all manner of dishes[46] and as a dip for bread or as flavouring to raw vegetables. *Tzir* was also made from the pickling liquid of locusts.[47] Locusts, like fish, were allowed to be cooked and served with milk products.

Fresh fish cooking is rarely mentioned. Nevertheless the Mishnah gives several ways of cooking fish. It could be coated with egg, probably after cooking to give it gloss, or coated with flour and fried in oil. The most intriguing fish dishes I found reference to were two dishes of stuffed fish: one using a mixture of crumbed, hard-boiled egg and the other a stuffing of mashed or chopped leek.[48]

OLIVES

The Bible numbers the olive[49] among the most important blessings of the promised land, the 'land of olive oil and honey' (Deuteronomy 8:8). Olive trees certainly dominated the landscape, clinging to the stony slopes of the Galilean hills. It is no surprise that the tree has gained a mysterious, symbolic and wise reputation. In the story of the flood, when God wants to indicate that he is at peace with man, he sends as his messenger a dove with an olive branch in its beak. When Joshua was planning the conquest of Israel, according to legend, he set ten rules, one of which was that olive trees should not be destroyed like all the other trees. The olive tree became a symbol of fertility, peace and continuity.

The origin of the tree is unclear, but most scholars agree that it was first cultivated in Syria and Palestine.[50] The tree, because of its deep rooting system, can survive in the most difficult conditions. It retains water with a shield of leathery leaves which are dark and shiny on the outer side and silver grey on the inner side. Being evergreen, it provides shelter all year round. The olive tree can live for generations.

Economically, the olive was the most important crop in the land. Israel was famous for the quality of its olive oil which was used not only for eating but also was essential to any religious ceremony, both for anointing and lighting. The skills which were developed to produce the special quality of sacramental oils encouraged the development of a lively industry which supplied local demands and also exports to the far corners of the world. King Solomon paid with olive oil for the wood he used to build the Temple (Kings 1, 5:25). He also used olive wood to build special doors in the Temple. Olive wood is especially beautiful in its marking and is hard and durable, making it ideal for carving. It was not allowed as firewood at the Temple and was used for fire only under severe restrictions.

The Talmud gives detailed instructions about maintenance, ways of grafting, growing, harvesting and using the olive tree. Instructions for the extraction of olive oil in the Talmud are numerous. The quality of the oil was not only judged by the quality of the olives but also by the way these were gathered and the technique of oil extraction. Olives for the best quality oil used only in the Temple were gathered almost ripe by hand. For the second quality the olives were shaken off the tree. For all other qualities the olives were beaten off the tree with long wooden poles. The lowest quality came from olives which fell naturally and were gathered off the ground. For the best quality oil the olives were crushed in a pestle and mortar. In Hebrew the word *katit* (crushed) is still used to describe best quality 'extra virgin' olive oil. The second quality was milled in a stone mill and then extracted to different grades of oil mainly for cooking and bathing. The poorest quality was extracted from the pulp of the olives, boiled in water and skimmed from the surface. The oil was used mainly for soup-making and domestic lighting. The exhausted pulp and the stones were finally used as fuel.

Olive oil was essential for maintaining personal hygiene and was used as a cleanser, softener and moisturising agent. The olive's connection with bath houses (*hamam*) was not only hygienic; special salted olives were softened in vinegar and sold in the bath houses, to encourage drinking. Oil[51] was an essential ingredient in the kitchen. Bread dipped in oil or vinegar was the staple food and it was eaten mainly for breakfast. In descriptions of the preparation of sacrificial food we read recipes for oil-rich cakes and bread. Oil was also mixed with fish sauce, probably to soften the concentrated flavour of the sauce. It was used to marinate and baste meats and added to boiled or roasted meats before serving. It was also indispensable in vegetable cooking and, together with water, salt and vinegar, for dressing all manner of salads.

The olive fruit was eaten both raw and processed. The poor often ate olives as their only other ingredient to accompany bread. Some species of olives when fully ripe can be eaten raw. Although bitter they leave a wonderfully fruity sweet sensation in the mouth. Normally the olive was preserved by brining or dry salting. Another method was to bury them, probably with salt, until they softened and lost some of their bitterness.

BREAD AND CAKE

Bread and grain dishes were still the most important items in the Mishnahic diet, eaten by poor and rich alike. A poor farmer's diet consisted mainly of bread dipped in vinegar and oil, sometimes accompanied by olives, cheese and raw vegetables. Symbolically the bread became an indispensable part of religious observance. Bread together with wine symbolised the sacrifice in the Temple. Of these two, bread is far more important. Indeed, when wine is unavailable it can be replaced by bread.

Honeys were used to sweeten and flavour a wide range of sweet cakes. The Mishnah lists[52] four kinds of sweet cakes. *Sufganin* (sponges) were probably made of a soft yeast mixture and were baked in a slow oven.[53] *Dovshan* (*dvash* means honey) was a honeyed cookie which was either kneaded with or boiled in honey. *Eskrytyn* was probably a kind of a thin cake or wafer which was baked on a pan or griddle and soaked afterwards with honey. The name of the fourth cake, *hallahth hmashereth*, probably indicates that the dough was poached or boiled in water in a special pan. Although proving the connection between them might be historically difficult or presumptuous, traditional cakes and sweetmeats which are made by the same technique and include the same kind of ingredients are served both by Ashkenazi and Sephardi Jews today.

One of the most curious dishes mentioned in the Mishnah is *knuvkaote* (the K is pronounced). It is probably the first time in history that a pasta-like dish appears in writing. Maimonides explains that it was made from bread dough which was kneaded with oil. After drying or baking, the bread was crumbled (and dried again) and used to make soups or softened and given to children as a porridge. This technique is similar to *tarkana* or *kishk*, which is made from sun-dried, pellet-shaped pieces of flour and burgul dough which are crumbled and made into tasty porridge-like soups. *Tarkana* can be easily bought in any Middle Eastern or Greek shops.

CHICKEN AND EGGS

Chicken is not mentioned in the Bible, although the *koreh*[54] is usually identified with a desert bird of the chicken family which was hunted in the wild. We know that eggs were eaten as the kosher laws instruct that only eggs of permitted birds are allowed. It is certain that the Hebrews encountered chickens in Egypt where they were kept for decorative or ceremonial reasons. Only ducks and geese were kept for food. It was only after the Babylonian exile that chicken started to play an important part in both Jewish lore and kitchen.

Both the Babylonians and Persians believed that chickens, especially cocks, had mystical powers. According to the ancient Persians, the cock was created to chase away the darkness associated with evil. The rooster with his special power over evil was an ideal subject for *kapparot* (expiatory sacrifice) practised on the Eve of Yom Kippur, the Day of Atonement. The tradition of *kapparot* stems from the ancient custom of *saeer la'azazel* or 'scapegoat'. This animal was burdened with man's sins and sent to the wilderness. The tradition of *kapparot* is still practised today amongst the very orthodox. On the eve of Yom Kippur a white cock* for males and a white hen for females are ceremonially waved three times around the heads of each member of the family. The fowl, which in the past was thrown into a river or released in the wilderness, is ritually slaughtered and either used by the family or given to charity.

The Mishnah indicates that chicken was eaten as there is a prohibition against eating chicken with milk products though it points out that chicken can be placed with cheese on the same table.[55] Although chicken was eaten, it was probably raised mainly for egg production. The importance of the chicken as a supplier of meat and cooking fat in the Jewish European kitchen probably did not occur until the late 14th century.

Hens' eggs take on a curious dual role in Jewish food symbolism,

---

* The tradition of using white cocks is probably very old and of pagan origin. The Mishnah forbids the selling of white cocks to non-Jews for fear they might be used for pagan rites (Avoda Zarah 1:5). Incidentally, the devil, according to Jewish lore, has a rooster's feet.

representing both life and death. Raw egg is a symbol of fertility and life and is given to newly wed women and newly born babies, especially girls, as a protection against evil and to guarantee their fertility. Boiled (dead) eggs and more specifically eggs roasted (*megulgalot*, rolled) in hot ashes, symbolise death and mourning and are eaten on return from funerals. They are also eaten on the ninth day of the Hebrew month, *off Av*, the traditional date for the destruction of the Second Temple. Only eggs of kosher birds are permitted and considered *parve* (neutral). They can therefore be used both for meat and milk dishes unless they are fertilised and have a blood spot. It is the duty of the cook to check each egg before use.

The Mishnah mentions several ways of cooking eggs. It differentiates between soft-boiled eggs or *tarmita*,[56] which were considered a drink and were probably used for medical purposes, and hard-cooked eggs or *megulgalot*, which were considered food. To cook the egg hard it was rolled in hot ashes or buried in very hot sand.[57] Eggs were also cooked or scrambled in a pot and mixed with spices and oil.[58] Hot, cooked ingredients were dipped in egg probably to give them an appetising gloss. Eggs were also included in a special Sabbath meat stew. The Mishnah also indicates that eggs were sold as snacks together with dried fruit by drink vendors in markets and bath houses.[59]

6

ALMONDS, SPICE AND SUNSHINE
Sephardi Food

RESEARCH MATERIAL on Sephardi cultural subjects is scarce. This is due to several reasons of which the most important is the deep prejudice against it borne by the dominant Ashkenazi culture; in a recent programme about British Jewry[1] the vital role of the Sephardi community on Anglo/Jewish life was completely ignored. Jewish cookery books published in Britain, North America and, more surprisingly, Israel ignored the existence of the Sephardi kitchen until the late 1950s.

Who are the Sephardim? Jewish communities existed outside Israel since the reign of King Solomon. The Bible hints at the existence of trade delegations to Spain and the coastal urban centres of North Africa; the Mishnah mentions both Italy and Spain. These ancient communities of Jewish Palestinian émigrés and converted Jews were continually revitalised by new waves of Jews from Palestine; diaspora Jews used to come back to Jerusalem to worship at the Temple, to marry and to be buried.

After the establishment of the Second Temple another community came into being, formed by some of the Babylonian exiles who chose to stay and start a strong and influential centre which until the 14th century played a major role in the religious life of all Jews.

The destruction of the Second Temple in 70AD sent forth yet another wave of immigrants which were absorbed by the already thriving diaspora communities.

The story of the Yemenite Jews is much more romantic. There is evidence that converted, warring Jewish tribes roamed Yemen and the Arabian peninsula well into the Islamic period, surviving until the first quarter of the 6th century. Those Jews are the ancestors of the present-day Yemenite community, and probably of the Ethiopian community also.

Yet the most remarkable tale is the history of the true Sephardim, the glorious Jewish community in Spain which flourished, on and off, until their expulsion exactly 500 years ago. After 1492, the expelled Spanish Jewish community spread to all the centres of the known world with their particular brand of nobility and wisdom.

Sephardi Jews share the fact that the majority of them lived in countries which were at one time or other under the influence of Islam. Islam and Judaism have a lot in common; both sprang from a Middle Eastern nomadic pastoral culture. They share many attitudes and systems.

The Jews were at home in the exciting scientific and intellectual hothouse of the ancient Middle East. When, at the beginning of the 7th century, Islam started to spread, Europe, which was still suffering from the chaos brought about by the deterioration of the Roman Empire and the setting of the Dark Ages, was easy prey for the warring Arab tribes. United under the banner of Islam these tribes conquered the whole of the Middle East, parts of Europe, all of the southern shore of the Mediterranean, and most of the Iberian peninsula. Although Islam did not accept Jews gladly, a certain *status quo* was achieved. Jews were tolerated, partly due to the similarity of their religious beliefs, and because of their similar ethnic and cultural background. Being stateless, Judaism, unlike Christianity, did not constitute a political and military threat to Islam. Moreover, the Arabs also understood the economic importance of the global trading and familial network which had been established by the Jewish community. Although Jews under Islam suffered periods of anti-Jewish activity, restrictive legislation and expulsion, living amongst Muslims gave the Jews a degree of freedom not experienced in Eastern and Central Europe.[2]

The success of the Arab and Jewish traders brought a general prosperity which manifested itself in a surge of intellectual, scientific and commercial activity. Eastern Jewish communities flourished, achieving new frontiers in philosophy, science, medicine and theology. Prosperity led to the establishment of a stratum of solid upper-class families who were connected globally.

Throughout the Arab world Jewish traders specialised in dealing with money, textiles, slaves, precious stones and metals. This led to the establishment of an artisan class which produced silver and gold jewellery, religious and secular ware, manuscripts and other *objets d'art*. These Jews also imported and exported durable foodstuffs, such as preserves, spices, scented oils and dried food, which were important for their religious observance.

The Jewish involvement in the movement of these foodstuffs was essential. Strict dietary laws demanded that food should be supervised, sold and transported under constant Jewish surveillance for fear of contamination. It was safer, if not obligatory, to buy food from a Jewish trader.

Spices were essential not only for achieving the highly spiced food favoured by the Jews, but also for the celebration of the Sabbath.[3] Until the opening of the trading routes by the Crusaders, Arab and Jewish merchants were the only suppliers of exotic spices to Europe. Jewish and Arab travellers amassed a vast amount of documented information (mostly during medieval times) which benefited the development of European culture. The constant travel also helped the Jews to further their global community; each part was aware of the other's development.

Travelling was also important for the religious life of the Jewish communities. Jewish religious study is done by repetition of old writings combined with a process of complicated, logical arguments and interpretations which illuminate and explain the writing. The process is called *pilpol* which means, literally, to add pepper, to spice. This process demanded a constant communication between the old and important theological centres of Mesopotamia and Israel and the emerging centres of Spain and elsewhere. The emphasis on study meant that a large majority of Jews was literate and numerate. Arabic was a convenient common language as it shares roots with Hebrew, the language of the Bible, and Aramaic, the language of the Talmud. These factors gave the Jews, as historian Paul Johnson observes, 'the ability to compute exchange rates, to write business letters and, perhaps even more important, the ability to get it delivered along their wide-spun family and religious networks'.[4]

For convenience I divided the Sephardi community into four bands of influence: Mesopotamian (comprising Iraq, Kurdistan, Syria and Persia); Arabian (Yemen, Aden and Ethiopia); North African (Morocco, Algeria, Tunis and Libya); and Iberian (which includes the northern shores of the Mediterranean (Italy, Greece, Turkey, and to a lesser extent Bulgaria and Yugoslavia, and all the Mediterranean islands).

PHILOSOPHERS AND BREWERS
Mesopotamia

For more than 1000 years the Mesopotamian Jewish community was the shining light of Jewish thought and knowledge. Yet the urban centres of Sura and Pumbeditha produced not only great philosophers; one of the greatest scholars, Rabbi Papa (375–420AD), made his fortune brewing beer.

The community was presided over by an 'exilarch', Rosh Galuta, who was, according to legend, a descendant of the House of David. These royal figureheads used to maintain a princely court. They certainly had the raw ingredients to maintain a sumptuous table as the whole of the twin river valley was an endless source of the richest raw material.

The Tigris and Euphrates were teeming with fresh fish. When stocks were depleted a network of fish farms was developed which specialised in fattening fish in man-made ponds. The orchards were full of exquisite fruit, vegetables and herbs. Exotic spices and cooking techniques, together with new philosophies and new scientific thoughts, arrived regularly from the East.

Historical evidence shows that Mesopotamian Jews travelled as far as India and China. We know little about the food of the Chinese Jews, but have more information about the foods eaten by *Bene Israel*, the 'sons of Israel' or the Jews of Bombay. In an article about Indian breads[5] the author mentions a special Jewish *roti*, a bread called *yehudi roti* or *khameeri roti*, which was introduced into India by Iraqi Jews. It is a thin, large, round pitta, which is baked in a *tandur*. Although most of these Jews have now migrated to Israel, this *roti* is still baked by the Muslim bakers who bought the Jewish bakeries. Moreover, the tradition of not baking the Jewish *roti* on the Sabbath is still maintained by the new owners.

Although I have not found any written evidence of medieval Middle Eastern Jewish food[6], judging by the Arab cookery books which started appearing in the 10th and 11th centuries they ate in a most sophisticated and magnificent manner. Although the food of the original Arab tribes was primitive nomad and peasant food, it underwent a radical transformation after being combined with the magnificence of Persian court cuisine. Muslim manuscripts mention fragrant dishes of aubergine and mutton, light starch puddings made from wheat and flavoured with the essence of pomegranates, oranges or roses. Delicate rice *pilavs* and sweet, fragrant meat and fruit stews were plentiful, all of which are still part of that cuisine today.

Yet for me the most remarkable feature of the Mesopotamian food is the imaginative way of cooking the staple rice in Persia and wheat, both burgul and *g'risha* (wheat groats), in Kurdistan. These were eaten either simply cooked to a gruel and served accompanied with fresh herbs, vegetables, fresh yoghurt and curds or made into complicated dishes. The Persians specialise in light, fragrant rice *pilavs* while the Kurds and Iraqi Jews have a profusion of recipes for wheat *pilavs*, *kibbehs* (wheat dumplings) and wheat salads.

POETS AND WARRIORS
Yemenite Food

Although probably as old as the Mesopotamian community, the Yemenite community was influenced by a different set of conditions. Arabian mythology is full of recorded stories of fierce and successful warrior tribes who adopted Judaism around the 3rd century AD. These tribes remained autonomous until the advance of the Byzantines, who with the help of the Abyssinians conquered some of the Jewish tribes. There is evidence that some of the Abyssinian warriors adopted the Jewish religion and they are probably the ancestors of the Falashi community. The Yemenite tribes suffered a further setback when, in the 7th century, they encountered the full impact of Islamic fervour.

Being desert people their food was basic. Staples were mainly made out of grains, wheat, both cracked and burgul — *haris* — which was served with *samna*, clarified butter. For breakfast different kinds of pittas were served to be eaten with *samna* and *hilbah*, a paste made from soaked fenugreek seeds which, as well as being nourishing, were considered essential for good health. Meat, mainly mutton and goat, was eaten on all celebratory occasions, and lamb and kid were especially favoured.

For the Sabbath a special yeasted bread called a *kubana* is made. It is cooked overnight, like *hamin*, and moistened with a large amount of fat. The result is a spongy mixture which resembles a cross between bread and a suet pudding. For Saturday lunch, the Yemenite serve a soup like *hamin*, mainly made of wheat and cheap cuts of meat such as head, tails and trotters. This simple basic food contrasts with the wealthy cultural life enjoyed by the Yemenite community. From the Yemen comes some of the best classical poetry in the Hebrew language and superlatively gifted silversmiths.

COOKING IN THE SUN
North African Food

In contrast to the desert qualities of Yemenite cooking, the North African communities of Morocco, Algeria, Tunis and Libya developed a cuisine which embodied all the colour and sunshine of that part of the Mediterranean. Strictly speaking, it is wrong to mention these four culinary traditions together as they represent two different bands of culinary influence. Morocco, Algeria and Tunis were influenced by France, while Libya was under Italian influence.

The most remarkable feature of the North African kitchen is the imaginative and varied use of vegetables. They appear in a large number of cooked and fresh salads and in countless crustless pies which Claudia Roden calls *eggah* and which are known under a variety of names (*elmachmar, elmegina, kuku* or *feritada*). These are mixtures of cooked vegetables and sometimes meats which are combined with eggs and baked in the oven until set. These dishes solve a number of particularly Jewish problems. Unless they contain either cheese or meat they can be served with both, or be the base for a milky dinner. It is also cheap as it can be starched easily by including bread, breadcrumbs or *matzah* meal.

The North African Jewish communities specialised in distilling alcohol, an occupation which was forbidden to Muslims. For generations they distilled alcoholic drinks called *boukah* or *mechaia*, made from fermented figs and dates.

The North African communities, especially the Moroccan community, celebrate a special holiday, the Maymoonah. The origin of the holiday is disputed. Some say that the name comes from the Hebrew word *emoonah*, meaning faith or belief, and it is celebrated as an affirmation of tradition. Others suggest that it is a commemorative day to the Cordoba-born Moshe Ben-Maimon, or Maimonides, who settled for a while in Fez in Morocco in 1160.

The one-day holiday starts on the last night of Pesach. It is celebrated by maintaining an open house in which the centrepiece is a sumptuous table groaning under the weight of dishes, mainly made with milk, butter, honey, dried fruit, wheaten flour and a special milky white couscous.

The Maymoonah gained an added impetus in Israel. It became the holiday on which the North African community affirms its cultural identity. It is now celebrated with public and private picnics in which gargantuan quantities of barbecued meats and salads are consumed in the open accompanied by singing and dancing.

THE GOLDEN KITCHEN
Spain

The importance of the Sephardi community was not only in its giving of a generic name to all Eastern Jews, it also played a vital role in the political, financial and religious life of the international Jewry. Its demise came with the general shift of power from the south to the north. The Jewish community which survived successfully the transition from Islam to Christianity in the 12th century AD was less fortunate after the expulsion by Ferdinand and Isabella in 1492. This coincided with a spate of expulsions which occurred between 1000AD and 1500AD all over Europe, and forced the Jews once again to pack up and start reshaping the map of Jewish Europe. The Spanish or Sephardi community managed to survive the expulsion rather well, establishing and reinforcing existing communities in Amsterdam, Germany, France, North Africa, Turkey, Greece, Egypt, Palestine and Damascus, some of them travelling as far as India and China.

As well as a common religion these communities shared a language — Ladino or Judezmo, which is based on old Spanish combined with Hebrew and Arabic words and written in Hebrew cursive.

It is safe to assume that during their Golden Age the Sephardi community kept a sumptuous and sophisticated table. A hint to the elaboration of this table can be found in a recipe, probably of medieval origin, which appeared in Lady Montefiore's book *The Jewish Manual*.[7] *Bola d'amore* is a complicated and rich sweet made from layers of almond paste flavoured with orange flower water, vermicelli-like egg threads cooked in boiling syrup, and citron cut into thin slices. All these ingredients are piled into a handsome, high cone shape which is then put into a gentle oven until it becomes a little set, with the last layer slightly crisp. It is then decorated with fresh myrtle leaves and gold and silver leaf.

Another prominent feature of the Sephardi kitchen is the profusion of little pies called *burekas, burekitos, shamizikos* or *kezadas*. These pies are usually made very small, from a variety of pastries; the most commonly used is filo. They can contain sweet or savoury fillings and appear in a large number of shapes.

Although ignored for a long time, there are signs that the Sephardi kitchen and culture is once again beginning to claim its rightful place within the global Jewish community.

7

ASHKENAZI FOOD

THE ORIGINS of the Jewish community in Central and Eastern Europe are unclear. The core of the community probably consisted of Jewish merchant settlements which were established during the Roman occupation. We know of large settlements in the Russian Crimea which date to the 1st or 2nd century AD. At the same time Jewish colonies were also established around the Rhine valley and along the Elbe river. The Jews probably started moving into Eastern Europe to escape the Crusaders who were exterminating anyone who was not Christian on their way to the Holy Land. There is an old legend which associates the name Poland with Jewish origins. The story tells of a group of refugees arriving during the time of the Black Death (1348AD) at an unknown territory east of Germany. They heard a voice telling them in Hebrew *Po-Lin* (rest here). *Polin* is also the Hebrew name for Poland. As well as such refugees the Jewish European community probably also absorbed converted Jews after the collapse of the Jewish khazar kingdom in 1016AD. The khazars were a collection of nomadic tribes, probably of Asian origin, who adopted the Jewish faith and lived as a self-determined kingdom for nearly 300 years in the fertile area between the Caspian and the Black seas.[1]

Life in Christian Europe was difficult for the Jews. Besides their general 'foreignness' they also had to cope with the stigma of being 'Christ killers'. As a result both of choice and necessity the Jews specialised in commerce and money lending. They were considered useful as long as their services were required and were therefore given shelter and a certain autonomy by interested rulers. However, whenever the debts became too large or there was popular unrest, the easiest solution was to turn upon the Jews. These sporadic, but constant upheavals meant that every few generations Jews were forced to pack their bags and look for a new shelter. This continuous mixing created a pan-European Jewish stock which, although influenced by some of the host country's customs, nevertheless maintained a defined, overall 'European Jewishness'.

One of the strongest manifestations of the European Jewishness was a common language — Yiddish — which was used with very few variations by all European Jews. Yiddish is a colloquial language derived from Middle High German with the addition of Hebrew elements and written in Hebrew characters. In each new setting elements from the local vernacular have been absorbed and modified to suit the Yiddish idiom.[2]

By the end of the 15th century there were Jewish settlements or ghettos in most major European towns in which many Jews, either out of choice or edict, lived. Yet the majority of the Jewish population lived in small rural communities known as *shtetls*, a diminutive of the Yiddish word *shtat* or town. The word also donates an environment and a cultural identity which was shared by most European Jews.[3]

One can safely assume that the origins of the Ashkenazi kitchen, like those of the community, lie in the rich and sophisticated kitchens of the Mediterranean Jewish community. From there, via medieval Germany, this food spread all over Europe. The German influence can be clearly traced both in recipes and in names of dishes such as *kugel*, *kneidel*, *chulent* and *eingemacht*, to name but a few. It is true that within the Ashkenazi community food differs, not only from country to country but also between towns and rural communities. Yet the following will describe a common element which defines a recognisable Ashkenazi food tradition shared amongst all European Jewry.

As everywhere else religious observance and study were the contributing factors in the life of the Jewish community. Study was the most treasured of the Jewish pursuits; the ambition to excel in study was instilled in every male baby from the moment he was born and led to an extraordinarily high literacy rate. The Jewish image captured in the holy writings belonged to a sunnier climate, to a land of milk and honey, olive oil, fatted lambs, dates, spices and figs, a very different world from the European reality of pork, rye and cabbage. The impact of this Biblical imagery is reflected superbly in a passage by the Israeli national poet Bialik,[4] who describes a boy sitting reciting sacrificial laws and superimposes this with memories of his mother's kitchen before a holiday:

> When I come to the description of head and forbidden fats, intestines and hind quarters washed in water, wrung necks and spilled blood, imme-

diately my mind drifts to a different image, mother's kitchen on the eve of a holiday. Mother and the maid, wearing aprons with their sleeves rolled up to their elbows, standing armed with long wooden pins rolling dough on the noodle board, beating eggs in mixing bowls, pouring sparkling, bright oil on to mounds of semolina . . . The cat is also there, hiding behind the salting board, eyes fixed on the 'best part of the liver', the kidneys, gizzards and chicken legs which lie in koshering salt in a pool of pink blood . . . from time to time the maid throws bits — intestines, a white fish bladder or a feather covered crop of chicken and such like to the cat, which momentarily distracts the cat from its watch. Pestle and mortar ring out in rhythmical harmony 'pound well, pound well'. To my nostrils wafts the good, soul reviving aroma of baking, the 'offering of semolina mingled with oil' and yolks of eggs; in my ears rings the sound of the hissing and plopping pan-cakes, sizzling in boiling oil, the same noises heard when the 'mingled with oil' offering was burnt in the temple. All other manners of delicacies come to my mind, the turnovers, the crumbles, the *farfels* which are made into puddings, *knuvkaote* with raisins, flavoured with turmeric and cinnamon . . . the word mingle tingles my appetite until my temples hurt and my cheeks are sucked in: 'meeeen-gle' . . . My mouth fills with saliva and my thumb, as if it has a life of its own, finds itself between my teeth.[5]

Life for the European Jews was a continuous battle for survival. The constant harassment by their Christian neighbours forced them into isolation. Home, within the boundaries of the ghetto and surrounded by the family, was the only place a Jew could feel safe. Home symbolised a haven, and tribal memories of constant hunger made food an obsession around which domestic life centred. 'To give food symbolizes not only maternal love but also the friendliness of the household to its visitors. Not to offer a guest "honour" in the form of food, or at least a glass of tea, would be equivalent to rebuff, and not to eat in another person's home would be equally bad manners.'[6]

Children, the hope of the nation, were of the utmost importance; their needs came first, taking preference even above those of the head of the household. They were fed constantly and food was used to pacify, encourage and reward. Food was a way of communicating feelings, giving security and expressing love. Well-stocked larders meant security and prosperity. The Jewish concept of a loved, healthy child was a fat child. Fat was considered the best protection against ill-health. It also protected from the evil eye and was considered to be an important reserve for difficult times. In a book published in 1939 Sir Jack Drummond, the father of modern British nutrition,[7] makes several interesting observations on the attitude of European Jewish immigrants to food in general and to the feeding of their children in particular. Summing up a health survey done amongst working-class Leeds schoolchildren in 1902, which found marked differences between Jewish children and their Gentile contemporaries, he concludes:

> It is certain that this was due to better feeding, for it is a well-known fact that the Jews as people take far more pains to give their children good food than do the English. For one thing, Jewish infants are nearly always breast fed. Secondly, the Jews have a sense of good living and even the poor will make almost any sacrifice to try to get wholesome food for their families.

The kitchen was and still is at the heart of every Jewish household. It was not only the place where food was prepared and eaten but also a congregating point which was constantly full of people. Organised meals were eaten only on the Sabbath. During the week, although there was a distinction between different kinds of meals, such as breakfast, lunch and supper, meals were not eaten in a formal way or at set times. Breakfast was a hasty affair consisting mainly of bread which was eaten with raw onions, radishes and turnips or a piece of brown bread probably rubbed with garlic and smeared with goose or chicken fat. In more prosperous times salt herring, smoked sausages and meats were also served. All this was washed down with copious hot drinks, such as fruit jellies dissolved in water, tea which was drunk usually black with lemon and sweetened with fruit preserve, or coffee and *chickoria*, a coffee substitute made from chicory root. What characterised breakfast, and probably all the other weekly meals, was that they were eaten in haste, 'on the hoof'. Children were fed constantly while adults ate when they were hungry.

Sitting down to a proper meal meant having to perform the full ritual blessing which should start every meal. It is not necessary to say a full blessing over snacks. This is probably why noshing (snacking) was so popular. Nosh can be leftovers, a slice of cake, cold potato or just a hot cup of tea and a spoonful of fruit preserve. Women and children snacked on sweet things which were generally considered feminine and childish, while men noshed on savouries.[8] There was always somebody in the kitchen. Older daughters, grandmothers or maiden aunts were constantly preparing food, surrounded by hoards of children. This hive of activity, like all the other activities of the household, was controlled by the omnipotent figure of the Jewish matriarch.

The Jewish mother carries with her a formidable image which is clearly defined in the Bible:[9] her price is dearer than jewels, she is to feed her household; she is described as a merchant ship travelling to the end of the earth to get food, she wakes in the middle of the night to prepare the meal for her kin. She is also good at business, looking for land, buying and planting it. She is a strong, hard worker and industrious; spins her own wool, makes her linen, weaves and makes clothes for winter. She also augments the family income by selling garments to merchants. On top of all those qualities, she is also beautiful, well dressed, clever and charitable.

This image is recited every Friday night as part of the celebration of the Sabbath and is implanted into the mind of every Jewish woman from early childhood. As if this were not formidable enough, Jewish literature is full of the images of martyr women; those who gave their lives for their nation, like Jephthah's daughter who was sacrificed by her father to free her people,[10] and Hannah who, when her seven children were killed by the Greeks for refusing to eat pork, encouraged them to face their maker with pride but not forgetting the rules of the Lord.[11] These formidable images have followed the Jewish woman through history and each generation embellishes and magnifies the image to fit the needs of the time.

The ambition of every Jewish father was to marry his daughter to a Talmid *chochem* (a scholar), whose purpose in life was to dedicate himself to a lifelong study of the holy writing. Although in theory the young couple were supposed to be supported by the wife's father at the beginning of their lives together, the reality was that the wife found herself lumbered with a useless husband who was solely dependent on her. In a large number of Jewish households the woman was the only breadwinner. These women earned their money by opening small grocery shops, cooking speciality goods, making cheese and fattening geese and chickens. They also had to run an organised kitchen which was made more complicated by the requirements of the kosher laws and the extra demands of preparation of the holiday food.

The Jewish woman was officially excluded, apart from three religious duties, from taking part in the religious life. Yet, apart from caring for all the needs of her family, she had a unique role in shaping the religious education of her children. The kitchen was the place for spiritual as well as practical education. Daughters were not supposed to be formally educated, but the complexity of the Jewish dietary and personal hygiene laws had to be taught. The mother had to instruct her daughters not only in the techniques of cooking and housekeeping but also about the maze of religious duties relating both to marital purity and to kashruth. The complex pattern of holiday food symbolism demanded a basic knowledge of Biblical writing and the vast treasure of folk tradition and stories. Daughters were encouraged to ask questions and the pattern of repeating simple versions of Jewish history, customs and religious duty was established. Not only girls were exposed to this kind of education. Boys, until the age of three, when they were sent to *chader* (school), were tutored by their mothers on laws of personal devotions. Being kept in the kitchen, they also absorbed the essence of Jewishness which manifested itself in the folk traditions repeated there. It is no surprise that according to Jewish tradition the religious affiliation of the child is passed on by the mother and not the father.

Cooking gave the Jewish woman an opportunity to express her creativity. Her esteem both in her own eyes and the eyes of her family depended on her domestic skills of which cooking was one of the most important. Running a Jewish home is very complicated. Preparation for holidays needs a large amount of pre-planning. For example, preparations for Pesach in April usually begin before Channuka in December. The additional work which meat and milk separation demands is immense. The kitchen has to be organised in such a way that cross-contamination between milk and meat is avoided at all cost. Contaminated food must be destroyed which could mean a whole family must go without food.

The strict observance of separation between milk and meat together with the economic reality of life in the *shtetl* meant that, especially during the week, the Jews survived on a diet consisting mainly of *parve* (neither milk nor meat) and *milchig* (dairy) dishes. Everyday food consisted mainly of starchy foods: bread, noodles and potatoes. Grains, such as pot and pearl barley, buckwheat and corn, were also used to make gruels and soups which were eaten almost daily. Pulses were important not only in the making of the Sabbath *chulent* but also in pottage and beans stews.

Dairy products were essential to the weekly diet of the *shtetl*. Milk was rarely drunk on its own but was used in coffee or as a base to soups. As milk is kosher only if supervised or milked by a Jew, most households kept a milking animal, usually a goat, although milch cows were occasionally kept. The milk was used for making various kinds of cream: sweet, sour and *smetana*. However it was mainly made into fresh curds which were incorporated into a vast range of dishes, such as sweet and savoury pasta dishes, feather-light dumplings and puddings and employed as stuffing for pancakes and cheesecakes. Butter, when available, was used lavishly, mainly in baking or for fish frying. Hard, mature cheese was rarely used.

Fresh vegetables, except carrots and beets, were rarely eaten, although pickled vegetables played an important part in the Jewish kitchen. As a rule, fresh raw vegetables, except for the ubiquitous onion, garlic and numerous members of the radish family, were never eaten. The reason for this might lie in an inherent abomination of raw ingredients. Rawness is associated with things which are bloody, pagan and forbidden. Therefore food had to be thoroughly cooked. Generally food was preferred soft,

71

spicy and served piping hot. The favourite way to describe good food is to say that it melts in your mouth.

LOKSHEN, FARFEL AND KREPLACH

It is difficult to ascertain when the Jews started eating noodles. It is even more difficult to make sense of the legends attached to the origins of pasta-eating. The frequently mentioned story is that Marco Polo brought back the knowledge of pasta-making from China in 1292AD. This is unlikely as there are records of pasta-eating in books published prior to his journey. The other popular legend says that pasta was brought to Italy by the conquering Ostrogoths and was passed to the populace by a love-sick kitchen maid.[12] Maimonides suggests that pasta-eating is an ancient Persian and Middle Eastern tradition.[13] The Mishnah mentions *knov-kaot*, which was similar to a rudimentary kind of pasta, and was made from a mixture of flour, water and possibly egg and subsequently dried in the sun. Noodles or *lokshen*,[14] to use their Yiddish name, became one of the most important standbys of the European Jewish kitchen. They are filling, cheap, and easy to make and therefore solved a lot of the problems of the impoverished Jewish kitchen. Being *parve*, noodles could be served both with milk and meat dishes. They were included as a substantial filler in soups and made into sweet and savoury puddings (*kugels*). They were also served with the addition of curd cheese, sour cream or more plainly with fried onions, almonds or poppy seeds as a main course in a milky meal. The basic dough recipe includes flour, preferably unbleached as it helped to enhance the desired rich yellow colour of properly made noodles, eggs, water and salt. The addition of water seems to be the basic difference between the Italian pasta dough and the Jewish *lokshen*. The other difference is that *lokshen* are generally served well cooked and not *al dente* as is usual with Italian pasta. The basic dough recipe can be made in times of scarcity without eggs, like the *farfel* dough described below, but the result is a tougher, rubbery noodle.

Noodles were traditionally made on Friday, some to be eaten with the soup on Friday evening, some to be made into *lokshen kugel* (noodle pudding) for Saturday lunch, and the rest to be dried and stored for use during the week. Every household had a noodle board — a plank of scrubbed wood kept only for noodle-making. The dough is rolled paper thin, left to dry for a few minutes, then rolled into a long sausage shape and sliced into noodles of various widths. The shapes of noodles used in the Jewish kitchen are limited. Most popular are medium and broad fettucini-like noodles which are served on their own or made into *kugels*. Also popular are thin vermicelli which are normally served in soup.

The *farfel* shape is specifically Jewish. The name *farfel* usually refers to irregularly shaped crumbs created either by tearing or chopping the dough to very small pieces or grating it on a rough grater. The dough crumbs are dried and lightly browned in an oven. *Farfel* has nothing to do with the Italian *farfalle* (butterfly). The word probably comes from the Yiddish *parfalen* which means 'to happen, to occur', which signifies their random shape. *Farfel* is also the name of a round-shaped, small noodle 'doughnut'.

As flour is not allowed during the Pesach there is a recipe for making *matzah* meal noodles. A thin batter is made from eggs and fine *matzah* meal and fried to thin pancakes, which are then rolled and sliced to resemble noodles.

Noodle dough is used for the making of *kreplach* or *varenikes*, ravioli-like stuffed turnovers which are used as a garnish in soups or eaten as a main dish, a sweet or a starter. The name *kreplach* probably comes from *krapen* which is Yiddish for 'to cram or stuff'. *Kreplach* for soup garnish are normally stuffed with minced meat of some kind, lung and liver being the most popular. When served on their own they can be stuffed with sweet or savoury cheese fillings, potato mashed with fried onion and *schmaltz*, buckwheat *kasha*, cherries, prunes and other good things. They are served piping hot, with melted butter or sour cream or crisply fried and garnished with fried breadcrumbs.

Kreplach are served traditionally on holidays in which flogging is a part of the religious ceremony: on the eve of the Day of Atonement when one beats one's breast for expiation; at the end of Sukkoth when one flogs the ground with willow branches;[15] and on Purim when, as part of the ceremony, every time the name *haman* (the adversary) is mentioned, he is flogged symbolically by loudly rattling a rattle. This brought about a jocular observation that when a woman serves *kreplach* on a week day, she has probably been recently flogged by her husband.

Kreplach are also traditionally served on Rosh Ha'shanah eve when they are made into rounded shapes by sticking together the ends of the crescent-shaped turnover, very much like tortellini. The round shape symbolises the wish for a rounded, smooth and prosperous new year.

MEAT

The use of the meat pot meant Sabbath, a holiday, a special event, sickness in the family or a very rich household.[16] Though rarely served, meat was preferred above all other foods. Indeed, as Shalom Aleichem observed: 'The best of milky dishes is a piece of meat.' The requirements of kashruth demand that meat should be koshered not later than 72 hours after slaughtering. Because this does not allow the meat to tenderise the Jews tend to prefer long slow cooking methods and fatty cuts which are cheap and suitable for long cooking.

The force of economic necessity meant that every available part of the permitted meat had to be used. There was also an ethical aspect: the killing of an animal was considered an essential evil; thus waste showed a sinful disrespect for the sanctity of life. For all the above reasons offal cooking, which is now looked upon with mounting alarm, became a developed branch of Jewish meat cooking. Offal also has the soft, melting texture loved by Jews.

Liver was used extensively, mainly chopped but also served fried with plenty of onions or cooked in a sweet and sour sauce. Cow, ox and calf feet were used in the making of *patcha* which was either served as a soup for Sabbath lunch or left to coagulate and served as brawn accompanied by lemon or vinegar for first course. The spleen (*miltz*) was hollowed and stuffed with a mixture of breadcrumbs and fat. It was stewed with onions and plenty of pepper. Puddings made from cow stomach were a measure of the culinary skills of the housewife. Bialik describes in his short story 'Aryeh Ba'al Guff'[17] the humiliation Aryeh's wife suffered after serving this acclaimed pudding which did not turn out right and retained a whiff of its original aroma.

Lung was used extensively either as a stuffing for *kreplach*, *knishes* and savoury strudels or stewed with plenty of pepper and onion to make a delicious savoury dark brown stew which was usually served with wide, flat noodles. Brains were prized for their soft, melting texture and for their alleged properties as a mind improver. Udders, the only way in which Jews could experience the effect of cooking meat with milk, were much liked and made into wonderfully delicate stews.

Although most communities adopted meat cooking techniques from their neighbours, there are some techniques and combinations of flavours which are shared by all Ashkenazi Jews. The most common flavour combination is the liking for sweet and sour which applies to fish as well as to meat dishes. The origin of the particular fondness for sweet and sour is difficult to establish. Medieval European cuisine certainly had an abundance of meat dishes which were flavoured with sugar or honey and included dried fruit, as did the Greek and Roman cooking tradition. Sweetened foods are traditional on Rosh Ha'shanah (New Year) when they symbolise the hope for a sweet (good) year. I also suspect that to the Jews dried fruit, especially raisins, represented memories of the lost and much loved Promised Land. Including those fruit in special holiday dishes brought them closer to that land. In Yiddish, to sweeten is *mach shmekedic* — to make tasty.

One popular recipe shows clearly its medieval origin. *Essig fleisch* (sour meat) is probably a simplified version of the German medieval dish *säuerbraten*, which is meat marinated in wine, vinegar, onions, bay leaves and pepper and finished, especially in the Rhine valley, with raisins and thickened with honey-cake crumbs. The Jewish version is much simpler and probably older: the meat is not marinated but simply cooked with a mixture of sweet wine and vinegar or just vinegar. Raisins, honey or ginger-cake thickening is sometimes included.

By far the most important and popular sweetened meat dish is the *tzimmes*. The word describes a large range of dishes which have one common denominator: a combination of meat, fruit and sweet vegetables.[18] The word *tzimmes* probably derives from the German word *zumuss* or seasoned vegetables, but the popular use of the word, which in Yiddish can mean 'mixed together', indicates that it comes from the German word *zusammen* meaning 'together', probably referring to the method of cooking many ingredients together — a meal in one pot. To make *tzimmes* a fatty cut of meat, usually brisket, flank or short ribs, is simmered very slowly together with dried fruit and vegetables, sometimes overnight. The vegetables and fruit change from community to community. The German Jews are famous for their *flaumen tzimmes* (prune *tzimmes*), the Polish and Russian Jews specialise in carrot and fruit *tzimmes* and the Romanians use chickpeas and pumpkin. All *tzimmes* are flavoured with generous amounts of pepper and sweetened either with honey or sugar. In colloquial Yiddish, to make a *tzimmes* also means 'to make a great fuss', usually without apparent reason.

Another favourite method of meat cooking, especially in Eastern Europe, is the *rosel fleisch* or, as it is usually called in the diminutive, *rossale*. The word *rosel* describes a gravy or liquid left after cooking meat or the brining liquid in which vegetables are pickled. The technique is basically pot-roasting (*poêlage*) where the meat is first seared in fat, then chopped onions and sometimes garlic are added. The process of slow frying is continued until the onions caramelise and turn dark brown. The pot is then tightly covered and left to simmer until the meat is perfectly tender. As little liquid as possible is added and most of the gravy is the natural juice of the meat. Sometimes potatoes are added towards the end of the cooking. They absorb some of the gravy and the results are wonderfully brown, meat-flavoured potatoes. The dish is finished with mashed garlic which is added towards the end of the cooking. Garlic is one of the most esteemed flavourings in Jewish cooking. Together with onion it is the base of almost all pot roasts and stews and it is also included in most pickles. As a result, the Jews used to be scornfully called garlic-eaters by their Christian neighbours.

SCHMALTZ AND CHICKEN SOUP

Although beef was rarely served, poultry was eaten more often. Killing poultry does not require the skills needed with beef.[19] To Jews, poultry farming occupied the same niche which pig breeding held among their Christian neighbours. Poultry served as useful consumers of household scraps which they turned efficiently into meat. More importantly, poultry supplied the essential cooking medium of the Jewish kitchen — *schmaltz*. Every part of the bird was utilised, even the droppings were used as a fertiliser.

Most households kept poultry, mainly chickens, for eggs, but there were women who specialised in fattening birds for their fat. They mainly kept geese which were traditionally bought in early autumn just after the holiday of Sukkoth (September) and were then forcefed on a rich diet of soaked oat gruel, millet, bread scraps and boiled corn. The geese were fattened until just before Chanukah (December), which usually coincides with Christmas, when they were slaughtered and processed.

The tradition of animal slaughter and rendering fat around Chanukah has a special Jewish significance.[20] Both the Chanukah celebration and its food are closely linked with oil and fat. The holiday commemorates the Jewish uprising against the Greeks in 165BC and is celebrated by lighting candles in a special candelabrum (*Chanukyiah*) for eight days. According to tradition, when the Jews wanted to light the eternal lamp after recapturing the Temple, they found that all the oil reserves were defiled except for one small pot of oil. Miraculously this small pot of oil lasted for eight days until a new supply was found. The association with oil and light is probably very old and belongs to a pagan ritual of fire and lights for warding off the approach of winter darkness.[21] The association with oil may also stem from the fact that Chanukah coincides with the end of the olive harvest when olive oil is plentiful. This association gave rise to the tradition of serving fried food on Chanukah.

Chanukah was a busy time in the kitchen and every available pair of hands was recruited for help. An added complication was the reserving of some of the fat rendered for Pesach use, which meant that the kitchen had to be koshered for Pesach by removing all leaven and flour products and the utensils used had to be koshered by dipping them in boiling water.

All parts of a slaughtered bird were used, but first it had to be cleaned, dissected, koshered and processed. Plucking geese was a hard and messy business. The feathers, used for brushes, feather beds and as stuffing for quilted winter garments, had to be sorted from the down and cleaned. All the innards were eaten. The intestines were washed well and served either fried or included in soups, as were the feet which added strong jelly to the stock. Even the goose tongue was fried and given as nosh to children.

Goose meat was and still is used in the Jewish kitchen in the same way that pork fat and meat is used in the European kitchen. The legs and thighs (*polkes*) were salted or brined and smoked like hams. The fat breast meat (*baylik*) was used to make pastrami. It was brined, coated in a mixture of spices and minced garlic, hot smoked, and eventually used like bacon, either fried, eaten cold or used for larding. Goose meat was also used in the making of salami-type sausages, strongly flavoured with black pepper and garlic and smoked to a concentrated savoury perfection. The skin of the neck (*helzel*) was stuffed with a mixture of flour, breadcrumbs and fat and then either roasted or boiled in soups. The rest of the skin together with the fat was used to make the ubiquitous *schmaltz*.

Schmaltz, made either from goose or chicken, was the identifiable flavour of the Ashkenazi Jewish kitchen as much as olive oil is that of the Mediterranean kitchen, butter of the French cuisine and dripping of the British kitchen. To make *schmaltz*, pieces of skin and fat were covered with water and simmered until all the fat was rendered and the water evaporated. The rendered fat was then strained through a cloth and poured into earthenware containers which were sealed and kept in a cool place until needed.

The crisp, wonderfully delicious bits of skin and fat left after rendering are called *gribenes*, *gribalach* or *caines* and were used to add interest, texture and crunchiness to a large number of dishes. Goose *gribenes* were also made as a special dish: pieces of skin 'as big as the palm of your hand', as one recipe instructs, were rolled and fastened with wooden skewers. The rolled skin was laid, closely packed, in a preserving pan and sprinkled with salt. Enough water to cover was added, after which the pot was covered and simmered until tender and all the liquid had evaporated. The pot was then uncovered and some soft goose fat added. The pot was then left uncovered for the *gribenes* to brown slowly for up to two hours. When brown and crispy they were lifted out, dusted with salt and pepper, and served either for lunch with rye bread, as a snack with drinks or covered with fat and preserved for later use. Unhealthy, but delicious.

Schmaltz was also employed as a general lubricating agent to soften chapped hands, as a chest rub against colds, for heartburn, as a base for cosmetic preparations and as a marital aid. *Schmaltz*, with its many associations, is one of the cornerstones of Jewish humour. It also entered the Yiddish vernacular: to have good fortune is 'to fall into a well of *schmaltz*'. To *schmaltz* means 'to add flavour or substance', yet like everything else in the Jewish culture the word can also be used in a negative sense. *Schmalzi*, for example, means over-sentimental or suspicious.

Chicken was used to create *the* dish of the Ashkenazi kitchen: chicken soup. This dish encapsulates everything that is good. It is described as a *goldene yoich* — golden soup fit for a king. A dish of limpid yellow nectar with a generous distribution of bright, sparkling fat droplets floating temptingly on top, garnished with all kinds of tasty morsels, such as *nokerles*, noodles, rice or *kneidlach*. These titbits are known in Hebrew as the content (*tochen*) of the soup. This liquid gold was served on every Sabbath, holiday and *simcha* (domestic celebration), and especially at weddings when the *goldene yoich* was served to the bride and groom, symbolising health and prosperity.

It is not known when Jews started to eat chicken soups. *The Jewish Manual* (1846) mentions chicken broth only in the chapter dealing with invalid cookery and Mrs Levy (1871) does not mention chicken soup at all. It probably came into common use in the medieval kitchens of Central Europe as a way of utilising old laying hens who had stopped producing eggs. There is a Yiddish proverb which states that if a poor man eats chicken soup either he or the chicken is sick. Chicken soup, the 'Jewish penicillin', is embedded deeply in the Jewish psyche. It conjures up an image of warmth, care and generosity, which is the reputation every Jewish mother would like to have. From time to time 'learned' articles appear which claim to have discovered the magical medical ingredient which accounts for the curative properties of the wonderful elixir, yet the curative importance of chicken soup is mainly due to its nourishing quality; it is easily digestible, sustaining and comforting, especially when taken hot after a period of fasting. Possibly even more important is the psychological effect of its image of love, care and recovery.

To make chicken soup one should use an old bird, preferably an old layer, which although tough is likely to be much more flavoursome. The chicken feet, cleaned by scorching over a naked flame to remove the tough outer skin, are included as they contain a large amount of gelatin. In the past the head was also included. The whole bird is covered with cold water which is brought slowly to the boil and skimmed thoroughly, only then are vegetables added. The mixture of vegetables changes according to the country and the season of the year. Most recipes include onions and root vegetables, such as carrots, turnips and, most important, *petrushka* (parsley root). Sometimes pumpkin and courgettes are used. The soup is flavoured with pot herbs, usually dill and parsley leaves, although sometimes celery leaves and a bayleaf are added. The soup is boiled for a long time — some recommend for up to eight hours — and served with a garnish which includes the vegetables. The boiled chicken was served, browned in chicken fat, for the main course.

SABBATH FOOD

An old legend says that when God gave the Law to the Israelites, he promised that if they kept His word their reward would be eternal life in Heaven. Being practical people, the Israelites wanted to know what life in Heaven would be like, so God gave them the Sabbath as a foretaste. For the European Jew the Sabbath was certainly Heaven on earth; it was the day on which they could escape the grim reality of life. On the Sabbath, which is referred to as the Queen, the bride, the Jew can become the King — a free man.

We know very little about Sabbath celebrations before the destruction of the Temple. The importance of the Sabbath gained momentum in the diaspora. The weekly celebration of the Sabbath has become the most important consolidating factor between the Jew and his religion. As Achad Ha'am observed: 'More than Israel has kept the Sabbath, the Sabbath has kept Israel.'[22]

The Sabbath is celebrated by complete rest. Any kind of work, *except in emergency*, is completely forbidden and the day is spent with the family in joyful religious worship, both at home and in the synagogue. Not only spiritual needs are cared for; the body has also to be satisfied. A mandatory stipulation is that at least three meals should be served. These are Friday evening dinner, Saturday lunch, which is eaten after the morning synagogue service, and *se'udah shlishit*, which means 'third meal' and is eaten on Saturday afternoon. Some communities also serve a fourth meal on Saturday evening. The food on the Sabbath should be extra spicy, especially rich and of ample quantity because the *neshama yeterah* (or extra soul which descends from Heaven) needs feeding also.

The Talmud relates a story about the spiciness of the Sabbath food. A Roman Emperor asked Rabbi Joshua Ben Chananya (80–110AD) why the Sabbath dishes had such a fragrance. The Rabbi answered that the Jews used a special spice called Sabbath. When the Emperor asked for some, the Rabbi replied that the spice is only effective for those who keep the Sabbath. To make the Sabbath extra special the Talmud, with typical wisdom, recommends that a husband should 'service' his wife on Friday evening, a time which was considered to be especially beneficial for conceiving a male baby.

Spices are not only used in food. The ceremony of escorting the Sabbath out, separating it from the coming week (*Havdalah*), involves smelling sweet spices (*besamim shel shabbath*). The tradition probably started with the habit of burning sweet-smelling herbs and spices as a part of any special meal. The folk explanation of the custom is that when the extra soul departs with the end of the Sabbath, the body is faint and should be revived with sweet-smelling spices. The traditions around the departure of the Sabbath were also connected with a widespread belief that demons, especially Lilith the she-devil, were more powerful on Saturday night. There was also a belief that the departure of the Sabbath was the time when lost souls went back to hell.[23] Smelling sweet spices was a protection against all those evil spirits. The spices used in the ceremony were usually nutmeg, cloves and cinnamon and were held in a beautifully decorated perforated or filigree silver vessel. This tradition played an important part in the shaping of a culinary tradition. In a time when spices and exotic flavourings were generally the privilege of the rich, spices were familiar and present in every Jewish home, even the poorest.

The Sabbath dictated the weekly rhythm of every Jewish household. The week was divided into two, the first of which was known as 'after Sabbath' while the end of the week was called 'before Sabbath'. Preparation for the Sabbath often began on Wednesday because Friday is a short day. The Sabbath starts an hour before sunset on Friday, which in winter can mean as early as just after lunch on Friday, and there are a lot of preparations to be done. The house must be cleaned, all linen changed and clean clothes provided for all the family. Bread has to be baked and at least three substantial meals must be planned and cooked for the day to come.

The Mishnah stipulates that both meat and fish are to be served at the Sabbath table. This provision used to impose an impossible burden on the meagre means of many Jewish households. People used to eat frugally during the week so they could afford to eat well on the Sabbath. The Yiddish literature is littered with Jewish men who positively sacrificed themselves to provide a proper Sabbath meal. The social shame of not being able to provide this was, and still is, immense.

Thursday was the shopping day and often coincided with market day. On Thursday night the dough for the *hallah* (Sabbath bread) and for the weekly bread was made. It was left to ferment until early Friday morning when it was shaped and baked. On the Sabbath and holidays (except the Pesach) two loaves (*hallah*) graced every table, the baking of which gave Jewish women a rare opportunity to take an active part in a religious ceremony. There are three religious duties which every Jewish woman must perform and two of them take place on the Sabbath. Every pious woman should purify herself after menstruation, separate the *hallah* and light the Sabbath light. The Mishnah decrees that if she does not comply with all three she runs the risk of giving birth to a stillborn child.[24]

HALLAH
The Ancient Symbol

The word *hallah* is of Biblical origin though its meaning is not completely clear. In the Bible the word has two meanings. It is used as a general name for a loaf, but is also applied to an unquantified portion of dough which was separated and given to the priests. After the destruction of the Temple, in the absence of a priestly sect, the separation of the *hallah* evolved into a domestic ceremony. A small piece of dough 'the size of an olive' is separated while saying a benediction. The ceremony takes place just before the *hallah* is shaped. The piece of dough is completely burned in the oven. The custom of burning a portion of dough is very old; it was and is still practised all over the Middle East as a protection against the evil eye.[25] The separation of the *hallah* is the duty of the woman or whoever bakes the bread, such as a commercial baker. The *hallah* is not considered kosher unless the separation is done.

Two *hallahs* are placed on every Sabbath table, but the reason for displaying two loaves is obscure. One of the traditional explanations associates the custom with the two kinds of bread mentioned both in the Bible and in the Mishnah as being used in the Temple.

Another explanation for serving two *hallahs* is that they represent the double portion of manna given to the Hebrews on the Sabbath. In fact, the reason might be simply culinary: according to the Roman etiquette of the day it was customary to serve bread with each dish. On special occasions like the Sabbath meal two courses were served instead of a single weekly dish, therefore two loaves were displayed.

The association of the two *hallahs* with the manna led also to the custom of covering the *hallah* with a special cloth, representing the dew which covered the manna. The cover, lovingly embroidered usually on a white background symbolising purity, is said to be there for another reason. On the Sabbath, the wine for once is blessed before the bread. Therefore, the cover is laid over the *hallah* so it is not shamed.

Hallah or *kitka*, *boulka* or *braches* as it is also known, with its familiar braiding which we eat today probably originated in medieval Germany. It is a light, delicious, slightly sweet bread that usually contain eggs and fat in the dough, making it almost cake-like. The name *braches* has an interesting origin. It probably derives from the name of the German goddess of fertility and vegetation, Berchta. The baking of plaited bread was one of the rituals associated with her worship. *Braches* also sounds like the Hebrew word for blessing, *brachah*. Braiding was usually done with six strands which represented the two rows of six loaves of the Temples' Shaw Bread. Today three or four braids are more common as they are easier to make. The sprinkling of sesame or poppy seeds on top of the *hallah* is a representation of the *manna*. The Sabbath *hallah* should have a dark golden-brown crust, the shinier the better. The crumb should be light, sweetish and as golden as possible. Saffron is sometimes used to accentuate the colour and to add that special spicy flavour loved on the Sabbath.

There were two interesting Ashkenazi traditions connected with bread baking. The concession for selling yeast in a large number of *shtetls* was held by the Rabbi as a source of extra income and the duties of the bath attendant's wife included helping the matrons, for a fee, in kneading the dough. In some communities the bath-house ovens were also used for baking bread.

GEFILTE FISH AND HERRING

Friday morning was thus associated with the smell of newly baked bread and the flavour of fresh buttered rolls. The smells in the kitchen changed as the day progressed. After baking the bread and making noodles, the fish had to be prepared. Fish, when available, was an important and popular source of protein in the *shtetl* diet. It was also better fitted to the demands of the kosher kitchen than meat. Although not decreed, fish was habitually salted, inside and out, and left for a while to drain all traces of blood.

To the *shtetl* Jews, as to all European peasants, salted herring was a life-saver. It was convenient, relatively cheap, long-lasting, nourishing and a healthy source of protein. Herring was probably the only ready-to-eat food which Jews were allowed to buy from non-Jews. Salt herring was first soaked in water to remove excess saltiness. It was then dressed with vinegar and oil and served with plenty of sliced raw onion and hot, boiled potatoes. Salt herring was also the basis for numerous dishes. It could be chopped, mixed with apples and hard-boiled eggs and served as an appetiser. It was also fried in butter or oil, baked, sauced and pickled.

Fresh fish for the Sabbath was cooked mainly in two ways, *sharfe* or *essig* (sour) or *gefilte*. The only mention in *Larousse Gastronomique* of dishes *à la juive* (in the Jewish style) is for four recipes for sweet and sour carp. All are variations of a basic recipe for stewed carp which are finished in different ways. The carp is sliced and cooked on a bed of onions which have been previously blanched in oil and sprinkled with a little flour. Salt, cayenne pepper and a bouquet garni of bay and parsley are added and the fish is almost covered with a mixture of water, wine and oil and cooked for 20 minutes. The slices of carp are then lifted and arranged to resemble the shape of a whole fish. The cooking liquid is reduced and poured over the fish and the dish is left to cool. The three variations are as follows: in *à l'oriental* a pinch of saffron and chopped almonds are added; in *au persil* an extra amount of parsley is added to the cooking liquid and the sauce; the final recipe is a fancy version of the favourite *sharfe* (sweet/sour) fish and the reduced sauce is flavoured with sugar, vinegar, seeded Malaga raisins, and Smyrna and Corinth raisins which have been previously soaked in warm water.

But by far the most popular way of serving fish on the Sabbath was *gefilte* (stuffed) *fish* which became the most identifiable dish of the Ashkenazi kitchen. Indeed, its notoriety is so great that in Israel the Ashkenazi Jews are dismissively called by the Sephardi Jews 'gefilte fish eaters'. As the name indicates, *gefilte* in Yiddish means stuffed, and it is a dish of boned fish, stuffed with minced or chopped fish forcemeat. The fish is then poached in rich fish stock and served cold, accompanied by the jellied stock and horseradish relish tinted with beetroot.

The origins and date of the dish are unknown, but may be traced to the kitchens of medieval Europe. Recipes for stuffed fish appear in most European medieval cookery books. The technique of mincing fish, both raw and cooked, enriching it with ground almonds and then binding the mixture with raw or hard-boiled eggs and breadcrumbs, was common-place. The forcemeat was usually flavoured with nutmeg, saffron, raisins and sugar. The fact that the fish was minced suited the Jewish kitchen perfectly. Fresh fish was expensive and in short supply, especially on Fridays when the Jews had to compete with Christians who also traditionally ate fish on that day. Mincing was an opportunity to extend the mixture with cheaper ingredients. With a lot of stretching a single fish could feed a whole family. Chopping the fish was also practical in other ways. Freshwater fish, especially pike and carp which were customary, are bony and chopping got rid of the bones. Moreover, chopping solved a particularly Jewish problem: picking bones is considered to be work and thus is not allowed on the Sabbath. In addition, *gefilte fish* appealed to the resourceful Jewish housewife who would keep back some of the fish stock to use as a base for soups and for making a delicious potato dish — *fish kartoffel* — which was traditionally served at Friday lunch.

It is curious that *gefilte fish* recipes were not included in the early Jewish recipe books published in English on both sides of the Atlantic. Both Mrs Levy[26] and Lady Montefiore[27] do not mention *gefilte fish*, although the latter gives a delicious-sounding recipe for fish forcemeat which she suggests might be used to make fish balls or used as stuffing.

The combination of the ingredients, flavourings and methods of cooking *gefilte fish* are subject to fierce argument among each ethnic group. The combinations vary depending as much on local availability as on personal taste and ethnic prejudice. It is generally agreed that *gefilte* is best made from a mixture of at least two kinds of fish: roughly one-third oily fish to two-thirds lean white fish. In Central Europe the mixture consists mostly of pike and carp. In North America, it is usually pike or carp with white fish, although pike is considered by some to be an inferior fish. Salmon is sometimes used. Thelma Barer-Stein, who was born on the West Coast of Canada, told me she thought *gefilte fish* was pink until she moved to the East because salmon was always included as a part of the mixture. In Britain, the mixture includes mostly cod, haddock and hake which makes the texture rather grainy and dry. Mackerel is sometimes used; this helps to keep the mixture moist but makes it darker. In Israel, carp is widely used and sometimes mixed with sea fish.

The colour of the dish is important. In Britain, it is preferred very white. Polish Jews like their *gefilte fish* brown, which is achieved by including a few onion skins in the cooking liquid. Others prefer it yellow, which is achieved by including carrots in the mixture and either saffron or turmeric in the stock. The question of flavouring is widely disputed. The Jews of Poland add sugar and sometimes raisins in the preparation.

Russian Jews look up on this with contempt as they prefer their *gefilte* well peppered and never include carrots in the mix; carrots are allowed only in the stock, sliced to thin rounds which are also used as the traditional garnish.

Originally, making *gefilte fish* was a laborious task. The fish was carefully skinned after which all the meat was removed and chopped by hand. Hand chopping was very important because the chopping motion helped to incorporate air into the fish mixture, making it lighter. The chopped flesh was mixed with breadcrumbs (*matzah* meal on Pesach) and other ingredients before being stuffed into the fish skin. The fish opening was sewn with a thread, wrapped in cloth or white buttered paper, and poached in a stock made from fish bones and vegetables.

Since *gefilte fish* now is rarely made in the traditional way the name lost its original meaning. The boning and stuffing are dispensed with and the dish is just poached fish forcemeat balls. Gone also are the days of hand chopping; the fillet of fish is either minced, processed in a food processor or bought ready mixed from the fishmonger. The mixture can also be fried, as is the preference in Britain, or baked in the oven. It is, however, always served with *chrain* (horseradish relish).

SHALOSH SE'UDOT
The Three Meals

The three Sabbath meals followed more or less a traditional pattern. The first meal on the Friday evening started after the blessing of the wine and the *hallah* with *goldene yoiech* (chicken soup). Sometimes in rich families, the meal started with appetisers of chopped liver, egg salad or *patcha* (calf or ox foot brawn). After the soup the obligatory fish is served, then the main meat course which, especially in poor families, included the chicken boiled in the soup, perhaps accompanied by *helzel*, a pudding made from the neck of the chicken and boiled in the soup. Rich families traditionally served both beef and poultry stews and pot roasts, accompanied by a variety of cooked vegetable dishes, potato or noodle puddings and various *tzimmes*. The meal was concluded with a sweet *kugel* or stewed fruit. After the meal, tea, cakes and sweetmeats were served. The evening was spent eating. Especially in winter the Friday evening meal was eaten immediately on return from the synagogue. This could be as early as 5 in the afternoon thus leaving a whole evening to be spent singing *zmiroth* (traditional Sabbath songs) and munching on all manners of delicacies such as cakes, cookies, and sweetmeats or just boiled, salted and peppered beans and chickpeas or dried pumpkin seeds. Black tea was also drunk accompanied by sweet fruit confitures.

Alcoholic drinks were served both at the meal and after. During the meal wine was served rarely. When served, the women drank sweet red wine diluted with water. The men usually drunk distilled liquors, vodka, schnapps or *slibovitze*. These are known in Yiddish under the collective name *yaash*. After the meals, sweet fruit wines and fruit liqueurs were served usually accompanied with *lekach* (sponge cake) or *mandel brot* (almond bread). The cakes were eaten dipped into the sweet liqueur.

On Saturday morning very little, if any, food was eaten. If a breakfast was required it consisted only of a piece of cake with a hot drink. Bread was not eaten as it needed a full blessing. Lunch, eaten immediately after returning from the synagogue, was substantial and normally served by late morning. This was known as the 'second meal'. The name gave rise to a tradition of serving two kinds of dishes in each course. The meal, especially in rich houses, could start with a few appetisers which might include some of the leftovers from the Friday meal. Then might come the first courses which could include a reddish salad flavoured with *schmaltz* and *griben* or an egg salad or perhaps just raw onions dressed with *schmaltz*. Then the serious eating began: first a hot liquid version of *patcha* might be served flavoured with garlic and pepper. Only then came the taste of Sabbath: the *chulent*, accompanied by a savoury *kugel*.

Kugel generally means a pudding, either sweet or savoury.[28] The word *kugel* in German means a ball or a globe. This possibly indicates the shape of the special pot (*kugel-topf*) in which it was baked. The pot was a round earthenware casserole with a very small base designed to minimise the area in contact with the oven floor, thus reducing the chance of burning. The rich *kugel* is notorious for sticking to the pot. The word might also originate, as Mrs Leonard mentions,[29] from the Hebrew *ke-igul* meaning 'like a circle'. In modern Jewish usage, especially in Britain and South Africa, the word describes a spoilt and pretentious Jewish woman known in the States as a 'Jewish American Princess'.

Whatever the meaning of the word, a *kugel* is a loosely defined cookery term describing a mixture of starchy foods — potatoes, noodles, bread or flour — bound with eggs and moistened with chicken fat, oil or sometimes butter, depending on whether it was meant for milk or meat meals. Fruit, vegetables and other fillings are sometimes added. The pudding can also be made exclusively from fruit and vegetables as in the case of carrot *kugel* and the famous and delicious German apple *schalet*. A *kugel* can be made either sweet or savoury, although a large number of sweet *kugels* include black pepper as flavouring in addition to the customary cinnamon, cloves and nutmeg. *Kugels* can be served as a main dish, especially in a 'milk' meal when the chicken fat can be replaced by oil, butter or, nowadays, margarine. It can also be served as a side dish with meat or as a sweet and may be served hot, cold or warm.

After such a meal a long sleep was needed to refresh oneself and prepare for the rest of the day's food. After waking up and having a glass of hot tea with maybe a slice of cake, it was the custom to visit family and friends. This usually meant having some more tea with 'something small to eat' which might include cakes and cookies. After the afternoon ceremony at the synagogue, just before sunset, the third obligatory meal was served. Mercifully it was a light one, usually consisting of purely milky dishes with cold, smoked or pickled fish and pickles or leftovers.

Amongst the *Chassidim*[30] a fourth meal became an important celebration; it is called *melave malka*, literally meaning to escort the Queen (Sabbath). The custom is that the *Chassidim* gather at their Rabbi's court and share his food. The Rabbi sits at a table surrounded by his disciples, the food is laid in front of him, and he blesses it. The Rabbi only tastes the food and leaves the rest to be shared amongst his disciples. It is a great honour to eat morsels of the Rabbi's table and his disciples are known to fight for the privilege. After the food is finished the rest of the evening is spent singing and dancing led by the Rabbi. Thus the Sabbath is over.

'If I Forget Thee, O Jerusalem'

The cooking of holiday food, although not a written law, was considered a *mitzva* (religious duty). As any cook will have experienced, cooking holiday food has a strange effect on the cook's mind. Throughout the meticulous planning, shopping and cooking, the cook has to focus her mind on the meaning of the holiday. Cooking holiday food was one of the main ways of passing on tradition. The preparation involved remembering a complicated set of food symbols, the logic behind which had often been obscured by hundreds of years of change. The symbolism of the food was carried from generation to generation by an oral tradition of folk tales and accepted 'truths'. Some are loosely based on historical happenings while others are wonderfully colourful inventions of the imagination. These are repeated in every kitchen, instructing the future generation in the ways of tradition.

Holidays always brought to mind past history and dead ancestors for whom the holiday food was cooked as much as for the living family. It seems that the action of kneading the *hallah*, probably because of the hypnotic rhythmical motion, stimulates a wave of memories and emotions. There are numerous description throughout Yiddish literature of women shedding bitter tears into the *hallah*. The same kind of emotion is also involved in lighting candles; the crying seems to become almost a folk tradition.

Except for the mention of *hamin* for Sabbath and lamb in connection with Pesach, there is no written evidence about specific holiday food either in the Bible or in the Mishnah, yet there is a general indication that the difference between everyday and holiday food was that the latter was fattier, more elaborate and probably sweet.[31] *Zevach* is the word which the Bible uses to describe both the sacrifice and the meal which celebrates the holiday. The word conjures up an abundance of food, especially of meat.

Most of the holidays are based on events or practices which took place in Israel. The country which is described in holy writing and folk tales (*zmiroth* or traditional songs) as a country of milk and honey, abundant in fruit, wheat and spices. In celebrating a holiday the Jews could feel closer to this Heaven on earth. Tradition decrees that the land of Israel should be remembered at every holiday table and that at least one fruit associated with Israel should be blessed. Purists maintained that only fruit actually grown in Israel should be used.

A holiday menu followed the same pattern as Sabbath food. Variants appear in the eve of holiday meal and differ greatly from country to country and sometimes from family to family. The holiday lunch follows exactly the same pattern as the Sabbath because work on the holiday is forbidden, except on minor holidays like Chanukah and Purim. Like on the Sabbath, slow-cooking *cholents* and *kugels* and *tzimmes* were served. Some dishes contained special ingredients which had a traditional association with the holiday and were not used during the year. The following pages will discuss the holidays and mention some of the foods used. The holidays are listed in chronological order according to their appearance in the Jewish calendar.

Rosh Ha'shanah   (New Year. 1 Tishri September/October)

The celebration of the beginning of the year on the first of Tishri is a relatively new custom. Although the Bible mentions a holiday around that time, it never refers to it as the New Year. The holiday was not celebrated in any particular way, but like all other holidays was the occasion for a sacrifice (*zevach*) and the sounding of the *shofar* (ram's horn). Modern scholars agree that the New Year was celebrated with the Pesach (April/May). In the diaspora, Pesach lost its importance as the beginning of the agricultural year and eventually the holiday which was celebrated on the first of Tishri took its place as the official beginning of the year. It is not a joyful holiday, but marks the beginning of ten days called Days of Awe. These lead to the most holy day of the Jewish calendar, Yom Kippur (Day of Atonement). According to folk tradition this is the time when God in Heaven sits in judgement, deciding the future of every individual. The final decision and the signing of the book is done on Yom Kippur.

The holiday is celebrated with contemplative activities which start a month before Rosh Ha'shanah, with prayers of forgiveness (*slichot*). The ten Days of Awe are the time for all Jews to settle their accounts with their maker and, more importantly, with their fellow human beings. The custom is to go around the neighbourhood and ask forgiveness for misdemeanours, both deliberate and unintentional.

This contemplative, hopeful mood is reflected strongly in Rosh Ha'shanah food. All dishes on the holiday table reflect hope for a better year. They are sweet, fruity and preferably round in appearance. The *hallahs* baked for this holiday are round and especially sweeter, more golden and richer than for the Sabbath. Sometimes the *hallah* is decorated with ladders, plaited crowns and birds in full flight, representing the wish that the prayers will climb and fly directly to heaven. The roundness is also present in the apple, dipped in honey, which is served as an opening to the meal, and in the round kreplach which are served with the soup. The dough covering of the kreplach represents the covered or veiled way in which God works his justice.

Sweetness features in almost every dish. The custom is to avoid any bitter or sour flavours. Some communities do not serve almonds and nuts as these are associated with bitter tastes. Almonds are also avoided because their shape resembles a teardrop. Anything which is associated with sadness is avoided; Algerian Jews will not eat fish as the Hebrew word for fish (*dag*) resembles the word for worry (*de'aga*).[32]

The agricultural tradition of the holiday is maintained by a special blessing over new fruit, preferably fruits which are mentioned in the Bible. Traditional fruits served include dates, figs, carobs and pomegranates. The pomegranate has a special significance as its many seeds are supposed to represent the 613 good deeds which a Jew has to perform during the year.

Dishes which include fruit and sweet vegetables are also made, especially carrot *tzimmes*, which are traditionally made on this day without meat. Carrots are used because when sliced their shape resembles gold coins (for riches) and their Yiddish name *mahren* sounds like the word *mher* (more, multiply). Sweetness is also present in the many honey cakes, cookies and honey confections which are served.

There is also symbolism in the main courses. Fish and meat, especially fowl, are served whole to represent hope for a wholeness of the coming year. Dishes made out of fish heads or a whole roasted lamb's head are traditionally given to the head of the family after which he shares morsels with the others. This tradition signifies the wish to be at the 'head and not the tail' of the nations. If a head is not available, the head of the family is served with a whole head of roasted garlic or a whole roasted onion. Fish being a symbol of fertility features strongly at the Rosh Ha'shanah table. It also symbolises purity because of its association with running water.

Yom Kippur (Day of Atonement. 10 Tishri September/October)

This most important of the Jewish holidays is a fast day. No food should be eaten after the last meal, *se'uda mafseket*, on the afternoon of the Yom Kippur eve until the fast is broken with the appearance of the first star next day. The pre-fast meal is usually bland so as not to induce thirst because drinking is forbidden. It usually consists of chicken soup with *kreplach* and a chicken meat dish. These are usually made from the *kapparot* chicken. Tea and sweet cakes are also served. The breaking of the fast is usually done with a milky dinner which will include pickles and a variety of herring dishes. Sweet cakes and cookies are also served.

Sukkot (Feast of Tabernacle. 14 Tishri September/October)

The holiday tradition commemorates the sukkot (*sukka* means singular) or tabernacles in which the Jews lived before they settled in Israel. During the holiday, which lasts seven days, every Jewish male above the age of 13 is required to eat his meals in the *sukka*. The *sukka* tradition might also be related to the peasant habit of moving to temporary huts erected in the fields before harvest to guard the ripening fruit.

The celebration of Sukkot maintains strong links with the original meaning of the holiday which was a celebration of the end of the harvest, and fruit and vegetables are used widely. Unlike Rosh Ha'shanah and Yom Kippur, Sukkot is a joyous occasion. Especially lighthearted is the last day which is called *simchat torah* (rejoicing of the Torah). From the 10th century AD it became the universal custom to finish the cycle of reading of the Torah[33] on that day. It is celebrated with singing, dancing and eating of sweetmeats. It is also traditional to drink alcoholic beverages on *simchat torah*.

The food reflects the mood of the holiday. Apart from soup with *kreplach*, a large variety of fruit and vegetable *kugels* and *tzimmes* are served. Stuffed vegetables, especially stuffed cabbage leaves which are known as *galuptzi* by Russian Jews and *holishkes* or *parkaes* in Yiddish, are traditional. The cabbage was believed to be good for prevention of alcoholic intoxication.[34]

Chanukah (Feast of Lights. 25 Kislev November/December. Sometimes coincides with Christmas)

Food traditions and other aspects of this holiday are discussed on pp. 76–7. The tradition of serving predominantly fried dishes and food which included goose fat and meat was probably medieval. The most famous of these are the delicious potato latkes (pancakes) and fried pontchikes (doughnuts). A medieval Jewish folk tradition associates Chanukah with the story of Judith, a daughter of the Hasmonean dynasty, who served cheese which was probably preserved in salt to a Greek commander. As a result he got very thirsty and consumed too much wine which put him to sleep. Judith used the opportunity to behead him, thus saving the nation from destruction. Thus cheese dishes are also traditional.

Tu b'shevat (15 Shevat January/February. Also known as Rosh Ha'shanah La'Ilanot or 'New Year of the Trees')

A minor holiday probably intended to celebrate midwinter's day. The food associated with it consists mainly of different kinds of fruit, fruit cakes and pies. Now the holiday is celebrated in Israel, mainly by children, with planting a tree.

Purim (14 Adar March/April)

Purim is the most joyous of the Jewish holidays although, as in everything Jewish, sadness is also present. The day before Purim is a fast day, *Ta'anit Esther*, which commemorates the refusal of Queen Esther to eat at the table of her husband, the King of Persia. The holiday is supposed to celebrate the Jewish victory over hostile elements at the Persian court which is told in the Book of Esther, but probably has roots in Persian mythology.[35]

The food reflects the mood of the holiday. A large number of sweets and cakes are made. One of the traditions of the holiday is *mishloach manote* (*shalach-monos*, sending of a gift), where households send each other platters of cakes and sweetmeats. Shalom Aleichem describes what might be included in the sweet gift:

The *shalach-monos*, which Red Nechama carried, covered with white cloth included: one large and magnificent *Hamantash* (turnover), filled with sesame; two sweet cakes, one with a dimple in the centre filled with sweet crumble, the other round, covered with pastry lattice work; a square piece of strudel; a small honey bun glazed with sugar, with a plump raisin in the centre; a well-baked sweet bun, two small Kings bread and a very large slice of rye honey cake, which this year was better than before: was it because the flour was fresher, or probably the honey was purer or, that the oven was heated just right, or it might have been that it kneaded better or longer? Whatever was the reason this year the cake came out of the oven magnificently baked, soft, light and plump as a featherbed.[36]

The most typical cookie of the holiday was *Hammantaschen* (Hamman's pockets) or *oznay Hamman* (Hamman's ears) as they are known in Hebrew. These are triangular pastries stuffed with sweetmeat usually made from poppy-seeds cooked in honey.

The main meal in Purim is known as *se'udat Purim*. It is usually typified by a gigantic plaited *hallah* which is traditionally sweetened with honey and raisins. Well-peppered fish and stuffed cabbage leaves are also served. Alcohol is drunk to excess. It is the only Jewish holiday on which excessive drinking is written into the traditional celebration. The holiday is also celebrated by masquerades and acting of traditional Purim plays (*Purim shpiles*).

Pesach (Passover, from the eve of 14 Nisan to 21 Nisan April/May. Sometimes coincides with Easter)

Pesach was the most important religious holiday of the Jewish year until it was replaced by Rosh Ha'shanah and Yom Kippur. Yet domestically and socially the Pesach remains the most popular of holidays. This is probably because it is celebrated at the beginning of spring, a more convenient time for travel. It therefore became the holiday in which the clans would gather. Families which were separated throughout the year would travel to the house of the head of the family for the celebration of the Seder. The preparations start a month before the holiday with a general spring-cleaning designed to purge the house of any traces of *chametz* (leaven). The special Pesach cooking utensils, crockery and cutlery, which are kept hidden throughout the year, have to be checked and koshered for the occasion. This is done by dipping them into boiling water. There is also a tradition of making new clothes and shoes for Pesach.

The original law forbidding the use of leaven evolved to a general ban on the use of cereal flour (except in *matzah*). In some communities certain legumes and rice are also prohibited. By some communities chickpeas are prohibited, for example, because their Hebrew name is *chumzah*, which sounds like *chametz* or leaven. This blanket-banning of all flour products gave rise to a specific cuisine in which *matzah* meal and later potato flour replaced wheat flour and a large amount of eggs are used to replace its thickening and binding qualities. When liquid only is added to *matzah* meal the resulting dough is hard and lumpy. It needs all the egg and fat it can absorb to make it lighter and edible. Potatoes were used extensively either on their own or mixed with *matzah* meal as a base for *kugels*, dumplings and fritters. Potato starch was used for baking and thickening. The making of potato starch at home was a time-consuming process. The potatoes were grated and washed repeatedly with water. The rinsing water was then left standing for a few hours to let the starch settle. Then the water was poured off leaving the starch at the bottom of the dish. This was collected and either used wet or left to dry and turned into fine powder.

Preparation of food for Pesach started as early as Chanukah, with the making of a *chametz*-free fat for use in Pesach. The real sign of the approaching holiday was the appearance of a specially kept wooden barrel in which *rasol* is made. *Rasol* is a fermented beetroot and salt water juice used as the base of Pesach borscht (soup). The beetroot was left in brine for a month to ferment. Every few days the scum collected on the top was removed, leaving at the end of the month a beautifully clear, bright purple, fragrant liquid which was also used for a number of special Pesach dishes. The beets themselves were included in the borscht or used for special dishes. My grandmother used to make a delicate, delicious sweet and sour chicken dish cooked with fermented beets and beet juice.

As everything is supposed to be strictly *kosher L'Pesach* (kosher for Pesach), jams and sweets were made as close to the holiday as possible. Finding raw ingredients in winter was difficult as fresh fruits were not available. In the *shtetl*, the problem was solved by making *eingemacht* (German for preserved), a ginger-flavoured jam made from root vegetables, beetroot, carrots or radishes, grated and cooked either in syrup or honey. Carrots and ginger were used to make another Pesach speciality, a fudge-like sweetmeat called *imberlach*; *imber* means ginger in Yiddish.

The main problem of Pesach was baking without either flour or leaven. The Jewish cook employed her usual resourcefulness and created a wide range of cakes and sweets which did not use any of the forbidden ingredients. The results are magnificent: cheese cakes made with layers of *matzah* which have been previously softened by dipping them into wine and brandy; light sponges made with *matzah* meal which is very finely ground *matzah*, starch (potato or corn) and numerous eggs.

Almonds were an important item in Pesach baking as a substitute for flour in cakes, sweets and stuffing. Almonds are the base of one of the most favoured Pesach sweets, marzipan. There is a charming, if unlikely, story about the origin of the word marzipan. It is said to have been invented especially for Pesach in medieval Spain, hence the name *mazapane* which is a combination of the two words *matzah* and *pane* (bread). Marzipan or almond bread, powdered almonds mixed with puréed fruit and dried in the sun, was a staple food of nomads all over the Middle East and North Africa. It was brought to Europe by traders, some of whom were Jews. Sephardi Jews serve a wonderful range of marzipans flavoured with rose or orange-flower water stuffed into traditional fruit like dates, nuts and figs.

Nuts in general played an important part in Pesach food and were used extensively in baking or as an addition to stuffing and sweetmeats. Nuts are also given to children as a part of the Pesach gift and are used for playing games.

Matzah meal was also the base for a large number of dumplings, fritters and *kugels*. No Seder meal would be complete without *knaidlach*, *matzah* meal dumplings which are served as a garnish for the ubiquitous chicken soup. The name comes from *knodel*, German for dumplings. *Knaidlach* are made from a mixture of *matzah* meal, eggs and fat; *schmaltz* is traditionally used. Each year the burning topic of dispute around the Seder table is the merits of this particular *knaidlach* compared with last year's effort. There are two opposing schools of thought about the making of these simple, delicious dumplings: one maintains that they have to be 'as light as a feather and quiver under their own weight' and the other, which is almost as popular, insists on a heavy, substantial *knaidlach* 'which will sink to the bottom of the plate'. The recipe in this book, which was given to me by Mrs Toby Kay, and comes from South Africa, is for *knaidlach* which are 'as light as a feather'.

Matzah meal was also used in the making of *chremslach*, which has almost as many ways of spelling as recipes. Basically, they are *matzah* meal fritters, sometimes stuffed with either sweet or savoury filling and fried to a golden crispness. The sweet ones are served sprinkled with sugar. *Chremslach* may get their name from the special frying pan called *chremzler* or *krimzler*, which has small depressions to take the individual *chremzel*.

Whole *matzah* was the base for the most delightful Ashkenazi Pesach breakfast dish, *matze brei* or *matze brineh*. The name comes from the Yiddish word *briehn*, to soak. It is a pancake made of broken *matzah* soaked in water or milk, mixed with eggs and fried in oil or fat. It is served either peppered and salted or sweetened with cinnamon sugar or jam. Strict observers of the law used to serve the dish only on the last day of the holiday. This strict observance is due to the fear that a *matzah* soaked in water might ferment. In some families any dishes which use *matzah* soaked in a liquid are avoided.

Shavouth[37] **(Pentecost, also known as Chag Ha'katzir — wheat harvest festival — or Chag Ha'bikurim — Festival of the First Fruit. 6 Sivan May/June)**
Originally this holiday marked the completion of the wheat harvest. It was celebrated exactly seven weeks after the beginning of the barley harvest. *Shavouth* means weeks in Hebrew. The ceremony of the beginning of the barley harvest involved presenting a sheaf of barley at the Temple on the second day of Pesach. In olden days the holiday was not of great importance and was probably observed only in Jerusalem at the Temple. However, the importance of the day was increased in the diaspora when it became associated with the giving of the Torah (Matan Torah or Simchath Torah) which is celebrated on the second day of Shavout. Tradition maintains that the Torah was given on Mt Sinai fifty days after the exodus from Egypt. The food captures the harvest element of the holiday. Dairy products, in particular curd cheese, are an important ingredient in the celebration of Shavouth. The origins of the custom are suggested in the Bible in the passages about 'lamb in its mother's milk' which always come in conjunction with harvest laws, indicating that an ancient pagan tradition of eating milk or milk products was associated with spring, the time when nature is at its most generous. The Jewish tradition absorbed the custom and gave it a new meaning associating it with the other significance of the holiday — the giving of the Law to Moses on Mt Sinai. Tradition tells that the Jews had to wait for a long time for Moses to come down from Mt Sinai and on their return to the camp they were too hungry to wait for the long process of preparing a meat meal so they drank milk.

The most popular dairy dishes are cheese cakes, cheese *blintzes* or *plachinkes* (cheese-stuffed crêpes), cheese-filled *kreplach* and cheese and semolina dumplings. *Kreplach* and fried stuffed cheese dumplings were made in a triangular shape. This tradition is a reference to the numerous times the number three appears in association with the giving of the Torah: three parts of which were given to Israel (Torah, Prophets and Hagiograph writings); it was given to a triple nation comprised of the Cohen, Levi and Israel classes; the nation sprang from the loins of the three

Patriarchs Abraham, Isaac and Jacob; the Torah was given to Moses who was the third-born in his family; and it was given in Sivan, the third month in the ancient Jewish calendar.

Following the harvest theme, fruit cakes (Sinai cake) and sweet fruit *tzimmes* are also served. Sinai cakes are conical-shaped, representing Mt Sinai. They were stuffed with cheese, honey, nuts and raisins. These cakes were given to children in Germany and Northern France as Shavouth was the traditional time for them to begin studying the Torah. Special long-shaped breads or *hallahs* are baked for the holiday. The loaves are sometimes finished with four raised corners, symbolising the four possible ways of understanding the Torah. Those four ways are known as Pardes, which is abbreviation of the Hebrew words for plain (as written), symbolic, homiletic and esoteric.

Traditionally the floors of both the synagogue and home are spread with green herbs and sweet-smelling green leaves. Green is also the colour of the traditional *shchav borscht* (sorrel soup) which was served enriched either with sour cream or egg yolk.

The creative activities which precede every holiday continue, but alas the life and culture of the Jewish *shtetl* is no more. Although the Ashkenazi food tradition still goes on, it is constantly changing. Even among the ultra-Orthodox, who are the last bastions of the Ashkenazi cooking tradition, the health message is starting to penetrate. The prevailing attitude now is while still maintaining tradition to create a lighter, healthier cuisine.

8

ORANGES AND LEMONS
Anglo-Jewish Food

IT IS more than possible that Jewish merchants arrived in Britain with the Romans. According to Cornish folk tradition, which is based on the existence of Hebrew-derived names in Cornwall, Jewish merchants arrived with the Phoenician ships. The first written evidence of the presence of Jews in Britain comes in a document dated 1075 which mentions 'a great number' of Jews in Oxford. A Jewish name is also recorded in the Domesday Book of 1086.[1] The majority of the Jews probably arrived in the wake of William the Conqueror's invasion, along with a large number of other Flemish immigrants. About half settled in London and the rest established communities in York, Winchester, Lincoln, Canterbury, Northampton and Oxford.[2] The Jewish arrival suited the community as Jews specialised in money-lending which was forbidden to Christians. Moreover, they were successful merchants with commercial contacts in all the European centres. Thus the Jewish community prospered. It was dominated by a few very rich families, the most important being that of Aaron of Lincoln (1123–86) who was reputed to be the richest Englishman of his day.

Such rich Jewish families lived well. Aaron's house, which still stands in Lincoln, is a fine example of a lavishly built stone dwelling. We know very little of what these people ate, but can presume that the food was similar to that which medieval Jews ate in Spain, Italy or the Rhine valley. Contemporary records show that the Jewish community followed a relatively peaceful and strictly religious way of life until the first blood libel which occurred in Norwich in 1144. This heralded a period of anti-

Semitic activity which peaked with the anti-Jewish riots during the coronation of Richard I in 1189 and the York massacre in 1190. The Jews were finally expelled from Britain by King Edward I on 18 July 1290.

After the expulsion, a Jewish community did not exist as such, but there are records showing the presence of individual Jews in England. The community started to re-establish itself with the arrival of a few Marrano[3] families after the expulsion of the Jews from Spain in 1492. Although outwardly the Marranos practised Christianity, they tried as much as possible to keep the kosher laws and celebrate the Jewish holidays.

The rise of the Puritans and the resulting change of attitude towards the Jews helped to establish the Marrano community in London. In Europe, the situation was not as favourable. New massacres and the refugee problems created in their wake prompted the Dutch Rabbi, Manasseh Ben Israel (1604–57), to present a petition to Oliver Cromwell in 1655 negotiating the return of the Jews to England. Thus began the Anglo-Jewish community which has, since then, played an important part in all aspects of life in the British Commonwealth.

In the beginning, although the Jews did not have legal rights, they were allowed to establish synagogues and cemeteries. The first Sephardi synagogue was founded in Creechurch Lane in the City of London during 1657. In 1701 this synagogue moved to larger premises, at Bevis Marks, St Mary Axe, London, EC3. It is still used today, making it the oldest active synagogue in Britain. The rich, well-established Sephardi community attracted some rich Ashkenazi families from Amsterdam and Germany.

Towards the end of the 17th century when the poor Ashkenazi immigrants started to arrive they were not welcomed by the established families who saw them as a threat to the *status quo*. It was feared that the impoverished newcomers would damage the image of the prosperous Sephardi community in the eyes of the British upper classes with whom they had developed close commercial and social links.

The Jewish upper class had a lot to protect. They lived in grand style, some establishing homes both in towns and on country estates. They ate and entertained lavishly. David Ricardo (1772–1823), son of an old Dutch-English Sephardi family, was a talented economist and Member of Parliament. He was famous for his 'Ricardo's breakfast' which he gave in his Upper Brook Street house.[4] The Rothschilds, after leaving the East End of London, established a residence in Piccadilly and maintained a magnificent table which was presided over by chef Grosstephen Senior, who ran up a yearly bill of £5,000 for fish alone.

It is almost certain that the Ricardo household did not serve kosher or

Jewish food; Ricardo married a non-Jew and left the community. In the Rothschild household kosher meals were probably served only during the Jewish holidays. At other times the attitude was to avoid the most offensive items, such as pork and to a lesser extent shellfish, but otherwise to eat normally. Upper-class and upper-middle-class Jews entertained and were entertained by non-Jews. In 1845 Eliza Acton found it necessary to include in *Modern Cookery for Private Families* both recipes and advice on Jewish food. Mrs Acton observes that as a result of keeping the kosher laws the Jews:

> have oil much used in their cookery of fish, meat, and vegetables. Pounded almonds and rich syrups of sugar and water agreeably flavoured, assist in compounding their sweet dishes, many of which are excellent, and preserve much of their original character; but we are credibly informed that the restrictions of which we have spoken are not at the present day very rigidly observed by the main body of Jews in this country, though they are so by those who are denominated strict.[5]

Mrs Acton's observations reflect the image Jewish food had at that time: a rich and sweet cuisine of predominantly Sephardi origin typified by the use of olive oil, sugar syrups and almond milk. Mrs Acton's summation was not shared by all however. The Reverend Edmund Nelson (a relative of Lord Nelson) comments in his diary about the food served at Morden, the country estate of Abraham Goldsmid (1756–1810), a leading member of the London money market: 'Did not like their dinner; Jewish.'[6] The Goldsmids were known for their philanthropic work and were very involved in the life of the Jewish community. One of them, Benjamin, gave a part of his land to the Chief Rabbi for growing special reserved wheat for the Pesach *matzah*.[7]

Among the recipes included by Mrs Acton is a dish which has become associated with Anglo-Jewish food throughout the world. The recipe is for fish done the 'Jewish way' — 'to fry salmon and other fish in oil'. The dish was different because it was fried in olive oil instead of the customary suet or lard. Also, although it could be served hot, it was preferred cold. Mrs Acton's recipe instructs that the fish should be fried in fresh olive oil without any coating until it is lightly browned, 'when the proper colour is attained the pan must be lifted so high from the fire as to prevent it being deepened'. The fish is drained and, 'when perfectly cold, is dished garnished with light foliage. The Jews have cold fried fish served at their repast.' Fish fried in oil is also mentioned in the first Jewish cookbook published in the English language, *The Jewish Manual*. This recipe differs from Mrs Acton's because the fish is dipped in egg and flour before it is fried. In Miss Tattersall's *Jewish Cookery Book* (1895) the recipe calls for the fish to be first dipped in plain flour and then in egg. This recipe also appears in Florence Greenberg's *Jewish Cookery* of 1947. In this version the flour for coating is flavoured with salt and pepper which is the recipe used today; *matzah* meal sometimes replaces flour. Mrs Greenberg also mentions that if it is to be served hot, the fish should be covered with fine breadcrumbs after being dipped in flour and egg.

The Jewish preference for flavoursome, sweet food certainly comes through in the first Jewish cookbook to be published in English. *The Jewish Manual* is attributed to Judith, Lady Montefiore. It is a fascinating record of her colourful and mixed background together with practical advice about running a kosher home in Victorian England.[8] The recipes in the book come from many sources, and include delicacies from both the rich Mediterranean Sephardi tradition and Ashkenazi favourites. The book is full of alternative methods by which classical European recipes can be converted for use in kosher kitchens.

Lady Montefiore was well qualified to write such a book. She came from a wealthy Dutch Ashkenazi family. Her father, Levy Barnet Cohn, a rich linen merchant, settled in London before 1778. In 1812 she married Sir Moses Montefiore (1784–1885), a son of a leading Sephardi family. Sir Moses retired from business at the age of 40 to become the most important Jewish philanthropist of his day. He died aged 101. In the first years of their marriage the Montefiores did not strictly adhere to the kosher laws. Their attitude changed after their first visit to Jerusalem which also resulted in their growing involvement with the Jewish community in Palestine. Lord Montefiore sponsored the building of the first Jewish settlement outside the walls of the Old City and opened the first Jewish girls' school in Jerusalem. The involvement of the Montefiores with Jewish education both in England and in Palestine probably prompted Lady Montefiore to publish her manual. The Montefiores also began to keep a strict kosher kitchen and even hired a special *shochet* (slaughterer) to travel with them in order to slaughter trapped venison and other game.[9]

Although her prime aim was to educate, Lady Montefiore wrote the book for the only kind of people she knew: upper and middle classes. She assumed that her readers would have both the money and servants to make her cooking possible. The price of the book, five shillings, limited her readership considerably.

At first glance the book is very much like many other domestic works of the time, containing a large number of Victorian favourites. A closer examination reveals that even the most mundane of dishes sometimes includes an extra ingredient which makes the dish a bit different. There is a recipe for stewed brisket which includes half a pound of stoned raisins as well as the customary onion. The stew is finished with a teaspoon each of sugar and flour which is mixed into the cooking liquid. Lady Montefiore's attitude to sugar reflects the Jewish liking for sweetness even in savoury dishes: 'Sugar is an improvement in nearly all soups, sauces, and gravies; also with stewed vegetables, but of course must be used with discretion.' Discretion is also recommended with the use of bought sauces; she maintains that ketchup, soy and Harvey's sauce are used too indiscriminately by inferior cooks.

Lady Montefiore recommends a kosher version of béchamel sauce which is made on a veal broth base, flavoured with smoked beef and thickened with egg yolks and a spoonful of potato flour. 'It will not be quite as white, but will be excellent.' She also gives a sweet sauce without butter for puddings served after a meat dinner, although in the book separation between milk and meat is not specifically mentioned. In place of bacon in stews she recommends using a kosher sausage which she calls *choriso*. Instead of larding she suggests inserting small pieces of fat of smoked (kosher) meat, truffles or tongue. She also gives a recipe for clarifying suet in which she recommends the addition of a few sprigs of rosemary or a little orange flower water while melting, assuring the reader that this 'is far more delicate and wholesome than lard'.

The recipes collected by Lady Montefiore could satisfy any epicure. Among the Ashkenazi foods she mentions are classical favourites like sweet and sour carp, Pesach *grimstich* (probably derived from *chremslach* and baked instead of fried) and a version of *lokshen kugel*.

Her recipe for *commean* (*hamin*) combines the Sephardi and Ashkenazi methods and also outlines what Lady Montefiore considered socially permissible to be served at the table. It includes a cheap cut of meat which she calls gravy meat (soup meat), marrow bones and a calf's foot as well as two kinds of beans: Spanish beans and Spanish peas. Spanish beans are probably a variety of scarlet runner beans;[10] Spanish peas probably refers to chickpeas, which are extensively used in the Sephardi kitchen. She emphasised that cheap cuts of meat were not to be served at the table as they were unseemly in polite society. The excessively sweet *kugel* (1 lb of coarse brown sugar to 1 lb flour, ½ lb of suet and a soaked slice of white bread) is flavoured with nutmeg, ginger, clove and allspice. The Sephardi influence appears in numerous dishes in the Dutch and Spanish style, especially sweet dishes. Lady Montefiore gathered a wonderful collection of Sephardi sweets, including recipes for various holiday specialities. She also includes three recipes for *bola*, a kind of cake.

A simple *bola* recipe is also mentioned by Henry Mayhew[11] in *London Labour and the London Poor*, published in 1861. Mayhew's book contains probably the most detailed description of the everyday life and occupations of the poor Jews. Although honest and brutal, Mayhew's description is also stereotypical and prejudiced, revealing the way in which the Jews were seen both by him and by Victorian society in general. One of the major problems faced by the Jews was that the law did not allow them to be apprenticed to a Christian master, thus excluding them from industrial employment. The trades which were open to the poor Jews were those of 'hawkers' or 'travellers' who went all over the country selling watches, gold and silver pencil cases and eye glasses. In London, he observed, the Jews were 'an integral, but distinct and particular part of street life'. As well as having a monopoly on the second-hand clothes trade, they were involved in the sale of foodstuffs, especially 'green fruits', such as oranges, lemons, grapes and walnuts, and dried fruits like dates, both wholesale and on the streets.

> Jew boys, and the feebler and elder Jews . . . had, until some twelve or fifteen years back, almost the monopoly of orange and lemon street selling, or hawking.

The Jewish pedlars did not sell only oranges and lemons:

> The callings of which the Jew boys have a monopoly are not connected with the sale of any especial article, but rather with such things as present a variety from those ordinarily offered in the streets, such as cakes, sweetmeats, fried fish, and (in winter) elder wine. The cakes known as 'boolers' [*bolas*] — a mixture of egg, flour and candied orange or lemon peel, cut very thin, and with a slight colouring from saffron or something similar — are now sold principally, and used to be sold exclusively, by Jew boys. Almond cakes (little round cakes of crushed almonds) are at present vended by the Jew boys, and their sponge biscuits and Jew's butter-cakes are in demand. All those dainties are bought by the street-lads of the dozen or so Jew pastry cooks, the most of whom reside about Whitechapel. The difference in these cakes, in their sweetmeats, and their elder wine, is that there is a dash of spice about them not ordinarily met with. It is the same with the fried fish, a little spice or pepper being blended with the oil. In the street sale of pickles the Jews have also the monopoly; those, however, are seldom hawked, but generally sold from windows and door-steads. The pickles are cucumbers or gherkins, and onions — a large cucumber being 2 pence and the smaller 1 penny and ½ a penny.

Mayhew also recorded a detailed and fascinating account of the diet and attitude to kosher food of the East End Jews:

They are generally too lazy to light their own fires before they start of a morning, and nineteen out of twenty obtain their breakfast at the coffee-shops about Hounsditch.

When they return home from their day's work they have mostly some stew ready, prepared by their parents or wife. If they are not family men they go to an eating house. This is sometimes a Jewish house, but if no one is looking they creep into a Christian 'cook-shop' not being particular about eating 'tryfer' — that is, meat which has been killed by a Christian . . . On Saturday there's cold fish for breakfast and supper; indeed, a Jew would pawn the shirt off his back sooner than go without fish then; and in holiday time he *will* have it, if he has to get it out of stones. It is not reckoned a holiday unless there's fish.

Mayhew records that the attitude towards eating kosher is ambiguous. Some of the traders admitted that they bought meat whenever it was possible regardless of the way it was slaughtered. One trader said that he ate only kosher in spite of the high price of kosher meat. A 12-year-old boy told Mayhew that he never ate pork: 'Never touched it; I'd as soon eat a cat; so would my father . . . I don't know why it should not be eaten, only that it's wrong to eat it . . . I don't think pork smells nice in a cook-shop.'

The period that followed the publication of Mayhew's book brought some changes to the Jews of the East End who prospered in their trades, especially in textiles and tailoring. Some families started to move from the East End and established communities in Dalston, Islington and Canonbury. By 1880 Jews had settled as far north as St John's Wood and Hampstead. In the same year, as the result of pogroms in Russia, a big wave of immigrants started to arrive. These Russian and Polish immigrants again upset the apple cart. The new Jewish middle classes, who were mostly of Western Ashkenazi origin from Germany and Austria, looked with horror at the flood of poor, primitive and fanatically religious Eastern Europeans. They tried to dissuade them from coming, but still they arrived. These impoverished refugees found the conditions in the East End difficult. They did not speak the language and were totally unprepared to deal with the realities of life in London. The years of struggle which started with the 1880 immigration and lasted until the end of the Second World War created a short-lived but colourful and active Jewish community which had a developed cultural life, Yiddish newspapers and a Yiddish theatre and music hall. Sadly this community has died almost without trace, being revived only in retrospective exhibitions and in the memories of few survivors who are disappearing fast.

The markets of the East End which maintained some Jewish character until as recently as the 1970s are no more. Instead of pickled gherkins, cold fried fish and kosher meats, Bombay duck, curry powders and *halal* meat are sold. The East End changed its character yet again when it accepted the new wave of Pakistani, Bengali and Bangladeshi immigrants. These people are involved in the same industries as were the Jews: the rag trade and the supplying of food with 'extra spice'.

The vast improvement in the living standard of the Jewish community was due not only to their industriousness, but also to an early realisation that the best and quickest way to succeed in the British society was to become Anglicised as soon as possible. One of the cultural casualties of this rapid progress was the traditional Jewish kitchen. To paraphrase a remark made by Dr Jonathan Miller's father: 'My father genuinely believed that American Jews were Jews but British Jews were British.'[12] American Jewish food is Jewish, British Jewish food is British. Although in some households traditional Jewish food is still cooked and British Jews do follow a certain 'Jewish' pattern, nevertheless Anglo-Jewish food has developed more or less on the same lines as the general British kitchen.

This development is reflected in the cookbooks which have been published. *The Jewish Manual* had little effect on the way British Jews cooked. It was followed by a number of Jewish cookbooks which also had practically no influence on the Anglo-Jewish kitchen.

Miss M.A.S. Tattersall's *Jewish Cookery Book* (1895) was designed to teach working-class Jewish girls the delights of British cookery. They were introduced to sausage rolls, jam roly-poly, toad in the hole and Yorkshire pudding made with water to comply with the kosher laws. Although there was an attempt to 'Judify' one dish — she calls bread and butter pudding 'Jacob pudding' — there are very few recipes of Jewish origin. All but one of the Jewish recipes mentioned are Ashkenazi and the only hint of the Sephardi tradition is in a recipe for almond pudding.

The cookbook which had the most profound effect on the Anglo-Jewish kitchen was Florence Greenberg's *Cookery Book*, first published in 1947 by the *Jewish Chronicle*. Five revised editions were printed until it was finally brought out in paperback in 1967. Mrs Greenberg's book was immensely popular as a wedding present to young Jewish brides, and thus influenced several generations of Jewish cooks. Although the book mentions some Jewish recipes, sadly it does not reflect any pride, love or understanding of traditional Jewish food.

The Anglo-Jewish attitude started changing towards the end of the 1970s and coincided with the general revolution in British food. Like the rest of the population, Jews improved their living standards and travelled more generally, particularly to Israel and the big Jewish communities in

North America. Their attitude to eating out changed and there was a larger variety of restaurants to choose from. Evelyn Rose became the food editor of the *Jewish Chronicle* and published *The Complete International Jewish Cookbook*. The book was unashamedly Jewish, although very Ashkenazi in emphasis. It contains a large number of traditional recipes which are explained and presented with their cultural background and common names.

Eating out has always presented a problem for Jews. Except for Blooms restaurant in the East End and Golders Green, London is not famous for its kosher eateries. Until recently the availability of good quality take away food was limited to a few highly populated Jewish areas. However the 1980s brought changes to the Jewish food market. New take away kosher food started to appear in supermarket chains, especially Tesco. The new Israeli immigrants began to open both kosher and 'American Jewish style' delicatessens which are flourishing, showing that there is renewed interest in traditional, though not necessarily kosher, Jewish food. The Israeli immigrants also opened a large number of beigel bakeries and restaurants serving 'Israeli' fare, thus re-establishing the Sephardi influence on the Anglo-Jewish kitchen.

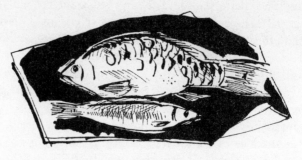

9

THE NEW JERUSALEM
Jewish Food in North America

IF JERUSALEM is the apple of the Jewish eye, the Big Apple is the crowning glory of the Jewish kitchen. There is no other place on earth, except for Israel, where Jewish food is so much in evidence. New York would not be the same without beigel and lox or pastrami on rye.

The history of the Jews in America started with the expedition of Christopher Columbus in 1492. The expedition's interpreter, a Marrano named Luis de Torres, was the first European to set foot in the new land. He was also the first man to make use of tobacco.[1] By 1654 a group of twenty-three Jewish refugees of Spanish and Portuguese origin had settled in New York which was then called New Amsterdam. They were the core of the American Jewish community and were soon joined by others who began to establish Jewish communities in other parts of the colony. The numbers were increased by the arrival of German Jews: 'Men of culture and substance, who had participated in the revolutionary movements of those years, or who were disappointed at the wave of reaction which subsequently set in, turned their faces in increasing numbers to the new continent, where equal constitutional rights and economic opportunity were open to all.'[2]

Most of these Jews belonged to the emancipated Reform movement which questioned the old religion and tried to update it. Amongst the first rules to come under scrutiny were the dietary prohibitions. The Reform movement maintained that those laws were only ritualistic and had nothing to do with the central philosophy of the religion and were therefore old-fashioned and unnecessary. In 1883 there was a notorious

106

scene at the first graduation dinner at the Hebrew Union College which was the main Reform-controlled Rabbinical seminary in the States. Shrimps and other non-kosher foods were served. There was uproar, and many Rabbis walked out in disgust.[3]

Both the Reform movement and the strong German influence were the dominating powers of American Jewry almost until the 1930s. Jews of German origin dictated the etiquette, influencing the way the Jews behaved, ate and dressed. They created a society which was dominated by rich and almost assimilated families whose lifestyle was as grand if not grander than that of the Anglo-Jewish upper classes. Kashruth figured very little in the life of the Jewish upper classes as the Reform movement left decisions about keeping kashruth to the discretion of the individual.

A strong reaction to this laxity of observance comes through in the first Jewish cookbook to be published in the States. Mrs Esther Levy's *Jewish Cookery Book on Principles of Economy, adapted for Jewish Housekeepers, with the Addition of Many Useful Medicinal Recipes, and Other Valuable Information, relative to Housekeeping and Domestic Management* states that although her book follows kashruth law, these rules were not followed by the majority. In the introduction Mrs Levy describes some of the basic rules of kashruth and some elementary precepts of Jewish observance, such as having a *mezuza*, lighting candles on the Sabbath and separating the *hallah*. Curiously she does not mention separation of meat and milk in her introduction. However in her suggestion for breakfast (Monday) she mentions, almost in passing, that if cold meat is served it should be put separately on the side table, while cold-boiled potatoes can be fried and served instead of the milk or buttered toast. Although in the extensive equipment list she advocates having different rolling pins, separate marble slabs for meat and butter and separate dish pans for washing meat and butter, there is no advice about keeping a separate set of utensils for meat and milk.

Mrs Levy's book also contains practical advice on running a household. She gives recipes for a large number of pickles, baking bread, cheesemaking, butter churning, how to fatten poultry in four or five days, salting and smoking meat. These practical recipes were probably included because Mrs Levy recognised the needs of Jewish housewives living in rural communities which, as a result of their isolation, had no kosher food suppliers so that the Jewish cook was forced to make all the necessary foodstuffs at home.

At the end of the book Mrs Levy gives menu suggestions for each day of the week. Sunday dinner (lunch) is the most sumptuous: 'This is the day the husbands are at home, then something good must be prepared in honour of the lords of the household. Ladies need not be at a loss to know what to have, when they have examined this book.' She honours her lords with mock turtle soup followed by a second course of roast turkey, goose, duck or lamb with mint sauce; this is followed by entrées of calf's feet and veal stew served with broccoli, mashed turnips and boiled onions. Finally there is strawberry pudding, fruit desserts, fruits, nuts and raisins.

If Mrs Levy was obscure in the matter of milk and meat, later cookbooks went even further. Collections of recipes which were published towards the end of the 19th century and the beginning of the 20th by Reform synagogues to raise money for charity abandoned kashruth altogether. Recipes for shrimp gumbos, crab cakes, dressed lobster, bacon, ham and even, in one case, pork chops, appeared side by side with recipes for *frimzel*, *scharfe* (sour) fish and *matzah chrimsel*. The attitude to pork is rather curious. Ham and bacon are mentioned freely, but the word pork or a recipe for a whole pork joint is rarely found. It is as if pork is acceptable so long as it is not recognised either by name or by shape.

The charity cookbooks on the whole were collections of recipes donated by members of the congregation and though popular, judging by the number published, did not play an important role in shaping the Jewish-American way of eating. Their importance or, according to one's point of view, their corrupting influence was that they legitimised in print the consumption of forbidden foods.

While the charity books reflected a well-established, almost assimilated society, the situation at street level was drastically different. The pogroms in Russia and Poland during the 1880s turned the trickle of immigrants into a flood. Between the years 1881 and 1914 almost 2 million Jews arrived in the States; most of them were from small *shtetls* of Central and Eastern Europe, Yiddish speaking, fiercely religious, superstitious and desperately poor. They clung in the beginning to their traditional ways of life and food, congregating in ghettos for safety in numbers but also because it was the only possible way to obtain essential kosher ingredients.

The health of the new immigrants was poor as the result of many years of hunger and the unbalanced fatty diet which they brought with them from Europe. The Jewish establishment realised that a drastic dietary re-education was essential. The situation is reflected in *Jewish Dietary Problems* published in 1919 by Mary Schapiro, who was the director of the Bureau of Home Economics and Dietetics of the United Hebrew Charities.[4] She observed that the diet of the newcomers was mainly based on cooked meats and fish, with no fresh fruit and vegetables; supplementing the children's diet with fresh milk was unknown.

The 1880 immigrants settled mostly in the Lower East side of

Manhattan. Although, there were some attempts by the established Jewish community to divert the immigrants to other centres, New York was the place they wanted to be. The stories of a 'new Jerusalem', with its streets paved with gold, in a country where even a poor tailor's son could become a president, spread through the *shtetls* like fire. Although the streets were not paved with gold, New York did become the new Jerusalem. By 1900 New York had the largest Yiddish-speaking community — one million — in the world. It also had the world's largest Yiddish Press. The Yiddish theatre flourished and gained an importance never achieved before. Synagogues and study houses popped up everywhere. Today, the Lower East side has changed; the Jews have moved to more prestigious pastures and China Town is expanding into the once purely Jewish areas. But even now, walking down the narrow streets where the Israel Etrog Centre exists next to Hong Kong Funerals Inc., it is not difficult to imagine what the streets were like at the beginning of the century, especially on Sunday. One can well imagine the sense of freedom and wonderment experienced by the new immigrants after the oppression of the European ghettos. The streets were lined with barrows groaning with piles of fresh fruit and vegetables, wooden tubs were filled with plump dill pickles, pickled tomatoes and pickled, red-lined juicy watermelon rinds.

> 'How much is this pickle?' asks an old Jewish woman holding a large pickled cucumber. 'A nickel,' answers the dealer. 'A nickel is too much,' she said, and put the pickle back into the barrel. She fishes in the barrel again and comes up with a little pickle. 'And how much is this little pickeleh?' she asks in a tender voice. 'That pickeleh?' answered the shopkeeper just as tenderly. 'Only a nickeleh.'[5]

There were herrings galore, *schmaltz* herring, bismarks, pickled, rolled with onions and sauced with *miltz* (soft roes), soaked in oil and full of flavour, not forgetting the pickled, smoked and spiced meats; the cheeses, the *varenikes*, the *knishes*. This is the stuff that dreams are made of, and all could be bought with pride and in Yiddish.

Such food, according to the home economics experts and dietitians, might be unbalanced and unhealthy, yet it was the taste of home. It was not only consumed in the narrow alleys of New York's Lower East side but spread high and wide, bridging cultural and religious barriers, all over the country. Although it was the Germans who introduced the delicatessen into the American food tradition, towards the end of the 19th century, the Jews made them into delis. These shops used to sell mostly cooked or peppered foods, breads, pickles and beers. The Jewish immigrants, graduating from being barrow boys, branched into the delicatessen business, introducing many of their traditional and well-loved foods. The shops which sold blood sausages, hams and *shpeck* were also selling corned (salt) beef, pastrami sandwiches and *gefilte fish* balls ready to eat.

The deli is not only a shop, it is also a place where you can have a nosh (a snack), a meal, a *fress* (gorge) or just come in to shelter from the rain, meet friends and exchange gossip. Delis are an institution, nay, places of worship, where quantity is as important as quality; the only place where a Jew can idolise other gods in the shape of gargantuan sandwiches, pickled tomatoes and large bowls of steaming chicken soup laden with matzah balls, *kreplach* or noodles, sometimes all three together.

They introduced to the American tradition of eating out not only mammoth portions, which probably led to the invention of the 'doggie bag', but also a few dishes which have entered the classical American repertoire. The most famous of these is undoubtedly corned beef (known as salt beef in Britain) and pastrami sandwich on rye: hot beef either just pickled (corned) or spiced and sometimes delicately smoked (pastrami), sliced paper thin and piled high between two slices of rye bread. Pastrami, a dish of Romanian origin, became so popular that a pastrami Olympics was held in New York in 1973 to decide on the best pastrami sandwich in town.

One version of the corned beef sandwich, the Reuben (pronounced rooben), even entered James Beard's definitive *American Cookery*.[6] He mentions two versions: a cocktail Reuben and the fully blown version which he describes thus: 'The old Reuben sandwiches I remember were made of thickish slices of pumpernickel, corned beef, sauerkraut, chicken breast or turkey breast, Swiss cheese, and Russian dressing. They were stupendous, but made a perfect summer meal and were also well fitted for picnics.' The modern version includes only corned beef covered with sauerkraut and topped with melted Swiss cheese. The origin of the Reuben is disputed. According to Evan Jones[7] there are two contenders for the title of inventor of this gargantuan culinary concoction. The first, which seems more likely, is the chef of Reuben's restaurant in Manhattan who first made it in 1914 for one of Charlie Chaplin's leading ladies; his version employed Virginia-baked ham instead of corned beef. The second is Reuben Kay, of Omaha, who invented a sandwich for his weekly poker game which included kosher corned beef, sauerkraut, Emmenthaler cheese and Russian dressing. One cannot get a Reuben in a kosher deli, but with the invention of non-milk cheese (also made for *parve* cheese cakes), the day might come.

In the beginning most delis were kosher and therefore did not serve any milk products. This inconvenient situation was solved by an invention which is purely Jewish: the dairy restaurant. These restaurants are usually attached to a bakery and serve a large range of meatless soups, *blintzes*, egg dishes, and vegetarian dishes as well as teas, coffees, cakes, breads and savoury pastries.

One cannot mention either delis or Jewish bakeries without mentioning beigels. The beigel or water doughnut (as Mrs Leonard, the Mrs Beeton of the Jewish-American kitchen, calls it) is probably the most popular Jewish contribution to the North American and international cuisine. Beigel, cream cheese and lox (smoked salmon) is the taste of Sunday breakfast/brunch to most New Yorkers. The beigel crosses more cultural barriers than any other Jewish food and is even sold tinted green for the celebration of St Patrick's day!

The history of the beigel is confused, but I found the most feasible story of its origin from Richard Yaffe.[8] In an article on kosher food he claims the beigel was invented in Vienna around 1683 when the city was under siege by the Turks and the Polish cavalry under the leadership of King Sobieski was called in for help. Some of the soldiers stayed and opened a coffee shop where they sold a stirrup-shaped pastry designed to symbolise the stirrups of the victorious Polish army. *Bugel* is the German word for a stirrup. From there the story becomes unclear. It is feasible that the *bugel* was brought to Galitzia by Jewish immigrants from Austria, gaining the Yiddish version of its name — beigel — and losing its stirrup shape to become the round, plump, shiny object which is eaten today. It arrived in New York with the Galitzian immigration at the beginning of the 20th century. Another version maintains that the beigel is named after Count Baigel 'who stuck them on his billiard cue so that he could munch while he played'.[9]

The New York beigel industry started in the basements of the Lower East side of Manhattan and the Williamsberg Bridge section of Brooklyn, both predominantly Jewish areas. The beigels were baked in coal-fired brick ovens, packed in sacks and peddled, usually by 'Jew Boys', on the sidewalks of New York. By 1964 (when Yaffe's article was written) the specialised beigel bakeries numbered thirty-six and had a union of their own: local 338 of the Bakery and Confectioners' Union. The union improved the lot of the beigel bakers and won, after a few strikes, a fringe benefit no other branch of the union has: each member receives a dozen beigels free every day.

Today's beigels are sold everywhere and are made in every conceivable combination of flour, flavour and size. One can find beigels made of rye, wholewheat, with egg, brown, black or green, flavoured with onions, caraway seeds, decorated with salt, poppy seeds and sesame seeds. As one beigel advertisement boasted: 'The healthiest food one can get. Made of gluten flour. All the starch boiled out . . . only 50 calories per beigel' — gold to figure-conscious America.

Beigels can now be found in miniature versions served at elegant cocktail parties. A recent product is beigel toasts, which started as a way of utilising stale beigels, but is now made specially. The beigels are sliced, dried in the oven, packed in fancy bags and sold to be eaten in the same way as Melba toasts.

Beigel bakeries also sell another speciality called by New Yorkers a *bialy* or bialystoker roll named after the Polish town Bialystock. It is known in Britain as a *platzel* or 'onion *platzel*' and is doughy, chewy and rounded, usually dotted with onion and slightly depressed in the middle.

There is constant dispute about which beigel is best. Torontonians maintain that theirs is better than the New York version as it is less sweet. The Jews of Montreal vie for first place as they have developed a special beigel which is larger in diameter, thinner and has a more chewy quality. There is also an Israeli beigel, or *beigaleh* or *ke'ach*, which is a large, thin circle of compact dough which is delicious hot.

The original beigel is a mixture of wheat flour, water, yeast and salt. The resulting dough, after short fermentation, is punched down and shaped by hand. After proving for 4–5 hours, the raw beigels are tossed into boiling water. Sometimes sugar is added to the water to increase the gloss of the beigel. They are boiled for 2–3 minutes or until they float to the top (the bad ones sink). When ready, they are taken out, lined up on narrow boards and put into a hot oven to bake for 15–20 minutes. Shaping a beigel is skilled work and as far as I know there is no machine which can do this. According to an old Jewish tale you must first take a hole and then shape the beigel around it.

When one talks about beigels one must also mention the lox. The name comes from the German word for salmon, *lachs* or the Scandinavian *lax*. Lox is smoked salmon but, as James Beard[10] notes, it is saltier than the best quality. It is also smoked at a higher temperature than the conventional smoked salmon and is usually made from Atlantic salmon.

Kosher food, especially in the States, is a billion dollar business. It covers food produced not only by Jewish manufacturers but also by most of the multi-national congolmerates who want their share of this lucrative business — the Jews are good consumers. At the beginning of the 20th century it was easier to determine what was kosher and what was not. The ingredients were rather simple and their origin was easily identified. With the introduction of food supplements, substitutes and reprocessed foodstuffs, the kashruth of ingredients has become almost impossible to define. The kashruth authorities are constantly faced with new ingredients that were never mentioned in the Sages' writing. The situation is not helped by the fact that the kashruth laws are not fixed and are subject to the interpretation of individual Rabbis.

Processed food may contain ingredients which are not acceptable and manufacturers are required to put an identifying symbol on all their products to signify that they are kosher. Looking at an average supermarket shelf in a Jewish area, one is overwhelmed by the number of symbols each belonging to a different branch of kashruth. One can find the letters K, MKU, U on its own, K in a triangle, U in a circle, OK, and so on.

The battle for kashruth does not take place only on the supermarket shelf. In the States the kosher authorities have also to face the spreading dominance of the Reform movement and the tendency of many young Jews to abandon the strict observance of the dietary laws. In an attempt to fight this corruption the *Jewish Examiner* announced a competition for kosher recipes. A collection of these recipes was published in 1937 in a book titled *Prize Kosher Recipes*, edited by 'Balabusta',[11] the editor of the women's page. In the introduction 'Balabusta' declares the purpose of the book: 'To bring back not only strict kashruth but also to help the fight against racketeers who declare that they are kosher when they are otherwise.'

To get a kosher seal of approval is complicated and in many cases also expensive. Payments to some Rabbis are high and the requirement of keeping a permanent *mashgiach* (religious observer) means that a salary has to be paid to an unproductive member of staff.

The fight became public with the publication of *The Kosher Food Guides: Organized Kashruth* in 1935. The declared purpose of the publication was to 'serve as a guide to observant Jewish women desiring to uphold the traditional dietary laws'. The magazine gave practical advice, advertised kosher products, restaurants and hotels and promoted blunt, forceful propaganda about the advantages of kashruth.

The OK (Organized Kashruth) Laboratories magazine was distributed free to hundreds of thousands of Jewish homes around the New York area; the income came from advertising and revenue from companies who sought their seal of approval. By 1952 a special announcement was published: 'Progressive firms will find it to their advantage to contact us and arrange for the use of our OK seal to further the sale of their products. Every Jewish buyer will select the kosher identified product especially if sold at the same price as the product that bears no kosher symbol of the OK laboratories.'

In the same year, as a reaction to the establishment of a rival publication,[12] OK released its most scathing comment:

> BE ON YOUR GUARD: OK Laboratories are the only genuine seal of kashruth. If you read the Yiddish press you will see the following: 'When you see the letter K on the package, you can be assured that the content was prepared under strict rabbinical supervision.' These are lies, and are inserted by the Joseph Jacobs Jewish Marketing Board Inc . . . They also inserted the letter K to fool the Jewish buying public into believing that the K is the OK laboratories . . . It is a fraud on the Jewish public . . . For your own protection be sure that the product bears our OK seal and not only the letter K which also appears on ham and other trefa.

Since then the situation seems to have become even more confusing with the recent popularity of the *glat* kosher. To make matters even more confusing, a new style food started to emerge called 'Jewish style' or 'kosher style'. This is a misleading term as it does not necessarily mean that the food is kosher, but only implies that the food is Jewish-oriented.

10

THE RECURRING CYCLE
Food in Israel

THE QUESTION which kept recurring in my mind even before I started writing this book was: is there an overall Jewish cuisine? The term cuisine has to be clarified. The Oxford Dictionary defines cuisine as a 'country's or establishment style of cooking: food which grows out of more or less one culture'. It is based on regional recipes which, with the help of talented chefs encouraged by enthusiastic and rich patrons, create a national style.

As my research progressed it became clear that although one cannot talk about a Jewish cuisine nevertheless a clear overall pattern of eating habits and attitudes to food does emerge. It is expressed by a common liking for certain ingredients which are either important for religious ceremonies or are written into the cultural or tribal memory. There is one more uniting element which is as important: a shared common experience. Although the Jews are not one cultural unit, as some ardently maintain, we are a group of people who share one terrible human experience. We all share the heinous memory of the loss of the most basic human right, the right to exist. The Jewish obsessive attitude to food, amongst other things, is the direct result of our mothers' memories of deprivation, famine and war.

The connection between the national palate and the effects of common historical and political events became even clearer when I started writing the chapter about Israeli food. To complete my research I went to Israel to look for original material, but mainly to talk to cooks, rekindle old memories and revisit favourite markets. Sadly this visit coincided with the occupation of Kuwait by the Iraqi army; the Middle East was at war

115

again. War in Israel is tangible, and you can feel it around you. It is manifested in a certain nervousness; basic foodstuffs such as oil, flour, eggs, sugar and tinned fish are bought in large quantities leaving gaps on supermarket shelves and starting rumours of shortages and panic. People congregate in tense groups, listening silently to news bulletins on the radio.

Food, like everything else in Israel, is the result of a unique, complicated set of circumstances which have been created by an accelerated evolutionary process, not so much a melting pot as a pressure cooker. Evolutionary processes which normally take hundreds of years to achieve have been condensed into just a hundred years. The accelerated process gives us a rare opportunity to examine the development of 'ethnic' food in a situation where people of diverse origins have fused together to create a kitchen which is specifically Israeli. The uniqueness of this process in Israel lies in the fact that all the stages of the development of national eating habits still exist in living memory.

The fusing of ethnic groups in Israel is unparalleled; intermarriage is essential for the survival of the Israeli Jewish state as no minority is big enough to maintain purity. This creates a situation in which the culinary heritage of one household is based on at least two origins, for food cooked at home must take into account not only the ethnic origin of the cook (the wife) but also that of her partner and partner's family.

Synthesis is a fascinating process. It can be seen all over Israel, in colourful well-stocked and exotic markets, enticing, delicious street food and some superb domestic cooking. The markets are at the centre of the process. Housewives like conversing when shopping and this is a wonderful opportunity to exchange opinions, gossip and recipes. When encountering a new ingredient they immediately enquire how to use it. The Israeli food market is changing at a phenomenal rate as new varieties are introduced and dropped at a lightning speed. The locals are used as a testing ground for the development of new products and new varieties of fruit and vegetables. Street food is yet another unifying factor because it is eaten by the whole community and bridges the barriers of religion, national affiliation, economics and ethnic origins.

From the onset I realised that my description of food in Israel would rely heavily on personal memories. Being a second generation *Sabra*,[1] I also realised that my memories of food would be totally different to those of the new immigrants who first encountered Israel in placement camps and developing settlements.

I was privileged to be born into an old, well-established Israeli family who emigrated to Palestine at the beginning of the century. Although the background of the family kitchen was Southern Russian Ashkenazi, the

116

influence of the Middle East was very noticeable. My mother, who is a talented and adventurous cook, learned her art not only from her mother but also from the Arab neighbours, both Christian and Muslim, amongst whom she was born in the old part of Haifa. Nor was the European influence only Southern Russian because although my grandmother, who was also a superb cook, was brought up in the southern Russian port of Odessa, she was born in Besarabia, which is on the border of Russia and Romania. Therefore the food my mother created was a rich and fascinating mixture of all those cultures. This open and imaginative kitchen was the foundation of my life-long interest in food. For this I am eternally grateful to her.

It is almost impossible to describe Israeli food in chronological order because subjects tend to overlap. For convenience sake I have divided this chapter into four broad subjects which I conceive to be the most important elements in the shaping of the Israeli palate: domestic cooking, kibbutz food, street food, and commercial and institutional food.

PALESTINIAN FOOD

There has been a continuous Jewish population in Palestine since the destruction of the Second Temple in 70AD. Although enjoying short periods of autonomy the Jewish community was generally small, isolated and very religious. Towards the middle of the 19th century it was concentrated around the holy cities of Jerusalem, Hebron, Safad and Tiberias and mainly comprised followers of various religious sects and pilgrims who came to be buried in the Holy Land. They lived in small, fanatically religious communities and strictly maintained the traditions they had brought with them from their country of origin.

This essentially rural community lived among sparsely populated and poverty stricken Arab areas. The indigenous population was made up of poor, struggling Christian, Muslim and Druze landworkers or *fellahs*. The countryside also supported a large number of nomadic Bedouins and some marauding warring tribes who roamed all the Middle East. Palestine was constantly at war and the food eaten by the poor villagers was a food of necessity.

It is difficult to pinpoint the origins of dishes around the Middle East, especially in Palestine, which was situated at a crossroads of commerce and pilgrimage. Obviously cross-fertilisation between cultures has been going on from the beginning of civilisation. Thus though one cannot deny the existence of defined national dishes, peasant food throughout the Middle East tends to be rather similar.

The villagers' diet was mainly based on grain, wheaten flour, *dora* (millet), olive oil, cheese and clarified butter. Rice, although liked and eaten when possible, was considered a luxury. These basic ingredients were supplemented by harvesting cultivated and wild plants. Sheep and cattle were slaughtered only for major celebrations. Otherwise the only meat to be eaten was game or domesticated pigeon. The villagers evolved a style of cooking which depended almost exclusively on locally grown ingredients. Foreign spices, although expensive, were available because the spice traders from the east used to travel through Palestine. The most used spices then were pepper, cinnamon (or *cassia*), allspice (pimento) and cardamom. But the favourite flavouring by far was *za'atar*, a herb which is traditionally identified as the Biblical hyssop (*ezove*, *Marjorana syriaca*), a small shrub with dark green leaves which grows profusely all around the Mediterranean coast and the Middle East. As well as having a savoury, pungent smell, *za'atar* is a potent disinfectant, relaxant and anti-inflammatory substance which is still used extensively in folk medicine. It is employed as a remedy for colds and stomach pains and is an effective wormicide and antiseptic.

Commercially bought *za'atar* is not pure hyssop, but a mixture of several species of wild marjoram, thyme and oregano.* Various proportions of those herbs are minced together and the combination used varies from village to village and sometimes from family to family. The minced herbs are mixed with a souring agent made from the minced dried pulp of the *sumac* fruit.† Salt and sesame seeds are added and olive oil is also sometimes included.

Za'atar is the flavour of Palestinian food and is used to flavour meat, fish, salads, cheeses and breads. It blends well with the local olive oil and complements the strongly flavoured fatty local mutton and lamb. One can find it in a pizza-like pastry called *fatir*, which is made from thin pitta dough sprinkled with olive oil and *za'atar* before being baked quickly in a very hot oven and served piping hot, a delicious and fragrant snack to be

---

* The most commonly used are the delicate, fragrant *za'atar el azale* (deer thyme, *Satureja thymbra*), the inferior *za'atar chmare* (donkey thyme, *Thymbra spicata*) and *za'atar farsi* (Persian thyme, *Coridothymus capitatus*).

† *Sumac* (*Rhus coriaria*) is the dark purple fruit of the *sumac* tree which grows in the wild all over the hills of the Middle East. It has a fruity sour taste and is used to add sourness anywhere a lemon is used. It also makes a deliciously refreshing summer drink. Its Hebrew name *oog ha'burskaim* (oog of the tanners) indicates its commercial importance as the acidity of the fruit was used as a tanning agent.

eaten while walking. *Za'atar*, especially when made from pure hyssop, should be used with discretion as it can impart a bitter, unpleasant flavour if used excessively.

The diet was supplemented by greens and vegetables, both cultivated and wild. Legumes were eaten both dried and fresh. Dry legumes were considered heavy to digest and were eaten mainly for breakfast or early lunch. The most important legume was, and still is, the chickpea. It is used as a base for stews, may be eaten roasted or deep fried as a snack, and is the main ingredient for the two most popular dishes of the area: hummus and falafel.

The most popular way of cooking vegetables was to sweat them in oil with plenty of onion and garlic, producing an effect very much like a single vegetable *ratatouille*. Tomatoes were sometimes included, but the vegetables were more usually cooked in their own juice until very soft, then served at room temperature, never hot, accompanied by lemon wedges and bread.

A large number of wild leaves and herbs were used. The most prized of the edible wild plants was a thistle called *akub* (*Gundelia tournefortii*). It has a delicate flavour and a texture slightly resembling asparagus. It was eaten either stuffed with meat or chopped and fried with eggs. The unopened flowerheads were eaten like artichokes. The most commonly used wild leaf which is still widely eaten is the *chubayzah* (mallow, *Malva sylvestris*). It is the most prolific and versatile wild plant of the area and can be found everywhere on deserted sites and roadsides all over the country. Its name both in Arab and Hebrew means bread, indicating the plant's importance and versatility. Most of the plant is eaten. Its fruit is flat and round, vaguely resembling miniature segmented loaves. They are eaten raw and known by children as 'little breads'. There is a Christian-Arab folk story about the origin of the name. When bread ran out at the house of Mary, Jesus told her to pay the baker with a branch of *malva* because money was short. He promised that for every loaf the baker would give her he would find a loaf (bar) of gold. And so it was that golden miniature loaves (the fruit) appeared on the *malva* and they sustain the poor even today. The leaves are eaten either as a salad dressed with onions, olive oil and lemon, or they are cooked in a variety of ways, in stews, or fried with burgul or rice. They are also used as stuffing for pastries or made into patties and can also be used instead of vine leaves for *mahshies* (*dolmas*).

Breakfast in the Arab village consisted mostly of bread dipped in olive oil, eaten with pickled olives. The olive tree, especially in Galilee, supplied the most commonly used fuel. Although olive oil was the most common

119

cooking medium, sheep's tail fat and *samna* (clarified butter) were also used. The latter was prepared mostly from sheep and goat's butter. Sesame oil was sometimes used; sesame seeds were mainly reserved for making tahina paste. Tahina is one of the most versatile ingredients of the Middle Eastern kitchen. It is used as a piquant sour dip for falafel, *dolmas*, and grilled meats and is also used to make hummus and as a sauce in many fish and meat dishes. Sesame paste is also the main ingredient for the manufacture of *halvah*, one of the most popular sweetmeats of the Middle East.

Meat such as lamb, mutton or goat was usually roasted on an open fire. Young animals were either put on a spit and roasted whole or sliced and skewered to form kebabs. Mutton and inferior cuts were chopped before being mixed with lamb or mutton fat. Herbs and spices were then added, mainly cinnamon, allspice, pepper and cardamom. The mixture was then formed into *shishlick* or *kuftas* (patties) which were skewered and grilled. Minced lamb was also made into *sania*, a dish which gets its name from the special round flat metal tray on which it is baked. In this dish the mince is flavoured with parsley, allspice and sometimes cinnamon before being baked until half cooked. It is then covered with tahina sauce and returned to the oven to finish cooking. The tahina sauce for this dish is made rather sour to counteract the fattiness of the lamb. The dish is served decorated with fried pine nuts which are the ubiquitous garnish of the Middle Eastern kitchen, adding crunchiness and a delicious, slightly resinous flavour to the food. The pine nuts are slightly browned in a small amount of oil to help maintain their crispness.

Chicken was eaten rarely because they were kept mainly for their eggs. Pigeons, however, were important and almost every household had a pigeon coop in the yard. The birds were usually barbecued, but could also be stuffed with rice or burgul flavoured with raisins, cinnamon and pine nuts before being stewed on a bed of onions.

Game was eaten a lot. Deer could be found in almost every part of the country and was hunted extensively. The meat was either used fresh or salted and kept for further use. Quail, partridge (*chogla*) and wild ducks were hunted.

Porcupine was also eaten and the Arab hunters evolved an ingenious way of cooking it. First the porcupine was cleaned, but not skinned, after which the whole animal was encased in a coat of wet clay or mud and put directly in the fire. When ready, the clay casing was broken, removing with it all the porcupine spines and leaving the delicate meat.

Fresh milk was rarely drunk as a beverage. Cow's milk was almost unknown and most of the milk used was from goats and sheep. It was made into several kinds of yoghurt and yoghurt drinks. The cheese was eaten either fresh as curds or made into hard cheese which was cured, dried and mostly used for cooking. The most typical and popular soft cheese of the area is the *labaneh*, which was originally made from goat or sheep yoghurt, though cow's milk is now used extensively. *Labaneh* is a fresh, piquantly sour, brilliant white soft cheese. It is either eaten fresh, dressed in olive oil and served with bread or shaped into small balls and preserved in olive oil.

Conditions in the urban centres were radically different. Especially from the middle of the 19th century Palestinian administrative centres flourished. The first rail link encouraged in both the Turks and various European powers an awareness of the economic possibilities of the Holy Land. The Turks also became aware of the importance of a coastal railway from Istanbul to Cairo to bolster the dwindling Turkish economy. The first rail link, completed by a German-Turkish venture, was destroyed during the First World War. The network was enlarged and modernised later by the British Mandate administration.

The urban middle classes developed a style of food which was cosmopolitan or rather Pan-Arabic with strong Turkish and Beiruti influences. Towards the end of the 19th century Beirut was rapidly becoming 'Paris on the Mediterranean'. It had famous casinos and was the place where rich Arabs came to escape the heat of the desert and to indulge themselves. It was famous for its elegant hotels and superb cooks and its reputation spread all over the Middle East. A large number of rich Palestinian families had a Lebanese cook and their influence on the Palestinian kitchen was mainly through the introduction of elegance, range and versatility.

The Turkish influence on Palestinian food is profound. The Palestinian *shawarma*, which is now popular Israeli street food, is a direct descendant of the Turkish *doner* kebab. This delicious dish used to be made from alternate layers of sliced and minced lamb flavoured with coriander and cumin and sometimes pine nuts and pistachios. The alternate layers of meat are skewered on a large spit which rotates in front of a heat source. When the outside layer is browned, it is thinly shaved to expose more raw meat, a process which is repeated until all the meat is cooked. Sadly *shawarma* now is made, at best, from a mixture of veal and lamb fat, but normally from sliced turkey meat flavoured heavily with lamb tail fat and turmeric.

It is in sweets that the Turkish influence can be most felt. It is found in filo-based pastries which are stuffed with custard or chopped nuts, baked to a golden crispness and soaked in delicately fragrant honey, sugar

121

and rosewater syrups. It is found in semolina cakes which look like amber, all translucent and glistening, and again in light and fragrant *sahleb* which are puddings made from special starch extracted from orchid roots,[2] flavoured with pomegranate cordial and sprinkled with cinnamon. The Turkish influence also appears strongly in a large variety of sweetmeats such as *halva* and *lukume*, which are still produced by both Arabs and Jews.

In coastal towns and some parts of Galilee fish was an important part of the diet. The most prized fish came from a species of the grouper family known locally as *loukos*, or *merou* in French. They normally appeared in the market weighing between 1 and 2kg (2 and 4lb) and have a firm flesh which is delicate, moist and almost translucent. It is well suited to the simple techniques of local fish cooking. The best flavoured fish of the area is a species of red mullet known locally as *Sultan Ibrahim* (*rouget* in French, *barabouni* in Greek). This small, bright red fish with a vivid yellow strip across its body has a uniquely gamey, fresh iodine flavour. When cooked its flesh is flaky and superbly fragrant. The best way to serve it is first to dip it in plain flour and then fry it crisply in boiling olive oil. Very small fish are not gutted as the intestines, and especially the liver, give the characteristic flavour. Wedges of lemon always accompany fried fish as the acidity of the lemon helps to reduce the oiliness of the frying. The lemon peel is then used as a cleanser because the fish is traditionally eaten with the fingers.

Fish cooking techniques were limited. The fish was either grilled or fried in olive oil, after which it could be finished in two ways. A sauce might be made from lemon juice, olive oil, garlic, salt and plenty of chopped parsley and dill. Sometimes chilli powder or chopped green and red chillies were added. This sauce was either served separately or was poured over the hot fish which was left to marinate for a few minutes. Its sharpness made it ideal for fatty fish, but it also goes extremely well with most fried and plainly grilled fish. Grilled or fried fish was also finished with a thin lemony tahina sauce after which the dish was put into the oven and cooked until the tahina was bubbling and slightly brown. For this dish the tahina paste is sometimes diluted with milk instead of water, creating a creamy, rich sauce which goes especially well with dry fish. The fish is finally decorated with chopped parsley and fried pine nuts.

These conditions were true until the arrival of the Jewish settlers towards the end of the last century. They changed the situation drastically, transforming forever the culture and therefore the food of Palestine.

ISRAELI FOOD

The first Israeli settlers were very different from the majority of poor refugees who had flocked to North America after the 1880-2 pogroms. Most came from emancipated, middle-class, urban Jewish families. All were educated and some were highly qualified. They were motivated to leave Europe less as a result of anti-semitic activity than because of a desire for change. Mostly of Russian and Polish origin, they were inspired by the intellectual socialism of the European revolutionary movements but, having encountered the inherent anti-semitism of the political establishment, realised that they could not affiliate themselves with the political mainstream. They therefore saw their way to freedom lay in changing the image of the Jew from the bourgeois, money-lending leech of the anti-semitic caricatures to that of a productive landworker intent on determining his own future. They wanted to create a way of life which would reject both the strictly dependent religious life of the Jewish *shtetl* and the bourgeois comforts of Central and East European urban society.

Some of those pioneers started to experiment with alternative ways of life, establishing different kinds of agricultural settlements which varied in their degree of communal living from semi-rural villages sharing only a communal distribution system, called *moshav* or *moshava*, to fully communal settlements known as kibbutz. A group of settlers established the new town of Tel-Aviv in 1909 and others established Jewish colonies in existing urban centres. Both movements developed their own style of food.

The biggest problem faced by the Jewish cook was how to adapt the traditional European diet, heavy in starch and *schmaltz*, to a lighter, healthier form more suitable for the hot climate of the Middle East. European Jews experienced great difficulty in becoming used to fresh vegetables, especially raw salad. The Jewish community is very conservative and most of the vegetables must have seemed exotic and very foreign. Culturally, raw salads had been considered animal fodder or rabbit food. Raw vegetables, the Biblical 'dinner of herbs' was also associated with poverty. The need for training and education was recognised very early and centres were set up mostly with the financial and active support of two Jewish women's organisations: Haddasa, established in the States in 1914, and Wizo, established in London in 1920.* The centres aimed to

---

* These two separate organisations started co-operating in 1930 to create a co-ordinated umbrella organisation which also included the Federation of Zionist Women (*Hestadruth Nashim Zionioth*) of Palestine.

educate and instruct newcomers in adapting to a new way of life.

The first cookery book to be written in Palestine appeared in 1935* and was published by Wizo. Originally written in German, it was translated into both English and Hebrew, the three languages appearing side by side in the same volume. In the introduction to her book Dr Erna Meyer recognises the importance of switching from animal fat to oil which was more suitable and easily available. She points out that oil is *parve* and can be used both with milk and meat. She also stresses the importance of using local Palestinian products.† Dr Meyer's book gave sound, realistic advice about all branches of cookery, especially recipes for vegetable cooking, salads and cakes. She also includes household management advice and instructions on proper European etiquette; kashruth is mentioned only in passing. It is very difficult to assess the impact of the book on the Israeli kitchen partly because it was aimed at a specific market — middle-class European newcomers. There is no attempt to include any Palestinian, Arab or Sephardi dishes. Moreover, shortly after the book was published came the Second World War when the problems of finding food for masses of starving refugees became more important than combatting bad food habits. Only towards the end of the 1940s did books start to appear which mentioned local and Sephardi recipes. The change in attitude is largely thanks to the work of one pioneering writer, Lilian Cornfeld.

Mrs Cornfeld was born in Canada. She studied nutrition and home economy in Columbia University Teachers' College and after graduation worked for Wizo as a supervisor of domestic science. After immigrating to Israel she managed all the food units of the US army in Tel-Aviv (1941–2) and the food services of American Red Cross (1942–4). Later she was chief dietitian for UNNRA Refugee Camps in Palestine and Egypt. She also wrote a food column in the *Jerusalem Post* and other Israeli papers and in 1938 began to broadcast about food.

The effect Mrs Cornfeld had on the Israeli kitchen was fundamental. Her books were to be found in almost every household and were the foundation upon which many young housewives based their food. Her books, although naturally based on Ashkenazi and the North American tradition, nevertheless acknowledged the importance of local dishes by

---

* *How to Cook in Palestine* by Dr Erna Meyer was published by the HNZ Federation of Wizo. The date appears neither on the front page nor with the copyright; 1935 is mentioned in an advert opposite p. 47. Although there probably are previously published recipe pamphlets, as far as I know it is the first cookery book to be published in Hebrew.
† One should point out that by Palestinian the good Dr means Jewish citizens of Palestine.

mentioning for the first time dishes which were to become Israeli classics: kebabs, *goulash mizrachi* (oriental goulash), peppers stuffed with meat flavoured with cinnamon and pine nuts, burgul, hummus and falafel. Her books also reflected the changing Israeli palate. The formidable work of the women's organisations started to bear fruit. They were concerned not just with technical training for the newcomers but were also the forerunners of a new kind of life. The following quotation from one of Wizo's publications declares this quite bluntly: 'We consider the knowledge of rational domestic management and nutrition one of the fundamental requirements for the upbuilding of the National Home. Accordingly we made the training of women and girls in this field one of our main aims.'[3]

Pioneers like Dr Erna Meyer and Lilian Cornfeld realised the importance of changing the eating habits of the European immigrants. The future of the nation could only be secured by creating a healthy and productive young generation. Thus bringing up healthy children became the patriotic duty of every Israeli woman.[4] Israeli youths were force-fed with all that was supposed to be good for them, especially raw fruit, salads of raw vegetables and milk foods which were still not eaten by their parents. The results of this change from the poor, starch-based diet of Central Europe were startling. The physical image of the Israeli Jew was transformed. The weak, thin, small, bent Jewish immigrant managed to raise a new generation of people bearing similar physical characteristics to those born American or Australian.[5]

Fresh salad became one of the most popular items of the Israeli diet. It was convenient to make because the raw materials were good, plentiful and cheap. In summer the salad consisted mainly of tomatoes, cucumber and onion. It was dressed with lemon juice, olive oil and plenty of herbs, such as parsley, dill and mint. Vinegar was rarely used because it was considered an unacceptable hangover from the Central European past. It was retained, however, for special purposes like dressing pickled herring or making special salads. It is only recently that wine vinegar has become popular again, promoted by a well-developed wine industry.[6]

Salad came to symbolise healthy living and was associated with everything young, new and Israeli. Making salads became a part of the 'macho' image of the male *chalutznic* (pioneer) who otherwise saw cooking as a woman's job. Great pride and time were taken to slice the vegetables, Arab fashion, into tiny, geometrically perfect squares. Many heated arguments were raised as to the merits of different oils and herbs.

Olive oil was rarely used in Ashkenazi households apart from in salad dressing. Until recently good olive oil was not available to the majority of the Jewish population as it was obtainable only direct from Arab villagers. Some of it is excellent, especially that produced from the local native olive which is sweet and very small. At its best, it is fruity, fragrant, dark green and smooth. Only recently has such oil reached the open market.

By comparison commercially produced olive oil was of very poor quality. The raw material was variable and had to be distilled and deodorised. The process of refining crude olive oil was started by one of the most important pioneers of the emerging Jewish-Palestinian industry. Nahum Vilbush was a Russian Jew who opened his first oil processing company 'Chadid' near the Arab town of Lod. The factory was later transferred to Haifa and in 1924 changed its name to 'Shemen'. In its time it was the most advanced oil and margarine factory in the Middle East. Its olive oil, although light, clear and superior to any other commercial oil available, had little olive flavour.

In the late 1970s a small number of well-made Israeli olive oils started to reach the Jewish market. Some of them are good but they are not always consistent; quality can vary within one harvest. Israeli olive oil tends to be rather heavy, dark olive green in colour, with a pronounced fruity flavour. Some oils have a slightly bitter, acid undertaste.

Oil is an important item in the Israeli food basket because it is used in large quantities, especially by the Sephardi community. Although olive oil is always preferred by the Sephardi cook, economics often dictate the use of other, cheaper oils, normally soya oil. Though fine when used cold, when heated it develops a 'fishy' aftertaste which has sadly become the characteristic flavour of a lot of street foods.

Two of the most important vegetables encountered by the new immigrants were the tomato* and the aubergine. Although tomatoes were used in southern Russia, they were rarely seen in Central and Eastern Europe. Tomatoes are of extreme importance in the kitchens of the Mediterranean and the Middle East. The local varieties are juicy and fragrant, almost minty in flavour and sweet, and are ideal as the base for a large number of sauces. Their slight acidity compliments fatty meats, such as the local mutton, and psychologically the red colour of the tomato suggests savour and piquancy.

Tomatoes are prolific in summer and several methods were used to

---

* The importance of tomato was so great that it entered early Israeli folklore. The word was used to describe newcomers in the same way that 'green' is used in English. This probably came about because the newcomers, who were mostly very pale and unaccustomed to the Middle Eastern sun, used to get very red on first exposures. Tomato was also the subject of a very popular folk song of the period.

preserve them for winter consumption. Firm green and red tomatoes were pickled in brine, while fully ripe red tomatoes were dried in the sun or first pulped, mixed with salt and then poured in a thin layer onto a clean mat and left to dry in the sun. The resulting tomato 'leather' was peeled off, oiled and rolled to be kept for further use when it would be hydrated with hot water. Tomatoes were also preserved in sugar, making a pleasant though somewhat insipid jam. The most important form of preserved tomatoes was, as in Italy, tomato concentrate. Sadly preserving tomatoes at home is a declining art.

The pioneering housewife not only faced problems of what and how to cook, she also had to invent the language to describe her food. Hebrew, chosen by the pioneers as the official language of the Jewish community in Palestine, was to all intents and purposes a dead language.[7] For almost two thousand years, although Hebrew was written it was used only in a religious context as the language of study and prayer. Only towards the middle of the 19th century did secular Hebrew literature begin to be written.[8]

Modern Hebrew is based on ancient Biblical Hebrew. The problems of re-vitalising the language were immense. The process of inventing a contemporary kitchen and food terminology started as early as 1903 with the publication of a list of seventy cooking terms and utensil names in the minutes of the committee for the Hebrew language. Although this list was the foundation of modern Hebrew cooking terminology it was short and incomplete.

In 1936 two committees[9] were set up to establish a standardised Hebrew culinary dictionary. The result of this work was published in 1937 in the first Hebrew culinary dictionary[10] which contained a comprehensive collection of old and new cooking terms and names of ingredients. Most of those terms were based on Biblical words, with some additional words which were translated either from Yiddish or other European languages, mainly German and English. Some of the words, especially the names of fish and vegetables, were taken from the Arabic. It is interesting to note that a large number of terms appearing in the dictionary are not used any more, having been replaced with new words and terms which evolved since the establishment of the Israeli state in 1948.

The first waves of immigrants, especially during the 1920s and the beginning of the 1930s, faced one more problem. Many were young and unmarried, and a disproportionate balance of males and females meant there were a large number of bachelors who could not fend for themselves. There was therefore a need for homely restaurants which could economically feed people who were mostly employed in hard physical labour. Food was also needed in 'working camps' which were temporary settlements for those employed to dry swamps and build roads.

In an attempt to solve this problem, the *Histadruth* (trade union) opened both mobile and permanent co-operative kitchens known as '*mitbach ha'poalim*' or workers' kitchens.[11] The main aim was to supply healthy, nutritious food made of 'Hebrew'[12] ingredients. The function of the kitchens went beyond this; they were also used as social centres and attempted to give all the care normally supplied by the family. They emphasised proper and up-to-date hygiene standards, supplying a medically supervised diet to whomever needed it. Especially in town, there was an emotional relationship between the kitchen and the eater.

The co-operative had to cope with supplying food to people from diverse ethnic backgrounds and social classes. It also had to overcome poor working conditions and competition from other eating establishments.[13] Conditions were difficult. There were problems of contaminated water supplies, low budgets and an untrained workforce.[14] Although these co-operatives were never successful commercially, perhaps because they were run by unskilled yet warm and caring Jewish mamas, they nevertheless became popular institutions. Those hard-working ladies supplied a mixed menu of soup and sympathy to generations of workers. *Mitbach ha'poalim*, for example, survived until the mid-1970s.

Conditions started to change rapidly after the declaration of independence in 1948. The country was in tatters, ravaged by the effects of long wars and many years of neglect. A major problem for the emerging state was how to cope with the influx of people* and their integration. The difficulties were immense because the country did not as yet have an established infrastructure. Apart from the expensive but necessary requirements of supporting a strong army, the pressure was to house and sustain people. One of the characteristics of a refugee society is an obsessive attitude to food; it is not surprising that memories of hunger and deprivation have a curious effect on behaviour often manifested by hoarding; the house must be full to the brim with food in case something happens. Abundance of food does not only mean prosperity, it gives security and a feeling of well being. This was not the time to create a national cuisine. Basic foods had to be heavily subsidised or given free.

The big wave of immigration also changed the ethnic balance of the

* In the first three years of the Israeli state 685,000 immigrants arrived, 304,000 from Europe and the rest from various Arab countries. The second wave of immigration (160,000) was mainly from Arab countries.

country. In 1949 the Sephardi made up only 21% of the population, but by the beginning of the 1960s they numbered 49%. Although the Sephardi immigrants were no strangers to conditions in the Middle East, they were foreign indeed to the culture of the dominant Ashkenazi population. The arrival of the Sephardis started a new and exciting phase in the Israeli kitchen.

The Sephardi community way of life and attitude to food was very different. Like their Arab neighbours they considered the honour of the family to be of utmost importance. Maintaining a lavish table is not only a way of showing social standing but also a matter of family honour. Sephardi middle-class Jewish families, especially in North Africa, Morocco, Algeria and Tunis, have developed a sophisticated, elaborate kitchen which has all the piquancy and imagination of Arab food mixed with the sophistication and elegance of the French kitchen.

Like their Muslim neighbours the whole family lived around a central court in a semi-communal way of life. Women were never allowed outside the confines of the family court. Cooking was done together, giving an important chance for social interaction. The hierarchical system meant that the oldest woman of the household was the 'head chef' whose duty was to instruct the younger members of the family and conduct the running of the household. The job of food preparation was shared by the rest of the women. Time was on their hands and it was used to create meticulously shaped, beautifully decorated foods for the men and their guests. Women were rarely allowed to go to the market. In very rich families the shopping was done by servants and in the less rich families shopping was done by the men. This created a situation whereby a large number of men who did not know how to cook were nevertheless aware of which ingredients were used.

The integration of the Sephardi community into Israeli society was difficult. A large number of the immigrants, especially those who came from rural regions, had to adjust not only to the Israeli reality but also to life in the 20th century. Their integration became even more difficult as a result of ignorance and misunderstanding of the Ashkenazi establishment.[15] However, when the Sephardi community finally established itself towards the end of the 1950s, its food became influential and started to change the Israeli palate.

The spread of Sephardi, Middle-Eastern-inspired food was helped by a particular set of circumstances. Most young Israelis are enlisted in the army when they reach the age of 18. It would be wrong to suggest that the army directly affects the Israeli palate, but it certainly has a major influence on the cultural heritage of almost all Israelis. Although army service is first and foremost a necessary tool of defence, it is also considered to be an important implement in racial integration by forcing youths of diverse ethnic origins to share a common experience.

Until the beginning of the 1960s there was no official attempt to satisfy the culinary demands of the growing number of ethnic Sephardi soldiers.[16] The eventual change in official attitudes was probably due less to a wider understanding than to the particular conditions in the army catering corps. Army catering suffered from the same attitude towards professional cooking which generally existed in Israeli society: kitchen work was considered the lowliest occupation, and being a chef was even less prestigious than being in the military police. The conscripts who were sent for kitchen duties were of sub-educational standard and normally could not be placed in any other branch of the army. A large number were of Sephardi origins. This created a strange situation in which the chefs cooked food which was culturally foreign to their palates. Yet those poorly trained and mostly uninterested chefs started an intriguing and far-reaching process. Under difficult circumstances, they created food which was inspired by the traditions they brought from their homes. A fascinating pattern started to emerge when it was found that chefs of North African origin, especially Moroccan, have a natural affinity to cooking. This is probably partly due to the highly developed food traditions of the North African community, and also to the French influence.

Army life also exposed most young people to one of the other most important elements in the shaping of the Israeli palate — street food. As a result of army service, young people travel extensively; army bases are dotted all over the country and one seldom serves near home. Eating on the go is sometimes the only food intake for a large number of the population.

Street food in Israel, especially out of the big urban centres, is still excellent and exciting. The variety is endless and changes throughout the day. The morning brings all the freshly baked goods, such as crisp rolls and fresh beigels, which are very different to those available in Europe or America. They are sold side by side with the Arab *ka'ak* (*kahk*) which is also beigel-shaped but much larger, thinner and covered with a thick coating of sesame seeds and a few nigella seeds.* *Ka'ak* is usually sold

---

* *Nigella sativa*, also called nutmeg flower or Roman coriander, are little black seeds with an interesting, warm, faintly spicy flavour. In Hebrew they are called *ketzach* (*kiza* or *kizta* in Arabic). The *ketzach* is mentioned in the Bible (Isaiah 28:25–27). They have been used since antiquity to flavour bread. Sometimes they are mistakenly called onion seeds. They can be bought in Indian shops, were they are sold as *kalonji* or *mungerela*.

accompanied by a little parcel made from torn newspaper, containing a mixture of *za'atar* and olive oil in which to dip the *ka'ak*. Or one can breakfast on Bulgarian *burekas* made of wonderfully thin filo pastry stuffed either with white brined cheese similar to feta, or spinach or potatoes. *Borekas* are usually served with brown, fragrant *huevos haminados* (hard-boiled eggs). For a tasty, simple breakfast one can have a Middle-Eastern pizza, which is made of pitta dough shaped into a thin flat cake, lavishly brushed with olive oil and sprinkled with *za'atar* before being baked in a very hot oven.

If you prefer a sweet breakfast you can choose from a large number of yeasted cakes, either plain like sweet buns, or shaped like large turnovers and stuffed with curd cheese. Sometimes raisins and grated lemon peel are included. The cakes can also be stuffed with apple, poppy seeds or fruit.

In winter, breakfast can be a bowl of wonderfully spicy sour *churba* which is a soup made especially by Jews from Thessaloniki and Bulgaria. It usually contains tripe, onion and garlic spiked with lemon juice or vinegar. There are numerous other soups based on offal (cow's foot and lamb trotters) and beans and lentils, which one can eat in the morning.

Towards lunchtime and in the evening the emphasis is more on meat. One can, for example, choose the ubiquitous *shawarma*. This is sadly now made from turkey meat crudely flavoured with cumin and turmeric and roasted with lamb tail fat to give it its characteristic flavour. One can occasionally still find well-prepared *shawarma*, in which case it is made from both minced and sliced lamb or a mixture of lamb and veal. It should be delicately flavoured with cumin and coriander and sometimes pine nuts and pistachios are added to the mixture. Other meats include a large variety of skewered meats, offal, *shiskuftas* (mince meat rissoles) and steaks. One of the most delicious offal dishes is a mixture called *meorave Yerusalmi* (Jerusalem mixture), a concoction of thinly sliced onions and mainly poultry offal (heart, liver, spleen, kidney and testicles). Sometimes veal or ox liver are included. The onions are first browned with a bit of fat, usually goose fat, on a flat metal griddle. The offal is added and the whole mass is scraped, fried and chopped with the aid of a wide metal spatula until the onions are sweetly caramelised and the meat is cooked. It is flavoured with cumin and coriander. Although laden with cholesterol, for offal lovers it is a delicious mixture of flavours and textures.

All these delicacies may be eaten either sitting down at a street restaurant or stuffed into a pitta with some salad and eaten on the hoof.

Perhaps the most distinctive and healthy Israeli street food is the falafel, a living relic of ancient Egyptian cuisine. In Egypt it is called *ta'amia* and is usually made from broad beans while in Israel it is always made from chickpeas. Falafel is eaten all around the Middle East and the eastern parts of the Mediterranean. Ingredients may change from country to country, but basically the falafel is a fritter made out of minced raw legumes flavoured with herbs and spices: parsley, fresh coriander and chillies, both green and red. The spices include coriander, cumin and sometimes turmeric. The mixture is shaped into variously sized rissoles and fried in boiling oil.

In Israel, falafel is king. For the last forty years it has been the first food young Israelis experience when they start eating out; it symbolises adulthood. It is therefore no surprise that in spite of all the changes, falafel is still the most popular street food in Israel. The salads which accompany the dish add interest and savour as well as vitamins and minerals. The sauces which are poured over add fire and moisture. All these good things are stuffed into a fresh pitta to be eaten with relish. Fortunately falafel is also nutritious and the addition of a salad and the pitta makes a perfectly balanced meal. It contains both legume and wheat proteins and is relatively low in fat though fried in oil. It also overcomes the tendency in Israel, especially amongst religious people, to avoid eating meat of unknown origin. Falafel, being vegetarian and *parve*, is considered a safe bet and can be bought anywhere.

Falafel stands in Israel demonstrate the affection in which the nation holds this dish. Until the mid-1950s falafel stands were run mainly to satisfy the Ashkenazi taste. Thus falafel was served in a pitta together with sauerkraut (a pure Ashkenazi addition), raw cabbage, gherkins and tomatoes, all of which were drowned with an anaemic tahina sauce. Towards the end of the 1950s, when the Sephardi immigrants established themselves, they opened falafel stands which evolved to the style which is so familiar today. A good falafel stand should be what the Israelis call *chagiga la'enaym*, a feast for the eye. The new style of stand, although not universal, is popular in most urban communities.[17] When you buy the falafel you are given a pitta with falafel balls inside and you can help yourself to a large variety of fresh, pickled and cooked salads. It is a feast of colour; purple pickled aubergine and radish next to bright yellow pickled lemons and the gold of pickled carrots and cauliflower. Black and green olives compete for attention with mounds of dark green chopped parsley, fragrant pale green, sliced fennel and a refreshing translucent onion ring salad speckled with purple flakes of the sour *sumac* fruit. Amongst all these are bowls full of fried sweet and hot peppers, fried courgettes and aubergines. Even the ubiquitous chips are not missing.

On another counter one might find sauces, some mild and piquant like tahina and some so fiercely hot they can burn the mouths of the uninitiated.[18] Normally there will be several types of hot sauce made from red chillies, sometimes fresh but mostly dried, mixed with garlic, oil and flavouring. They are known under the general name *hariff*, meaning hot, but are sometimes referred to as *schug* (Yemenite) or *charisa* (Moroccan). The Yemenites make a refreshing green version of *schug* from pounded fresh coriander, fresh green chillies, garlic and oil. Another sauce which is likely to be found at most falafel stands is *amba*, a turmeric yellow, thin, hottish sauce made from dried green mango powder. The name probably derives from the word amber which describes its colour. Its full name *amba hindy* (*hindy*, from India) probably indicates that it originated in India. It was introduced to Israel by the Kurdish and Persian (Iranian) communities.

These culinary Aladdin's caves hit you with their sheer opulence. It is difficult to resist all this temptation, especially as so much can be had for just over 70 pence at 1990 prices.

Chickpeas are also the base for *hummus-bi-tahina*, to quote its proper Arabic name, a paste of mashed, cooked chickpeas — hummus* — flavoured with tahina, lemon juice and garlic. The use of garlic is disputed by purists who maintain that its addition detracts from the earthy flavours of the chickpeas and the tahina. Hummus without garlic seems to be of Turkish origin.

Hummus probably originated in the northern parts of the Middle East, possibly in Syria or Lebanon. It became one of the most popular legume dishes eaten in the Middle East and the Eastern part of the Mediterranean and is now enjoyed all over the world. Like the falafel, it is both popular and nutritious; eaten with bread, salad and pickles it provides a well-balanced meal. It is also cheap and extremely delicious.

Nowadays many Israelis, including restaurants, buy their hummus from commercial manufacturers. At best these are mediocre, at worse they are a travesty. Individually prepared hummus is very different. Although all versions of hummus contain more or less the same ingredients, the proportions of tahina and flavourings are much disputed. In Jerusalem the tendency is for the hummus to contain less tahina — about a third. The hummus is therefore thicker and yellower. In the north, probably because of the Lebanese influence, more tahina is included — up to half — making the hummus paler.

---

* Hummus is the Arabic name for chickpeas which are called *humtza* in Hebrew. Both words are derivations of the word for sour. It refers to the acid sap which the green chickpeas emits when damaged. This can irritate the skin of the harvesters, therefore the chickpea pods are left on the plant to dry and only then they are harvested.

In some restaurants, especially in East Jerusalem, hummus is made to order. When a portion is required the chef transfers a measured amount of cooked chickpeas into the serving bowl, moistens it with mixed tahina sauce and mashes it to a smooth paste with a wooden mallet. The paste is then pushed from the centre to create a crown of hummus around the rim of the dish. Traditionally the hollow in the centre is sprinkled with olive oil and paprika. For decoration a small mound of whole cooked chickpeas is placed in the middle and the dish is sprinkled lavishly with parsley. The centre can also hold a variety of other ingredients. Sometimes it is filled with extra tahina, sometimes with fried pine nuts and olive oil. At its most elegant, the hummus is mixed with a large amount of chopped parsley and the centre is filled with tiny cubes of lamb, flavoured with coriander and fried quickly in olive oil. The dish is then decorated with fried pine nuts and sprinkled with chopped parsley. Hummus is always served accompanied with a bowl of pickles (*hamutzim*), which include pickled aubergines, cucumber, turnip, olives and hot peppers. Sometimes fresh hot peppers, raw onion, raw cos lettuce, fresh mint and parsley are also served.

With the introduction of French baguettes into the Israeli market a new street dish gained popularity: a baguette 'sandwich' stuffed with a variety of fresh vegetable salads, hot sauce, hard-boiled eggs and cooked (or more likely tinned) tuna. The sandwich is known as 'sandwich Tunisai', indicating its origin in Tunis. It derives from a dish called *fricassee* which consists of a freshly fried bread roll stuffed with olives, pickled peppers, boiled potatoes, hard-boiled eggs and tuna.[19]

Recently the quality and nutritional value of street food has begun to deteriorate. Economic pressures are pushing small operations out of the market place which is becoming monopolised by large distribution chains. Salads, dips and sauces are being mass produced and sold at prices which street food vendors cannot afford to refuse. Mass cooking creates problems of preservation and dictates the use of preservatives which drastically affect the nutritional value and flavour of the food. Everywhere you go you tend to find the same menu with exactly the same flavours.

Street food is also changing as the result of a shift in the ethnic balance of the population. The new Russian immigration will mean that the Sephardi community becomes a minority again. Signs of change are already present. For example, items like *pirashki* and *knishes* which, until few years ago, were done only domestically have begun to find their way into the market place. Who knows what the shape of street food will be in five years' time? I would guess, judging by the impact the Russian immigrants have had on Jewish food in New York, and knowing their inherent love for good food and drink, their contribution will be immense. The flavours preferred, especially by Southern Russians, are similar to those of the Middle East so that at least in terms of food, their integration into Israeli society will be comparatively easy.

SALAD AND PHILOSOPHY
The Influence of the Kibbutz

The kibbutz movement* is undergoing a crisis as the influence it once had on Israeli culture diminishes. Up until the early 1970s the kibbutzim represented an alternative culture with a particular ideology, a way of life and of cooking. The kibbutz movement set out to create communal farming settlements replacing the traditional family unit where all members were totally equal and shared in the advancement of the kibbutz. The philosophical ideals of the kibbutz were hatched amongst intellectuals in the middle-class salons of Central Europe, and became a reality when the first settlers arrived in Dgania in 1909. The problems the settlers faced were not philosophical; they had to start to produce food. They found that the land of milk and honey, in reality, was a swampy, malaria-infested, barren landscape populated by poverty-stricken Arab villagers who had suffered war, famine and neglect by a succession of corrupt, oppressive administrations. The pioneers — philosophers, chemists and schoolteachers — were totally ill-equipped to deal with problems of food production; they had never had to boil an egg, let alone use a spade or grow their own food.

Unfamiliar with the conditions, they turned to the Palestinian villagers for advice and local knowledge. The Arabs, not yet filled with any national aspirations, saw the newcomers as fellow-oppressed and welcomed them. Although there were skirmishes over water, the relationship was cordial. The shared danger came from bands of robbers and starving Turkish soldiers who supplemented their meagre income by robbing both the Arab and Jewish villagers. In the first few years the pioneers were plagued by natural disasters, malaria and malnutrition.

---

* Talking about the kibbutz movement as a whole is somewhat misleading. The political and cultural colour of the kibbutz varies from the ardent left to (very rarely) the far right. Conditions and attitudes differ according to the political affiliation of the kibbutz. The majority of *kibbutzim* have affiliations with variants of the labour movement.

Their food was basic. The memories of the first settlers of Dgania are vivid:

> 1916 was a difficult year . . . the chickens and cows gave very little eggs and milk, almost the whole yield was given to the children and the sick. When a member was seen eating an egg, everyone sympathised and inquired after his health. The main food was a kind of brown porridge made out of lentils which never left the table during that year; a bit better was the *megadara*, a mixture of wheat (burgul) and lentil served with fried onions. But the real treat was a bowl of boiled whole *hummus* (chickpeas). Their bright, light colour pleased the eye and gladdened the heart of the eater, after the brown doldrums of the lentil porridge and the *megadara*. Chickpeas were also given as a restorative food after sickness.
> Breakfast was bread, olives, salt herrings and jam. Lunch — *megadara*.
> To vary the menu and ease the digestion we drank a lot of 'tea' without any sugar. The tea was an infusion of roasted dry fig, which tinted the hot water and left a faint flavour (of burnt fig). Often we sweetened the 'tea' by chewing pieces of *kamardine* — a paste made of apricot pulp — people in the know said that the 'machine' for making *kamardine* was the bare feet of Arabs . . . this miraculous product looked like pieces of shoe leather.

Some of the early settlers left to return to their comfortable homes, but those who stayed set about adapting to their new conditions. The kibbutz was a totally original historical experience requiring a new rule book on which the communal life would be based. A culture was in the making.

Food in the kibbutz created a strange incongruity. Even though the basic idea of the kibbutz was to produce foodstuffs, cooking was looked down upon as a non-productive occupation because a pair of hands in the kitchen meant one fewer in the field. Cooking was left to the women, and this brought a fierce reaction from both men and women. The women complained about the 'restrictions of a low budget, complaints of the poor quality, monotonous food. The detachment from agriculture and field work caused a lot of bitterness. The women demanded that the men should work in the kitchen so they could experience the degrading conditions.'

Their frustration was shared by some of the men: 'Kitchen work was considered unproductive, yet someone had to do the cooking . . . with misgivings we observed the work of the women, bent over large copper cauldrons which rested on stones in the yard. The uncontrollable damp wood fire burned the food, emitting acrid smoke which irritated the eyes and dirtied the face; while we (the men) breathed the sweet air of the fields, they were inhaling smoke and soot. Is that the fate of women even in communal life? We must plan a kibbutz in which the women find more creative work.'

In the kibbutz food had changed from being an expression of love and familial security cooked by mother to simpler fodder which only supplied the necessary energy for survival. Diminishing the responsibility of the family unit to supply its own food created a special problem which is clearly identified in accounts written by the first settlers of Dgania:

> Although conditions in the kitchen are improving, the food is still poor and boring . . . The reason for the poor food is mainly the high price of the ingredients and the disregard of the chaverim (comrades) for the value of food products. We have to change radically the attitudes of the members towards food. When one lives alone, one knows the limits of one's personal budget and tailors one's food consumption according to his means. This is not the case in the kibbutz. Living together releases the individual from taking responsibility for one's own expenditure. The improvement in the kitchen should be, in my opinion, that it would run like a commercial restaurant so everyone will have the possibility to control their own expense. We as a co-operative should allocate an amount of money that is proportionate to our income.

This ignorance of the monetary value of food plagued the kibbutz for years to come. The waste was, and still is, especially in prosperous kibbutzim, enormous.

The process of the development of kibbutz cooking was described to me by Chaim Cohen, the head chef of the kibbutz movement training college and a member of kibbutz Na'an. Although the picture drawn relates to his own kibbutz, conditions in most of the kibbutzim were similar.

'Kibbutz Na'an was established in 1930. The first settlers were of Russian and Polish origins. Later they were joined by Hungarians and Yemenites. The first kitchen was in a hut, the only cooking facilities available were a few oil-burning primus stoves. The cooking was done mostly by untrained women, usually elderly or convalescing. Cooking duties were allocated on a rotating basis of bi-weekly shifts. Buying was done by the man who was also responsible for the general purchasing. The criteria for shopping was not so much what was required but whatever was available within a price range. Co-ordination with the cooks or projected planning was impossible due to the bi-weekly shift system.

'As the kibbutz established itself, conditions improved and occasionally a willing volunteer would take it upon herself to cook. Some of those cooks were magnificent, managing to create food which satisfied most palates within a budget. But in a large number of kibbutzim, as a result of lack of training, the quality of food was poor and the wastage criminal. As the kibbutz grew the organisation of the kitchen became more and more complicated; an expanding and ageing population meant illness and special dietary requirements.

'It was only at the beginning of the 1960s that organised training started. It was initiated by Kupat Holime, a health care organisation which is affiliated to the *histadruth*, the trade union movement. The training, which consisted of a two-week course, aimed not at teaching people how to cook, but rather at teaching them what to eat. The kibbutz movement agreed on a standard food 'basket' which became the guideline to kibbutz cooking. It was based on large amounts of carbohydrate — potatoes, rice and legumes — with very little meat. The course set out to help kitchen organisers solve the problems of feeding hard-working people cheaply and nutritiously, aided only by a largely untrained workforce.

The 1970s and beginning of the 1980s brought prosperity to a large number of kibbutzim whose kitchens now began to include all the modern equipment of an industrial kitchen. Indeed, some were grossly over-equipped. Modern industrial kitchens can cope with vast numbers of meals per day. In order to recover installation costs, a kitchen would have to be continuously operational. The kibbutzim found themselves with kitchens which had the capacity to feed thousands of people operating to half that and sometimes less. In an attempt to justify and utilise such big kitchens, it was suggested that each group of kibbutzim should have a central kitchen. The central kitchen would prepare food which would be either frozen or delivered in heated containers to each kibbutz where it would be reheated or dished up.

'This experiment failed due to a totally unforeseen reason. The members of the kibbutzim disliked the centralised food intensely, although the recipes and menus presented nothing new or vastly different. All the complaints insisted that the food did not taste the same as before. It was discovered that each kibbutz had developed, in spite of constantly changing cooks, a unique style of flavouring, dictated as much by the personality of the cook as the collective palate of the kibbutz.

'Until the late 1960s cooking was done by women. It was only with the change of serving methods and attitudes that men began to work in kibbutz kitchens. Until then food was cooked and served in relatively primitive conditions. Tables were set with the appropriate basic utensils and few basic condiments such as salt, pepper, oil and vinegar, salad ingredients, jam and margarine. The hot main courses were distributed by moving trollies and usually arrived at the table cold and unappetising. This changed dramatically when, in the beginning of the 1970s, a revolutionary self-service system was introduced. This very soon stream-lined most of the kibbutzim kitchens.'

Although kitchens became modernised and food generally improved, the number of members actually using the central kitchen began to decline. More and more members were eating at home; communal life could not suppress the natural instinct towards familial bonding. Women especially found that the denial of their parental responsibilities also denied them the important bonding role of 'mother the food supplier'.

It is difficult to determine exactly when private cooking started in the kibbutzim. People used to help themselves to food both from the communal kitchen or directly from the field. Although the practice of pilfering food was looked at with dismay, it was accepted as a part of the kibbutz sub-culture; food was not stolen, it was pinched. When pinching started to become an issue, it was decided that food rations should be available for those who wanted them. The demand was so great that eventually it had to be regulated to prevent waste; it was decided that raw ingredients would be sold by the communal shop which up to that time sold only a few luxury items such as soaps, cigarettes and sweets.

Economic improvements also led to a change in attitudes towards the possession of private property. The first things the *kibbutzniks* bought were radios and record players, then they bought basic cooking equipment. The most versatile and cheap cookers were fuel-injected primus or oil-burning wick stoves called *Ptiliyot*. Although efficient and easily regulated, oil stoves emitted a faint odour of burned petroleum which permeated all food cooked on them. For years this faintly unpleasant flavour was the trademark not only of domestic kibbutz cooking, but also domestic cooking in Israel. This was because until quite recently, oil burners were the only affordable stoves for a large number of Israelis. Even now, some cooks maintain that oil stoves are best for long, slow cooking.

Cakes were the first items to be tackled at home probably because they represent something special and are a luxury. Basic cakes need only minimal equipment — a mixing bowl, spoon and a baking utensil — and use basic available ingredients — flour, sugar, fat and eggs. The problem of baking on a single top burner was solved either by placing a Dutch oven contraption over the flame or using the famous wonder-pot. A wonder-pot is an aluminium or enamelled pot with a tight-fitting lid. A funnel runs through the middle, like a kugelhupf mould, facilitating the even distribution of heat. The wonder-pot was an important item in most Israeli households. This clever, practical device, which could bake as well as cook, dictated the shape of Israeli cakes for several generations. As a child I thought that a cake must always be round with a hole in the centre. It is even possible to bake bread and *hallah* in the wonder-pot. I find myself feeling very sentimental about this miracle pot. It conjures up the memory of the most deliciously spicy *babka* which my Grannie used to bake every Friday. *Babka*, a cake of Russian origin, is made with a rich yeasted dough flavoured with cinnamon and sugar. It was left to rise to a magnificent height and was baked in the wonder-pot to a beautiful, rich golden hue.

With these friendly, versatile implements the kibbutz woman set about inventing a distinct cookery sub-culture. The opportunity to create something at home allowed her to express herself in a way denied otherwise. Cooking gave her the opportunity to specialise, excel, and lift herself from being just a member of a commune to being a mother and a wife. Communal life attempted to ignore the cultural importance of the Jewish mama; it did not succeed.

Observance of kosher laws was problematic from the beginning of the kibbutz movement because atheism, or rather non-religiosity, was almost written into the kibbutz 'bill of rights'. The predicament of the first kibbutzim was how to survive; kashruth did not play any part in its life. As the kibbutz movement began to develop and established itself it was realised that some concession towards religion was necessary. In the majority of the kibbutzim, kashruth is a flexible term. It is seen as an unavoidable restriction which is rarely discussed. Most kibbutzim are very lax, though maintaining an official kosher policy. For example, they buy their meat from a kosher source, but do not salt it. Milk and meat are not served together though they are available to anyone who wishes to eat them at the same meal. Dishes and utensils are not usually separated and very few kibbutzim have separate dish-washing facilities. This kind of double standard is necessary because *Tnuva*, the kibbutzim's central distribution system, has an official kosher policy as a result of political and market pressures.

Although the problems of meat and milk separation were not so important, pig was a different issue. Some kibbutzim, partly for ideological but mainly for practical reasons, found pig breeding a profitable line. The market was there, both Jewish and Arab. Also, unlike cattle, the pig is not a fussy eater and is therefore an economical solution to the problems of kitchen waste. Some kibbutzim achieved great success in growing pigs, and one of them, kibbutz Mizra, established a meat-processing factory which produces a consistently good and wide range of non-kosher specialities. These products are sold through a chain of franchised shops in various urban centres in Israel and by a large number of independent butchers. The still-flourishing Israeli pig industry is, however, under threat. The pig law proposed by the religious minorities will forbid Jews either to rear, sell or process pork.

Absence of an official religion also required a change in the customs for holiday celebration. The religious holidays were meaningless to a large number of kibbutz members. As these lost their synagogue and family significance, they began to evolve into a tribal celebration. It is rather significant that by creating a secularly based tradition of celebration, the kibbutzim managed to capture the ancient original essence of the holidays.

The Sabbath is still important for it is a well-deserved day of rest when only essential work is done. Friday's meal is very important. The tables in the dining room are covered with white tablecloths and there are flowers on them. In some kibbutzim, though very rarely, wine is served on Friday. On the whole the meal is based on an Ashkenazi menu. It starts with a chicken soup garnished with either rice or vermicelli. This is followed by meat,* cooked vegetables and potatoes, rice or pasta. The meal is finished with stewed fruit (*liftan*) and/or cake. Some kibbutzim have also developed a ceremony which includes poetry reading and communal singing.

At Pesach a large number of kibbutzim adapted the traditional Haggadah to include topical items and a personalised history of the kibbutz. The food mostly remained traditional Ashkenazi fare.

It is in the new holidays like Yom Ha'azmauth, Israeli Independence and the Kibbutz Founders' Day and holidays with a direct agricultural association, such as Shavouth and Sukkoth, that the kibbutzim have created traditions which are exclusively their own. These holidays are celebrated very much in the spirit with which our forefathers celebrated theirs. The whole of the kibbutz is gathered in the open, celebrating with nature the passage of time. Food for these celebrations evolved also on similar lines to those of our forefathers; with the exception of Shavouth, which is celebrated by a mainly milky picnic, the other holidays are celebrated with a barbecue.

The association of the kibbutz barbecue with sacrifice is probably only coincidental. It is more likely that the barbecue simply suits the rural atmosphere of the occasion and is practical. The barbecue is an old tradition within the kibbutzim. From the beginning special occasions

---

* During the week meat used to be served disguised, i.e., minced with pasta, in *kugels* (*pashtidot*, baked puddings) or *mussakas*. Friday is the only time meat was served in a large piece — a quarter of a chicken or sliced, pan-baked roasted beef. In the past the chicken would have been one the soup was made of, lifted out, drained, basted with chicken fat and browned in the oven.

were celebrated by organising a barbecue, usually around a campfire. These celebrations were known as *Kom-Zitz*, a combination of two Yiddish words which mean 'come' and 'seat'.

The major contribution of the kibbutz tradition to Israeli cuisine is the inspiration for the famous Israeli hotel breakfast. In most hotels this consists of a buffet table covered with a fascinating array of food. Baskets full of fresh rolls, mounds of sliced fruit and vegetables, eggs, olives, curd cheese dips, sliced hard cheeses, various pickled, preserved and smoked fish, salads, butter, yoghurts, sour cream, jams and honey. All this splendour has its humble origins in the practical kibbutz breakfast. People arrive at breakfast at different times and the custom was to set the table with various ingredients, mainly fresh vegetables, cheeses and hard-boiled eggs. Each member could combine and dress his or her own salad. The same style of breakfast was also served in the kibbutzim guest houses and became very popular.

Hopefully the kibbutz movement is going to survive its ideological crisis. Being the supreme producer of agricultural products, I would guess that in the future it will also be a hothouse of original Israeli-style cuisine.

KASHRUTH IN ISRAEL

Today kashruth is a flexible term. The fundamentalists adhere to it blindly, but the rest of the population observes it only to varying degrees. Some will not allow non-kosher food at home, but will be laxer when travelling or eating out. Some will not eat pork or obviously non-kosher fish, but will drink a glass of milk with a hamburger. Some will eat shrimps and lobsters, but would never touch pork.

With the advance of Jewish religious fundamentalism, particularly in Israel, kashruth stopped being a religious issue. With the threat of the pig and the Sabbath laws it became a major issue of fundamental human rights. The rights which are in danger are the same rights which the Jews fought so hard to maintain; the prerogative of each individual to live according to his or her conviction.

This is an explosive subject which is not documented at all. There is no Kinsey report about eating non-kosher food, and even if there were one I doubt the results would have any credibility. The Jews feel more guilty about kosher-keeping than about sex

Being born in Israel of a non-religious family, I was not much aware of a kosher kitchen, nor were a large number of my contemporaries.

Although many households would not use pork, in most there was no separation of milk and meat and no concern about eating in Arab, therefore non-kosher, restaurants. In our house pork was eaten, but while there was no guilt attached, it was not discussed outside the family circle. The attitude in the street was the same. Until recently non-kosher food was readily available but never advertised. On the menus of many restaurants pork was referred to as white meat.

This ambiguity about pork started early in the history of modern Israel. Even the ardent non-religious labour movement found the subject too sensitive to discuss. The abhorrence of pig is deeply engraved on the Jewish mind. To most Jews, especially those who come from Central and Eastern Europe, the pig conjures up the memory of everything which is oppressive and threatening. At the time of writing this book, there is no constitutional ban on the sale of pork by Jews in Israel, although it is the right of every municipal authority to impose such a law.

At best the situation relating to kosher food in Israel can only be described as confused. Every section of the ultra-religious population has a kosher authority which vies with other authorities over control of the market. As food production is one of the major expanding industries of Israel, kosher is big business. The various rabbinical courts fight viciously and continually for supremacy; whoever controls the kashruth supervision is assured of a safe and lucrative income. Kosher supervision means maintaining a vast army of inspectors, mostly religious functionaries, who are wastefully paid by the community.

Hopefully the characteristic Jewish logic and sense of fair play will win so that the religious parties will not be allowed to have things all their way. Pork eating, as well as weddings, burials and education, should be left to the individual decision of every citizen.

FOOD INDUSTRY

In an article complaining about the poor quality of restaurant food in Israel, Bernard Levin, the Jewish-British critic and writer, jokingly asks: 'Doesn't anyone here have a Jewish mother?'[20] In a way Mr Levin is right, although I would identify the cause of abysmal restaurant food as the presence of too many Jewish mothers.

On the one hand the Israeli food industry is highly modernised, sophisticated and enjoys a good reputation all over the world. The dark side lies in the proportionally large number of 'cowboy' operators. One of the most striking examples of success is a company called Tivol whose imaginative and tasty vegetarian range of products is sold all over Europe and North America. Israeli agricultural exports, though expensive, are of a high quality both in flavour and in shape and are bought all over the world. The Israelis specialise in a large variety of exotic fruits, melons and citrus fruit and their agriculture is supported by original research done by various agricultural institutes.

New products appear almost daily. Few are likely to become classics and the majority disappear after a short time, never to be seen again. There is a constant nervousness in the market. Today's favourite, eaten by the whole population as a result of an aggressive advertising campaign, can be forgotten within months.

Economic realities for Israelis mean that their reliance on ready-made food is one of the highest in the world. As the extended family structure rapidly breaks down, long and elaborate food preparations are becoming a thing of the past. Moreover, the majority of women now go out to work in order to supplement the family income. Food eaten during the week is mostly convenience food supplemented by vegetables and fresh salads. The low prices of convenience foods also mean that sometimes it is cheaper to buy ready-made food than to prepare it at home.[21]

The Israeli palate has suffered as a result of this fast-moving, lively industry. The pressure of catering for such a diverse public dictates that the food should appeal to all, i.e. be bland. Flavour is mainly added at home with the aid of salads and hot sauces. Its useful blandness is probably one of the main reasons why turkey meat is the most widely eaten meat in Israel.

Turkey is an Israeli success story. Turkeys were almost unknown in Israel until a few kibbutzim found intensive turkey breeding highly profitable at the beginning of the 1960s. The birds grow well and are cheaper to raise than beef, lamb or chicken. The meat of intensively raised turkeys has the soft texture much loved by Jewish people and its size makes it convenient for large families although whole birds are rarely seen in the market; they are mostly sold jointed as many people do not like the dark leg and thigh meat which tends to have a strong flavour. Turkey meat goes into everything. The dark meat and fat are used in the making of various sausages and minced dark meat is also used to bulk more expensive meats in hamburgers and other meat products. The breast is cured and smoked like ham or made into pastrami. It also forms the base for the most popular dish in Israel: turkey schnitzel. Schnitzel appears on almost every menu commercially and at home, and it can be bought in most fast-food outlets where it is usually served stuffed into a pitta and flavoured with all kinds of *harrief* (hot sauces), tahina sauce and fresh vegetable salads which add moisture and flavour.

Although one might criticize some of the big industry products for their lack of flavour and tendency to use too many additives,[22] their products are honestly made, with meticulous attention given to hygiene, quality control and presentation.

Conditions are quite different amongst the large number of small- to medium-sized operators who produce food under unhygienic conditions for scandalously high profit margins. The high profit is mainly achieved by exploiting a cheap labour force mostly made up of local Arabs. Until recently a growing number of Asian migrant workers, especially Filipinos, worked in most Israeli urban centres. Migrant workers are used in the kitchens not just for obvious economic reasons but because Israeli workers tend to be temperamental and independent, creating problems of discipline detrimental to the smooth running of a professional kitchen.[23]

Bernard Levin's plea, written in 1982, reflected quite correctly the situation at the top end of the restaurant industry at the time. During the same period 'popular' restaurants flourished. Their renaissance was partly due to the relative peace and prosperity which were the results of the Six Days' War, and as all over the Mediterranean, good weather makes eating outside a favourite pastime.

Arab restaurants were and still are very popular. Some are excellent, serving the usual fare of hummus, tahina and kebabs together with local specialities like stuffed pigeons, stuffed vegetables and various *sania* dishes. The Jewish restaurants represented every conceivable ethnic group. These restaurants normally opened outside urban centres, usually in jerry-built structures, converted houses or private yards. They were mostly run by Jewish mamas, who supplied beautifully cooked traditional dishes. One could choose between Romanian and Bulgarian speciality grilled meats; spicy well-prepared salads and couscous from the North African coast; hot and earthy Yemenite dishes; elegant, light and fragrant Persian and Kurdistani food or the heavy, well-flavoured, unsuitable, but nostaligic food of Russia and Poland. In coastal towns like Jaffa/Tel Aviv, Haifa and Acre one can still find a good range of fresh fish, simply fried or grilled.

Popular restaurants still thrive in Israel though finding them without local knowledge is difficult. As a result of market pressures a large number change hands often or close down. Quality also seems to deteriorate when they become over-popular and start franchising.

At the top end of the market the situation is different. From the beginning the influence on the kitchen has been that of the international

145

haute cuisine. This style is mostly a hangover from British colonial influence which became established in the 1930s with the arrival of professional chefs and hotel and restaurant workers of Central European, mainly German, origin.

The German Jews' attitude to cooking as a profession was different, probably because of their long and respectable involvement in the food industry. Being a chef, especially a *chef pâtissier*, was considered respectable and proper. All over Central Europe many Jews were involved in the catering and hotel-keeping industries. Many Jewish-owned pâtisseries and catering establishments were amongst the best in Germany and Austro/Hungary. These highly qualified professionals came to what they considered to be an Asiatic wilderness. They set out with typical German determination to convert the barbarians to proper European gentle folk.

Some urban centres were turned into little versions of Berlin or Vienna where coffee and whipped cream were drunk with beautifully made pastries, *tortes* and *kuchen*. All would be served by a polite yet friendly waiter clad in a white jacket. The walls of the cafés were lined with heavy wooden panelling and the windows with velvet curtains, totally alien to the hot Palestinian weather. The customers were either German refugees trying to capture a bit of the old country or, before Independence, officials of the British administration and army. The majority of Israelis looked upon sitting in cafés and eating out as a decadent bourgeois pastime.

After the creation of the State of Israel there was pressure to create a representative Israeli style of food which would appeal mainly to experienced Jewish travellers. French *haute cuisine* was the foundation of the style, but created a problem where kashruth was an economic reality; thus hotels had to be kosher to cope with the demands of Jewish tourists.* Making kosher 'classic' French food is, if not an impossibility, surely a contradiction in terms. Even now, with the use of good quality margarine, artificial *parve* cream and other substitutes, the results are a pale imitation of the original French version. It was, however, possible to deal successfully with meals like breakfast, which contained a representation of typically Israeli products, fresh vegetables and fruit, interesting salads and spreads, breads and pastries.

Some Israeli food experts maintain that there is no Israeli cuisine. Their misconception is built on the generally accepted definition of a national cuisine formed of regionally inspired dishes. Yet one can look at other

---

* It is interesting to note that some of those tourists expected to be served kosher food in Israel though they would not normally insist on kashruth.

patterns of national food, such as in South Africa and the United States, where as well as regional variations the style comes from incorporating radically different and unconnected cultural origins. Israeli-style cuisine does exist, as Ya'akov Lishansky, the most knowledgeable Israeli food expert, rightly said: 'Whatever I create in my kitchen, using a locally grown product, is Israeli and is my heritage.'

THE RECIPES

INTRODUCTORY NOTE ON
THE RECIPES

THERE ARE no technically difficult recipes in the Jewish repertoire yet they are, if done traditionally, time consuming. The collection below is a mixed bag from a fascinating variety of sources. A large number of the recipes have been kept in families for generations and their true origin is obscured by time. The rest come from a treasury of cookery books, both Ashkenazi and Sephardi, written in the last 150 years.

For the uninitiated there are a few points one should remember before attempting a recipe.

1. Jewish portions are much larger than usual; therefore a recipe for 6 will serve approximately 8.

In this book the recipes are given in three separate measurements: metric, imperial and American. You should use only one set of measurements within a recipe. The important thing to remember is that when you cook using metric, teaspoons and tablespoons should be heaped, while using imperial and American they should be scant.

2. The amount of oil and fat used in traditional recipes is excessive; it indicated your social status. In the recipes below the amount of fat and oil has been reduced, but it can be minimised even further without affecting the flavour of the food.

3. The same comments apply to sugar.

4. Salt should be used discreetly when flavouring koshered meats as they retain some of the salt used for koshering.

I do hope that you will enjoy cooking and eating the dishes as much as I have. *Be'te'avon.*

11

BIBLICAL AND HISTORIC RECIPES

THE ACTUAL details of Biblical and historic recipes are a matter of speculation. Although ancient Jewish literature is full of descriptions of food and cooking methods, no recognisable recipe was ever recorded. Even if one were to be found, it would make little sense to the modern cook as both palate and food conventions have changed drastically.

The following recipes came from various sources, mainly Yemenite, Kurdistani, Palestinian, Egyptian and Greco-Roman. These recipes, some unchanged for hundreds of years, give a good idea of what the Jews could have eaten in ancient times. For convenience, I have divided them into two broad timescales: the early period, which includes dishes which might have been eaten from the beginning of the nation (Patriarchs 1900BC) to the destruction of the First Temple in 586BC, and the late period, which covers dishes which might have been eaten between the return to Israel in 516BC and 400AD when the Jerusalem Talmud was completed.

EARLY PERIOD

MEGADARRA
Burgul and Lentil Gruel

Serves 6–8

This dish is described in the Bible as Esau's favourite and is most likely to be the red lentil stew which was served by Jacob to Esau. Claudia Roden in *Middle Eastern Food* dates it to medieval times, but it is probably much older.

Though still widely prepared all over the Middle East it is nowadays usually made with rice instead of burgul.

250g/8oz/1 cup brown lentils, washed well and drained
75ml/3fl.oz/⅓ cup olive oil
1 small onion, chopped
250g/8oz/1½ cups coarse burgul
2 large onions, sliced into thin rings
1 litre/2 pints/5 cups water
Salt
Pepper (optional)

Cover the lentils with water and boil for 45 minutes or until they are almost cooked. Drain and reserve the cooking liquid.

In a heavy bottomed pot, heat 1 tablespoon of the olive oil. Add the chopped onion and fry until it starts to brown. Add the burgul, the lentils, salt and half the cooking liquid. If it is too dry, add some water. Cover tightly and simmer very gently for 20–25 minutes or until all the liquid has evaporated. Remove from the heat and allow to stand for 10 minutes.

Heat the rest of the oil in a large frying pan. Add the sliced onions and fry gently until they are dark golden brown, being very careful not to burn them. Pile the *megadarra* on a serving dish, top with fried onion and serve either warm or cold. The dish can be eaten as a salad either on its own or accompanying meat or a vegetable stew, or as a main dish moistened with yoghurt.

SHREET ADAS MAJOOSH
Lentil Soup with Cumin

Serves 4–6

The following soup appears in *Middle Eastern Cookery* by Arto der Haroutunian. It may also be the red pottage of Esau.

500g/1lb/2¼ cups red lentils
1500ml/scant 3 pints/7½ cups stock or water
1 onion, quartered
1 stick celery with leaves, chopped
1 clove garlic, coarsely chopped
50g/2oz/½ cup clarified butter
1 tablespoon onion, chopped
2 teaspoons ground cumin
1 teaspoon salt
¼ teaspoon black pepper
Lemon wedges for garnish

Rinse the lentils. Place the stock or water in a large saucepan and bring to the boil. Add the lentils, onion, celery and garlic and stir. Reduce the heat and simmer for 30–45 minutes or until the lentils are tender. The length of time will depend on the quality of the lentils. Meanwhile, in a small pan melt half the butter and fry the chopped onion until golden. Remove from the heat. Purée the soup in a liquidiser or by rubbing through a sieve with the back of a wooden spoon and discarding any remaining bits of vegetables. Return the soup to the saucepan and cook for a further 5 minutes, stirring all the time. Add the fried onion, cumin, salt and pepper. Just before serving, stir in the remaining butter. If you like a light soup, add a little more water, otherwise simmer for a few more minutes.

BASIC BURGUL PILAV PREPARATION

Serves 6

Burgul gruel was the main staple of Palestinian peasants for thousands of years. It was served either moistened with clarified butter or accompanied by yoghurt. It is extremely tasty and can be used instead of rice to accompany meat or vegetable stews.

350g/12oz/2¼ cups coarse burgul
50ml/2fl.oz/¼ cup olive oil
1 small onion, chopped (optional)
750ml/1¼ pints/3 cups boiling water
Salt to taste

Rinse the burgul several times until the water runs clear. Leave to drain and allow to dry. Heat the oil in a shallow pan. If onion is used, add the onion and fry gently until soft and golden. Add the burgul and fry for 2–3 minutes until some of it starts to brown. Stir frequently. Add the boiling water and salt and stir well. Bring to the boil, reduce the heat and cover closely. Simmer very gently for 15–20 minutes until all the water is absorbed. Leave to rest covered for 10 minutes and serve.

TABOULEH

Serves 8–10

One of the simplest, most refreshing and probably most ancient Middle Eastern dishes. The original recipe calls for fine burgul, but I have found that coarse burgul gives more interesting results. In Israel, chopped hot green chillies (1 or 2, finely sliced) are added. This salad is traditionally presented in an impressive mound and decorated with a variety of raw vegetables. It is served with a cos lettuce for each person to use to scoop up the salad.

250g/8oz/1½ cups coarse burgul
300–400g/12–14oz/1½–2 cups coarsely chopped mixed herbs (parsley and mint are a must, but spinach, sorrel and rocket or *arugula* are also used)
1 bunch of spring onions, including the green leaves, or 1 large onion, finely chopped
7 tablespoons olive oil
Juice from 2 lemons
Salt and freshly ground black pepper

Soak the burgul for one hour. Drain and squeeze out any excess water. This is best done by laying a flat layer of burgul on a clean kitchen towel, rolling up the towel and wringing it well. Mix the burgul with the herbs and onion and dress with lemon and olive oil. Leave for about an hour so that the burgul soaks up the lemon and oil. Taste to see if it is lemony enough; burgul has the ability to neutralise acidity and can therefore sometimes taste bland.

BURGUL WITH CHARD

Serves 6–8

500g/1lb/3 cups coarse burgul
250g/8oz onion, chopped
75ml/scant 3fl.oz/⅓ cup olive oil
500g/1lb Swiss chard or beet greens,* washed and chopped coarsely
1 litre/2 pints/5 cups boiling water
Salt and pepper to taste

Wash the burgul in several changes of water. Fry the onion in oil until it starts to change colour. Then add the chopped chard and fry for a few minutes to soften. Add the burgul and fry for a minute or two longer. Pour in the water, bring to the boil, cover and simmer on a very low heat until all the water is absorbed. Season and serve hot instead of rice, or on its own, accompanied by yoghurt or curds.

* The green leaves of sugar beet. They can be obtained at Greek, Middle Eastern and Indian grocers.

CUBBEH OR KIBBEH
Burgul Dumplings

Serves 6–8

Cubbeh is a generic term describing wheat dumplings which are generally stuffed with a variety of fillings, after which they are boiled in soup or fried in oil. Such dumplings are called *levivot* in Hebrew and may be the dish which Tamar made for Amnon (Samuel 2 9–22). The recipe below is time-consuming, but the results really justify the effort.

For the soup:
1kg/2lb soup meat (chuck or shin of beef) and bones, washed and cut
   to chunks
2 litres/4 pints/10½ cups water
1 large bunch of spring onions, trimmed and sliced lengthwise, retaining the
   green part
250g/8oz garlic chives, trimmed and sliced*
6 celery sticks, sliced†
500g/1lb beet greens, chard, or a mixture of sorrel and spinach, chopped
   (if sorrel is used the amount of lemon juice has to be reduced)
Juice of 2–3 lemons

Lay the washed meat and bones in a large stockpot and cover with cold water. Bring to the boil, reduce the heat and simmer for 1½ hours, skimming frequently. Add the onion, garlic chives, celery, beet greens, and lemon juice. Simmer very gently for 35 minutes.

For the dumplings:
500g/1lb/3 cups fine cracked wheat or burgul, soaked in water with a pinch
   of salt added
500g/1lb/3 cups semolina

Drain the wheat and squeeze dry. Knead with the semolina until a stable, softish dough is achieved. Some more water may be needed. Let the dough rest for at least 1 hour to lose its elasticity.

---

* Garlic chives are obtainable at Chinese grocers. They can be substituted with garlic, in which case use 5–6 fat cloves.
† One can successfully use ordinary celery sticks, but a much better result is obtained with the leaves of root celery which can be bought in most Greek and Turkish grocers.

For the stuffing:
500g/1lb meat cut in chunks (the meat should be rather fatty; if lean meat
   is used, add 3–4 tablespoons oil)
2 large onions, chopped
5 fat cloves of garlic, chopped
8 celery sticks and leaves, chopped
Salt

Put the meat, onion and oil, if used, in a heavy bottomed pot. Fry until
the meat starts to brown, stirring frequently. Coarsely pound or chop the
garlic and celery before adding them to the frying meat. Cook until the
meat is well done and all liquids have evaporated. Season with salt. I have
found that adding the celery and garlic mixture raw to cooled, fried meat
results in a more herby, fragrant *cubbeh*.

The Cubbeh:
Take a lump of dough the size of an egg. Roll it into a ball and make an
indentation with your thumb. Fill with 1 tablespoon of stuffing. Close the
hole by pinching the dough together. Flatten the *cubbeh* to a patty about
6cm (2½″) round. Continue to make patties with the rest of the mixture.

Place the dumplings very carefully in the boiling soup, being careful not
to break them for they are fragile. Bring the soup back to the boil, reduce
the heat and simmer very gently for 10–15 minutes, shaking the pot for
time to time to prevent the *cubbehs* from sticking to each other. Serve very
hot.

FUL MEDAMES
Egyptian Broad Beans

Serves 6–8 as a main course

This dish almost certainly originated in ancient Egypt and similar dishes
were probably a staple food of poor farmers all over the Middle East. *Ful
medames* is still eaten widely in Israel, usually for breakfast. Indeed, there
was a time when it was impossible to get *ful* in a restaurant after 11 a.m.
It is served either on its own with pitta bread and pickles or together with
tahina sauce or hummus.

1kg/2lb/5 cups Egyptian broad beans,* soaked overnight, and drained
3–4 cloves garlic, crushed
50ml/2fl.oz/¼ cup fruity olive oil
Juice of 1 lemon
Salt and freshly ground pepper
Parsley or mint, chopped
Lemon wedges, for decoration

Cover the beans with fresh cold water. Bring to the boil and simmer gently for 2–2½ hours. The boiling time will depend on the quality of the beans. In a pressure cooker it takes around 45 minutes. At the end of the cooking time the beans should be soft but not broken up. Drain the beans, discarding the cooking liquid. Mix in the garlic, olive oil, lemon juice, salt and pepper. Sprinkle with plenty of chopped parsley or mint. Decorate with lemon wedges. Serve warm, with pitta bread.

LACHUCH
Yemenite Sour Dough Pitta

Makes about 25 pittas

The following is probably one of the oldest versions of leavened pittas. It has an interesting, slightly sour flavour.

500g/1lb/4 cups strong unbleached flour
Water

Mix the flour with enough water to make a thickish, runny batter. Leave in a warm place for a few days to ferment, or until the batter is spongy.

Heat a frying pan and pour on a small quantity of batter as though you were making pancakes. Bake until golden on one side, turn and bake on the other. Serve hot.

* *Ful medames* can be bought at Greek or Middle Eastern stores. One can use other varieties of broad beans, but the *ful* has a nutty, slightly bitter, earthy flavour which cannot be duplicated.

MIDDLE EASTERN PIZZAS

Makes about 15

500g/1lb/4 cups strong unbleached bread flour, sifted (keep aside
  1 teaspoon)
½ teaspoon salt
50ml/2fl.oz/¼ cup olive oil for the dough
15g/½oz/1 tablespoon fresh yeast or the recommended equivalent in
  dry yeast
250ml/8fl.oz/1 cup water
Olive oil for brushing
Za'atar or dried oregano

Mix the salt and flour, add the oil and mix well. Dissolve the yeast in a
little water. Sprinkle this with the 1 teaspoon of flour and leave for 10
minutes in a warm place to ferment. Add the yeast and water to the flour
mixture and mix to a soft, unsticky dough. Knead well on a floured board
until the dough is smooth and elastic. Coat well with a little oil to prevent
the formation of a dry skin. Cover the dough with a damp cloth and leave
to rise in a warm place for 2–3 hours.

Knock down the dough and knead for 1 minute. Divide the dough into
50–75g (2–3oz) pieces rolling each one into a ball. Flatten the balls on a
floured surface and roll each one out to round 5mm (⅓″) thick pittas.
Transfer onto a baking sheet. When all the pittas have been rolled, stub
each one with the tips of your fingers so that the whole surface is covered
with small indentations. Brush liberally with olive oil and sprinkle with
a generous amount of *za'atar*. Leave to rise for about 25–30 minutes in a
warm place.

Pre-heat the oven for at least 20 minutes until it is very hot (gas 8–9,
240°C, 465°F). Sprinkle the risen pittas with a little cold water. Place in
the hot oven and bake for 5–8 minutes or until they are golden at the
edges. Serve hot. The same dough can be made into mini-sized pittas and
served with drinks.

MPUCHTA DAD KZEBEH
Date Honey

I found the following recipe in a book about Kurdistani Jewish cooking.
The technique is probably similar to the one employed to produce the
Biblical fruit honey. The result is a rich, nutty, sweet, thick syrup which

can be used to flavour icecream or be added as a fragrant sweetener anywhere honey is called for.

1kg/2lb/5 cups moist dry dates
1 litre/1¾ pints/4 cups water

Stone the dates. Cover with water and simmer for 30 minutes. Cool. Put the mixture into a muslin bag and gently squeeze out the liquid. Add some more water to the squeezed pulp and repeat. Put the resulting liquid into a clean pan and boil for 30 minutes to reduce. Pour into clean jars and seal.

LATE PERIOD

APICIAN STUFFED DATES

This recipe is from Barbara Flowers' *Apicius, Roman Cookery*. Although it sounds a bit odd, it makes a fascinating, though very sweet, dessert.

To stuff 50 fresh dates you will need:
100g/4oz/¾ cup lightly roasted almonds
100g/4oz/¾ cup roasted hazelnuts
100g/4oz/¾ cup roasted pine nuts
100g/4oz/¾ cup roasted pistachio nuts
2–3 tablespoons good quality honey, for the filling
100g/4oz/¾ cup honey, for the sauce
1 teaspoon powdered cinnamon
½ teaspoon freshly ground black pepper
Few drops of orange blossom water

Put the roasted nuts into a food processor and process to a fine powder. Add the honey and flavourings and process for a few seconds longer. Take out and knead well. If the mixture is too sticky, add some finely ground almonds or nuts. Stone the dates and stuff each with the sweetmeat (about 15g/½oz/1 teaspoon per date).

Boil the honey for the sauce in a large frying pan. Flavour with orange blossom water and add the stuffed dates. Heat gently until the dates are piping hot. Transfer them to a serving dish, moisten with some of the cooking liquid and serve with clotted cream.

'ANOTHER SAUCE FOR PIGEON'
A Sauce for Boiled or Roasted Pigeon

It is impossible to replicate this ancient recipe precisely as we do not know the precise quantities used, and some of the translated names of ingredients are also in dispute. However, I have made the sauce, which is interesting, if strong tasting. It compliments game or other strong tasting meats. The flavours of rue and lovage are exceedingly strong and should be used with caution. The term *liquamen* is disputed; some translators think that it means a fermented fish sauce (use bottled anchovy sauce as a modern equivalent), while others translate *liquamen* as stock or broth.

    1 teaspoon ground black pepper
    3–4 lovage leaves, chopped or pounded
    3 tablespoons parsley, chopped
    ½ teaspoon celery seeds, ground to a fine powder
    1–2 small rue sprigs, chopped or pounded
    100g/4oz/¾ cup pine nuts, pounded to a smooth paste
    100g/4oz/¾ cup moist dates, de-seeded, minced or pounded
    1 tablespoon honey
    50ml/2fl.oz/¼ cup vinegar
    2 tablespoons anchovy essence
    1 tablespoon mustard seeds, pounded
    50ml/2fl.oz/¼ cup olive oil

Either purée all the ingredients in a blender or pound them together. Transfer to a small saucepan. Bring to the boil. Reduce the heat and simmer very gently for 10 minutes. Pour over roasted pigeons or any other game bird.

HONEYED OMELETTE

Serves 4

    4 eggs (size 3)
    250ml/½ pint/1 cup milk
    Pinch of salt
    25ml/1fl.oz/2 tablespoons olive oil
    Oil for frying
    75ml/3fl.oz/⅓ cup honey

Beat the eggs, salt and milk well. Heat the oil in a frying pan. Pour in the mixture and fry until cooked underneath and almost set on top. Turn onto a serving dish, pour over the honey and sprinkle with black pepper.

CHAROSET

Charoset is a direct descendent of the Greco-Roman sweet-sour sauces which were served at the beginning of a feast as a dip for raw, bitter salad herbs. They were eaten to refresh the palate and tantalise the appetite. Today *charoset* is served as an indispensable part of the Seder (the Pesach ceremony) to commemorate the clay that the Jews used in Egypt. The following three recipes are from different communities. The consistency of *charoset* should be like a thick porridge. It can be diluted with wine or thickened with fine *matzah* meal or ground almonds or nuts to achieve the required effect.

YEMENITE CHAROSET

Serves 5–6

150g/6oz/¾ cup pitted moist dates
150g/6oz/¾ cup dried figs, soaked for a few hours
2 tablespoons sesame seeds, roasted in a dry frying pan
1 tablespoon honey
½ teaspoon clove powder
½ teaspoon ground cardamom
½ teaspoon powdered ginger
3–4 tablespoons sweet Pesach wine

Mince the dates and figs. Add the rest of the ingredients and mix well.

ASHKENAZI CHAROSET

Serves 10–12

250g/8oz/1 cup sweet/sour apples (Granny Smith, russets), peeled
   and grated
150g/6oz/¾ cup seedless raisins, minced or chopped
150g/6oz/¾ cup almonds or walnuts, finely ground
50ml/2fl.oz/¼ cup sweet Pesach wine
1–2 tablespoons honey
1 teaspoon powdered cinnamon
¼ teaspoon powdered clove

Mix all the ingredients together.

IRAQI CHAROSET

Serves 8–10

150g/6oz/1 cup ground almonds
150g/6oz/1 cup ground walnuts or pecan nuts
150g/6oz/¾ cup moist stoned dates, minced
75ml/3fl.oz/⅓ cup sweet wine or pomegranate juice
1 teaspoon black pepper
½ teaspoon ground cardamom

Mix all the ingredients together.

FISH STUFFED WITH LEEKS

Serves 4

Indications for this dish appear in the Talmud, in a discussion which tries to ascertain if a stuffing is to be considered a separate dish.[1] It mentions fish stuffed with *kapelot*, a relative of the leek. The word *kapelot* means 'head' which suggests that only the bulbous root end of the vegetable was used.

4 trout
50ml/2fl.oz/¼ cup olive oil
500g/1lb/ white part of leek, washed well and shredded
4 hard-boiled eggs, chopped
Salt and pepper
Fennel or dill
4 thin slices of lemon
4 sheets of aluminium foil or heavy parchment

Clean and gut the fish. Heat the oil in a heavy bottomed frying pan. Add the shredded leeks and fry for few minutes until they are transparent and beginning to colour. Remove from the heat and add the chopped eggs, salt and pepper. Stuff each fish belly with the leek mixture. Brush each piece of foil generously with oil and place a fish in the centre. Lay a slice of lemon and a few sprigs of fennel or dill on each fish before dusting with salt and pepper. Fold the foil loosely into a neat, tightly sealed parcel. Bake in a medium oven (gas 5, 190°C, 375°F) for 15–20 minutes. Serve hot.

GREEN OLIVES

Fresh olives may be bought in season at the beginning of winter, from many Greek and Turkish stores.

1kg/2lb fresh green olives
2 heaped tablespoons coarse salt
1 tablespoon coriander seeds, coarsely pounded
6 cloves of garlic, crushed
2–3 red or green chillies
2 lemons, sliced into small rings
50ml/2fl.oz/¼ cup olive oil
1–2 small sprigs of rue (optional)

Crush each olive with a mallet or a hammer. Place in plenty of cold water. Leave for three days, changing the water each day. Rinse and drain. Transfer the olives into a pickling jar. Add the rest of the ingredients, mix well and seal tightly. Leave in a cool dark place for 3–4 months, shaking the jar from time to time.

BLACK OLIVES

1kg/2lb fresh black olives, washed
Salt for brining
1 heaped tablespoon coarse salt
3 tablespoons olive oil

Lay the washed olives in an enamel or glazed dish. Strew a handful of coarse salt over them and mix well. Next day, drain away all the accumulated liquid, add a small handful of salt and leave to marinate. Repeat this procedure for five days. On the sixth day, rinse the olives well in a few changes of water. Put them into a clean pickling jar. Add the coarse salt and the oil, shake well and seal. The olives are ready after one week.

PUMPKIN COOKED WITH RICE

Serves 6–8

Both pumpkin and rice were probably introduced into the Israeli kitchen after the Babylonian exile. The following recipe originates from Northern Iraq.

50ml/2fl.oz/¼ cup olive or sesame oil
500g/1lb yellow pumpkin, peeled and cubed
500g/1lb/2 cups rice or burgul
Salt and freshly ground pepper
1 litre/2 pints/5 cups water

Heat the oil in a heavy bottomed pot. Add the pumpkin and sweat for few minutes over a medium flame. Add the rice, salt, pepper and water. Bring to the boil before covering tightly. Reduce the heat and simmer very gently for 15–20 minutes until all the liquid is absorbed. Adjust the seasoning and allow the dish to stand for 5 minutes before serving.

SWEET WHEAT PUDDING

Serves 8–10

500g/1lb/3 cups cracked wheat, washed and soaked overnight
Water
500ml/1pint/2½ cups milk
1 tablespoon honey
A few pieces of orange peel
50g/2oz/¼ cup sultanas
Pomegranate or rose syrup
50g/2oz/¼ cup slivered almonds, lightly roasted
A little cinnamon powder

Cover the wheat with plenty of water and simmer until perfectly tender, adding more water only if necessary. This could take up to 3 hours. Otherwise, cook in a pressure cooker for about 1–1½ hours. Add the milk, honey, orange peel and sultanas. Simmer very slowly, uncovered, until the mixture is thick and creamy (1–1½ hours). Stir often to prevent scorching. Transfer to individual ramekins. Cool and refrigerate overnight. Pour a thin layer of syrup over each pudding. Decorate with slivered almonds and sprinkle with cinnamon. Serve cold.

HAMIN OR CHULENT

Hamin used to be the taste of Sabbath. It is a dish which was cooked with local variations by most Jewish communities. The *hamin* is usually cooked in the oven on a very low heat overnight. It is impossible to cook *hamin* in small quantities. Leftovers freeze rather successfully.

SCHINA DEZERA
Moroccan Wheat Hamin

Serves 8–10

500g/1lb/3 cups wheat, washed and soaked overnight
3–4 tablespoons oil
1kg/2lb chuck steak or brisket
2 large onions, chopped
8 large cloves of garlic, peeled and crushed
8 eggs
8 small potatoes, peeled
350g/12oz/1½ cups chickpeas, soaked overnight
100g/4oz/½ cup raisins
½ teaspoon cinnamon
1–1½ litres/2–3 pints/5–7½ cups water
Salt and pepper

Drain the wheat and put into a piece of muslin. Tie the ends loosely to create a parcel.* Heat the oil in a large, heavy bottomed pot and sear the meat well. Lift out and keep warm. Add the onions and garlic and fry until they start to brown. Put the wheat parcel in the centre of the pot and arrange the rest of the ingredients around it. Add the water, salt and pepper, and bring rapidly to the boil. Simmer gently for about 2 hours. Cover tightly and transfer to a cool oven (gas 1, 140°C, 285°F). Cook overnight. Add more water if the stew gets too dry. For special occasions a savoury pudding is added to the *hamin*.

---

* A chicken-roasting bag can be used instead of muslin. Prick all over to allow penetration of moisture and do not tie too tightly so as to allow room for expansion.

———— Moroccan Sweet Pudding for Hamin ————

Serves 8–10

This recipe comes from Mrs Levy-Mellul's *Moroccan Cooking*. The sweet, hot flavour is rich and very special.

250g/8oz/2 cups coarsely ground nuts (walnuts, pecan nuts or almonds)
350g/12oz/1½ cups minced, fatty lamb
50ml/2fl.oz/¼ cup peanut or sesame oil
2 eggs (size 3)
3 tablespoons breadcrumbs or *matzah* meal
2 teaspoons cinnamon
1 teaspoon black pepper
¼ teaspoon ginger
2 tablespoons sugar
1 teaspoon mace
½ teaspoon nutmeg
1 teaspoon salt

Mix all the ingredients together and knead well. Shape into a fat sausage. Wrap in a piece of muslin and tie at both ends. Wrapping is necessary, otherwise the pudding will crumble. Cook together with the *hamin*.

———————— Ashkenazi Chulent ————————

Serves 8–10

50g/2oz/¼ cup *schmaltz* or vegetable shortening
2 large onions, chopped
1kg/2lb beef — chuck, short ribs, brisket or shoulder
250g/8oz/1 cup white beans (navy, lima or haricot)
150g/6oz/¾ cup pearl barley
500g/1lb potatoes, peeled and quartered
Salt and pepper
Boiling water to cover

Heat the fat in a large, heavy bottomed cooking pot or Dutch oven. Add the onions and fry until golden brown. Remove the pot from the heat. Place the meat on top of the fried onion in the centre of the pot. Arrange the rest of the ingredients around the meat and cover with boiling water. Simmer very slowly for 1½–2 hours. Check the liquid and add some more if too dry. Transfer to a cool oven (gas 1, 140°C, 285°F) and cook overnight. Stuffed *kishke* (*derma*), *helzel* or dumplings can be added and are cooked with the *chulent*.

HAMIN WITH AUBERGINES

Serves 8–10

Ya'akov Lishansky, one of the 'fathers' of Israeli cooking, told me that in his family stuffed aubergines were cooked with the *chulent* instead of *kishke*. The following is my version of stuffed aubergines.

8–10 small aubergines or 1 large aubergine
1 medium onion
350g/12oz/1½ cups minced lamb or beef
50g/2fl.oz/¼ cup olive oil
5 tablespoons chopped parsley
100g/4oz/½ cup rice, soaked for a few hours in cold water and drained
½ teaspoon cinnamon
Salt and freshly ground pepper

Slice the tops off the aubergines and put to one side. With the help of a spoon or a sharp knife, scoop out the aubergine flesh, being careful not to damage the skin. Chop the flesh.

Heat the oil in a heavy frying pan, add the onion and fry until just golden. Add the aubergine flesh and fry for a few more minutes until the aubergine has softened. Remove from the flame and add the rest of the ingredients. Mix well and stuff the aubergines with this mixture. Cover with the reserved tops and secure these with wooden toothpicks. Arrange in the *chulent* pot and cook as usual.

Yemenite Soup Hamin

Serves 6–8

This *hamin* is more liquid than the others and is served as a thick soup.

1½–2 litres/3–4 pints/10½ cups water
1kg/2lb calf's feet, cleaned and sawn into smallish pieces (ask the butcher to do this)
350g/12oz/1½ cups wheat berries (either whole or cracked), soaked overnight and drained
1 large head of garlic, peeled and crushed
1 large soft tomato, peeled and sliced
1–2 teaspoons *chwage**
Salt

Bring the water to a boil in a large heavy bottomed pot. Add the meat and simmer for 20 minutes, skimming well all the time. Add the rest of the ingredients and simmer gently for a further 1 hour. Transfer into a cool oven (gas 1, 140°C, 285°F) and cook overnight. Serve with *schug* (see recipe on p. 261).

---

* *Chwage* is the standard Yemenite flavouring mixture. To make this, grind to a fine powder 2 tablespoons black pepper, 1 tablespoon cumin, 1 tablespoon coriander seeds, 1 teaspoon cardamom, 1 teaspoon cloves, 2 teaspoons turmeric powder. Keep in an airtight container.

TABIT
Iraqi Chicken Hamin

Serves 6–8

A light and delicate *hamin*. The recipe appeared in *Israeli Flavour* by Mrs Pascal Perez-Rubin.

1 ×1½–2kg/3–4lb chicken

Stuffing:
3 tablespoons oil
1 medium onion, chopped
The chicken's innards (liver, gizzard, heart, etc.)
150g/6oz/¾ cup rice
½ teaspoon salt
½ teaspoon powdered allspice
½ teaspoon pepper
¼ teaspoon cinnamon
½ teaspoon dried mint, crumbled
1 teaspoon cardamom, powdered
1 egg, beaten
1 tablespoon tomato purée or 1 soft tomato

For the hamin:
3 tablespoons oil
250g/8oz/1 cup rice, soaked overnight and drained
2 large onions, peeled and coarsely chopped
2 large potatoes, peeled and cubed
2 medium courgettes, washed and cubed
3 medium carrots, peeled and cubed
Salt and pepper
1–1½ litres/2–3 pints/5–7½ cups water

Clean the chicken and have on hand a needle and thread to close the neck opening.

To prepare the stuffing: heat some oil in a frying pan and brown the onion. Add the chicken innards and the rice and mix well. Remove from the heat and add the rest of the stuffing ingredients. Fill the chicken cavity and close the opening by sewing.

For the *hamin*: heat the oil in a large heavy bottomed pot. Add the onion and stuffed chicken and brown slightly. Add the rest of the ingredients. Cover with water and bring to a rapid boil. Reduce the heat and simmer very gently for 1–2 hours. Transfer to a cool oven (gas 1, 140°C, 285°F) and cook overnight.

171

12

ASHKENAZI FOOD

FIRST COURSES

─────────── Soffy's Bean Salad ───────────

Serves 6–8

Mrs Soffy Boume arrived in Israel as a middle-aged, widowed refugee from Romania. Having survived the Holocaust, she was later forced to flee to yet another oppressive regime. Like many others at the time (1949), she was given shelter in houses of established Israelis in exchange for domestic help. As luck would have it, she finished up in our house. Soffy was a natural cook, and created elegant, tasty food, both traditional Jewish and Romanian, from the meagre resources available. Her presentation was impeccable and she spent a tremendous amount of time and patience on fine details. Soffy's memory lives on in many of the recipes which are presented in this book. The following is one which she often used to cook. It was always referred to as 'bean hummus'.

> 350g/12oz/1½ cups white beans, (haricot, navy or butter beans)
>   soaked overnight
> 50ml/2fl.oz/¼ cup good light olive or peanut oil, for the salad
> Juice of 1 lemon
> Salt and pepper
> 100ml/4fl.oz/½ cup good oil, for frying
> 500g/1lb onions, sliced into thin rounds
> Chopped parsley or mint and sweet paprika, for decoration

Either boil (for 1–1½ hours) or pressure cook (for 30 minutes) the soaked beans until perfectly soft. Drain and reserve some of the cooking liquid. Pass the cooked beans through a fine sieve. Add 50ml/2fl.oz/½ cup oil, lemon juice, salt and pepper, and mix well. The purée should be soft, but keep its shape. If it is too thick, dilute with a little of the cooking liquid. Keep covered.

Heat the oil in a heavy pan and fry the onions until they are evenly golden brown and some are crispy. Arrange a crown of purée around a serving platter or on individual plates. Pile a mound of fried onions in the centre. Sprinkle with some of the frying oil and then with herbs and paprika. This is best served warm.

PATCHA, PITCHA OR SULZE
Calf's Foot Jelly

Serves 8–10

The dish was a favourite standby for starting a holiday meal. We served it with horseradish and beetroot sauce (*chrain*) or mustard. It can also be served as a soup, being cooked in the oven for Saturday lunch.

1kg/2lb calf's or cow's feet, cleaned and sawn to fit the pot
Cold water to cover
1 large onion, stuck with 3–4 cloves
3 bay leaves
Salt to taste
2–3 tablespoons vinegar or lemon juice
3–4 cloves of garlic, mashed with a little salt
Freshly ground black pepper
2 hard-boiled eggs, sliced into thin rounds
Sliced lemon and parsley for garnish

Put the perfectly clean and washed feet in a large pot. Cover with water. Bring to the boil and boil rapidly for 10 minutes. Skim well. Add the onion and bay leaves. Cover and simmer very gently for 3 hours or until the bones stand away from the gristle and meat. Discard the onion and bay leaves and strain the liquid into a clean pot. Chop the usable meat and gristle into fine cubes before adding them to the strained liquid. Return to the heat and bring to the boil. Add salt, pepper, vinegar and garlic. Boil rapidly for about 5 minutes.

Turn into an oblong glass dish about 5cm (2") deep. Let the liquid cool until it is partly jellied. Push egg rounds into the surface and chill thoroughly.

Serve cut into squares and decorated with parsley and lemon wedges.

To serve as soup: prepare feet as before, but ask the butcher to saw them into serving portions. Add water, bring to the boil and skim well. Add onion and bay leaves, bring to the boil again. Cover tightly and place in a cool oven (gas 1, 140°C, 285°F) overnight. Next day discard the onion and bay leaves before adding vinegar, salt, pepper, garlic and 1 tablespoon mustard. Mix well and serve very hot.

GEHAKTE LEBER
Chopped Chicken Liver

Serves 6

500g/1lb liver (chicken, calf, goose or a mixture of poultry offal)
3 tablespoons *schmaltz* (vegetarian or otherwise)
120g/4oz onion, chopped
Salt and pepper
2 hard-boiled eggs
Hard-boiled eggs for decoration (white and yolk separated and sieved)
Parsley

Heat the fat in a heavy frying pan. Fry the onion until nicely browned. Add the liver and fry until it is done to your liking.* Add salt and pepper. Either chop by hand, process or mince the liver and onion together with the hard-boiled eggs. If the liver is too dry, moisten with some melted *schmaltz*. Arrange on a flat platter and decorate with alternately coloured stripes made from sieved egg yolks and the white. Border with parsley sprigs. Serve chilled.

BAKED HERRING

Serves 4

Herrings are one of the most important ingredients in the list of appetisers. Those known as *schmaltz* (fat) herrings are preferred and usually contain either soft or hard roes. The soft roes are used to sauce the herrings while the hard roes are used to make *ekra* (see recipe on p. 237). *Schmaltz* herring should be soaked in cold water or milk for at least 12 hours to remove excess saltiness. This recipe for baked herring is an adaptation of a recipe

---

* In some communities, the liver is boiled in water separately and then minced with the browned onion.

which appeared in the *International Goodwill Recipe Book*, published by the Johannesburg Women's Zionist League — probably the most widely read South African Jewish cookery book.

2 herrings, soaked for 12 hours, cleaned, skinned and filleted
2 onions, thinly sliced
2 tart apples peeled, cored and sliced
12 peppercorns
1 teaspoon mustard seeds
2 bay leaves
50g/2oz/¼ cup raisins
300ml/½ pint/1½ cups vinegar
50ml/2fl.oz/¼ cup water
100g/4oz/½ cup brown sugar or 4 tablespoons golden syrup

Butter a glass or enamel baking dish. Line with half the sliced apple and onion. Lay the cleaned herring, either as a whole fillet or sliced into bite-sized pieces, on top. Cover with the rest of the onion and apple. Scatter over peppercorns, mustard seeds, bay leaves and raisins. Dissolve the sugar in water and vinegar and pour over the dish. Bake for 20–25 minutes at gas mark 5 (190°C, 375°) until the onion is tender and the dish browned slightly. Serve hot or cold.

GEHAKTE HERRING
Herring Salad

Serves 4–6

2 large herrings, soaked overnight, skinned and filleted
2 hard-boiled eggs
1 tart apple, peeled and grated
1 small onion, very finely chopped
2 tablespoons lemon juice or 3 tablespoons vinegar
2 tablespoons salad oil
2 tablespoons sugar, or to taste (optional)
3 tablespoons dry bread, honey cake crumbs or cracker crumbs
Pepper

Chop, mince or process the herring fillets and eggs to a smooth pulp. Grate in the apple and onion. Add lemon juice or vinegar and oil. Taste and add sugar if liked. Stir in dry crumbs and add pepper. Cover and allow to rest in the refrigerator for at least 1 hour. Served chilled with *kichlach* (see recipe on p. 273).

PICKLED HERRINGS

Serves 4–6

2 large salt herrings with soft roes, soaked overnight, skinned and filleted
1 large onion, sliced into thin rings
2 sweet pickled gherkins, sliced into thin rings
2–3 bay leaves
5 allspice berries, crushed
1 teaspoons whole black peppercorns, crushed
Few juniper berries, crushed (optional)
100ml/4fl.oz/½ cup vinegar
1 tablespoon sugar or to taste
50ml/2fl.oz/¼ cup water

Slice the herring fillet to bite-sized slices. In a large glass jar or bowl arrange layers of herring, sliced onion and gherkins. Place spices here and there. Bring the vinegar, sugar and water to a rapid boil, boil for a few seconds, skim and allow to cool. Mash the soft roe and mix with the liquid. Pour this over the herrings and allow them to marinate for at least 24 hours. This dish can be kept in the refrigerator for up to 1 month.

EGG AND ONION SALAD

Serves 4–6

This is one of the simplest and most delicious of Jewish appetiser salads. It is traditionally made with *schmaltz* and *gribens*, but is just as tasty, and healthier, made with good oil.

6 hard-boiled eggs
1 small onion or 1 bunch of spring onions, trimmed and finely chopped
2–3 tablespoons chicken *schmaltz* and *gribenes*, or 3 tablespoons oil
Salt and freshly ground pepper
Sliced tomatoes and parsley sprigs for decoration

Mash the eggs rather coarsely with a fork. Add the onion. Moisten with melted, cool *schmaltz* or oil and season. Decorate with sliced tomatoes and parsley sprigs. Serve chilled.

Radish Salad

Serves 4–6

The radish used is the large Continental red or black variety. A good substitute is the long white variety known as *mooli* which can be obtained in some supermarkets or at Chinese and Indian greengrocers. I recommend grating the radish near a window or in a well-ventilated kitchen because it emits a dreadful smell when freshly grated.

500g/1lb radish, peeled and grated coarsely
1 small bunch of spring onions, trimmed and finely chopped
2–3 tablespoons melted *schmaltz* and *gribenes* or 3 tablespoons olive oil
Salt and plenty of freshly ground pepper
A few drops lemon juice or vinegar (optional)

Salt the grated radish lightly and leave it to drain in a colander for 1 hour. Add the rest of the ingredients, add more salt if necessary and serve. A few drops of lemon juice or vinegar may also be added.

Holishkes, Parakes or Galuptzi
Stuffed Cabbage Leaves

Makes 12

Cabbage has a reputation for being a restorative for hangovers. It was usually served on holidays like Purim and Simchat Torah when drinking was a traditional part of the celebration.

12 white cabbage leaves, blanched for 3 minutes in boiling water

For the stuffing:
500g/1lb/2 cups minced or chopped beef
1 medium onion, chopped
50g/2oz/¼ cup rice
Grated rind of 1 lemon
Salt and pepper

For the sauce:
50g/2oz/¼ cup brown sugar, or more to taste
Water, stock, sweet white wine or tinned tomato juice to cover*
Juice from 1 large lemon, or more to taste
Salt and pepper

* Originally tomato juice was not used.

Trim the cabbage leaves and remove any hard veins. Mix all the stuffing ingredients well. Put some stuffing on each leaf. Roll once or twice, folding in the ends until a neat cigar-shaped parcel is achieved. Lay these closely in a heavy bottomed pot.

To make the sauce: dissolve the sugar in the water (or other cooking liquid) and lemon juice and cover the stuffed leaves. Bring to the boil, reduce the heat and simmer gently for about 1 hour or until most of the cooking liquid is absorbed. Serve hot or cold.

NAHIT
Chickpeas Snack

Serves 10–12

Boiled, spiced chickpeas were served as tasty morsels to have with drinks at almost every celebration.

300g/12oz/1½ cups chickpeas, soaked overnight
1–2 teaspoons each of salt, pepper and paprika to taste

Boil or pressure cook the chickpeas until they are soft but still maintain their shape. Drain well before returning them to the pot to dry over a high flame for few minutes. Shake the pot vigorously while this is happening. Cool the peas and dust with salt, pepper and paprika. Serve warm.

ACCOMPANYING DISHES

The recipes below are to accompany main dishes. They played an important part in Jewish cooking because they were used as cheap fillers: the more of these you had, the less meat needed to be served.

POTATO KUGEL

Serves 6

500g/1lb potatoes, grated, rinsed and squeezed dry
1 large onion, grated
3 eggs (size 3), well beaten
75g/3oz/⅓ cup flour (approximately)
Freshly ground black pepper
50g/2oz/¼ cup melted chicken fat, butter or *parve* shortening
Salt

Peel and grate the potatoes. Rinse well, and then squeeze them dry. Add all the other ingredients. The resulting batter should be thick enough to hold its shape. If it is too thin, add a bit more flour. Grease a round baking tin or a glass casserole. Pour in the batter and bake in a pre-heated moderate oven (gas 5, 190°C, 375°F) for 45–60 minutes until set and nicely brown and crispy. Serve hot.

POTATO LATKES

Serves 6–8

This dish is traditionally served for Chanukah. The original version is fried in goose *schmaltz*. It is served either as a main part of a meal with apple sauce and sour cream or to accompany meat dishes.

1kg/2lb peeled, finely grated potatoes
250g/8oz grated onion
150g/6oz/1¼ cups *matzah* meal or flour (use 1½ cups)
4 eggs (size 3)
2 teaspoons caraway seeds (optional)
Salt and pepper
Oil for frying

Wash the grated potatoes in a few changes of clean cold water. Mix with the rest of the ingredients. Salt and pepper well. Heat the oil in a large frying pan. With the help of a tablespoon drop a spoonful of the mixture in the hot oil. Flatten each spoonful with a metal spatula into an unevenly round, flat, small pancake. Fry on medium heat for 3–4 minutes on each side or until each pancake is a pale, golden brown and perfectly crisp. Drain well on absorbent paper and serve very hot.

APPLE SAUCE

500g/1lb cooking apples, peeled, cored and sliced
2–3 pieces of lemon peel
1 cinnamon quill
4–5 cloves
1 large teaspoon honey or sugar
About 25ml/1fl.oz/⅛ cup water
½ teaspoon salt
100g/4oz/½ cup cold butter

Put the apple, flavourings and water into a thick bottomed pan. Cook rapidly for about 10 minutes or until the apple is a smooth pulp. Remove from the heat, lift out the flavouring and beat in the salt and cold butter. Serve at room temperature.

MEATLESS CARROT TZIMMES

Serves 6–8

This dish is traditionally served as part of the Rosh Ha'sanah eve meal. In some communities black pepper is omitted as no hot, sour, bitter flavour or black colour is served at the meal.

> 1kg/2lb carrots, peeled and sliced into thickish discs
> 250ml/⅓ pint/1 cup water
> 50g/2oz/¼ cup honey, sugar or golden syrup
> Salt
> 2 tablespoons *schmaltz*, butter, solid vegetable fat or peanut oil
> 2 tablespoons flour
> Freshly ground pepper
> 1 teaspoon powdered ginger
> Orange juice (optional)

Simmer the carrots with water, honey and salt until they are almost soft. Make an *einbren* (roux) by heating the fat in a small frying pan, adding the flour and frying until the flour is slightly browned, mixing all the time. Add the *einbren* to the carrots, season with pepper and ginger, mix together and cook for 5 minutes or until the sauce is thickened. If the sauce is too thick, dilute with some orange juice. Serve hot.

TZIMMES NAHIT
Chickpeas Tzimmes

Serves 6–8

This recipe is my grandmother's, Mania Dostrovsky, née Levinson. It originated in Besarabia, on the border of Romania and Russia.

> 250g/8oz/1 cup chickpeas, soaked overnight
> 2 tablespoons *schmaltz*, vegetable fat or oil
> 2 tablespoons flour
> 50g/2oz/¼ cup honey, brown sugar or syrup

Boil the chickpeas until just tender. Drain and reserve 300ml/½ pint/1¼ cups of the cooking liquid. In a small pan, melt the fat, add the flour and mix well. Add the sweetener and fry until the mixture starts to caramelise and turns light brown. Add the reserved liquid, bringing it to the boil while mixing all the time. Fold in the cooked chickpeas. Flavour with salt and pepper and cook for 10 minutes, stirring often to prevent sticking. Stir gently to prevent the chickpeas losing their shape. Serve hot.

——————————— LOKSHEN ———————————
Basic Recipe for Noodle Dough

Makes approximately 500g/1lb noodles or 6 kreplach

Noodles were of the utmost importance in the Ashkenazi kitchen. They were served on their own as a substantial dairy meal or as an accompanying dish with main courses. They were baked into sweet and savoury *kugels* or served with soups. The following recipes have been selected for their flavour and ease of preparation.

350g/12oz/3 cups sifted flour
3 small eggs (size 3)
2–3 tablespoons cold water

Sift the flour onto a kneading board. Make a well in the centre. Add the eggs and start mixing in the flour. Sprinkle with the water and knead well into a stiffish elastic dough. Divide the dough into two equal parts. Roll into balls and cover with a moist tea towel to rest for about ½ hour.

Flour the board well and roll the dough very thin. Dust the rolled dough lightly with flour and roll up the sheet of dough into a long sausage-shape. Slice across into noodles of the desired thickness.

Traditionally the noodles were sliced into three widths: 15mm (½″), 7mm (about ³⁄₁₀″) and thin vermicelli 1–2mm (¹⁄₁₆–⅛″) (served in soups or baked into *kugels*). Unravel each strand of dough and leave to dry, hanging on a clean broomstick or draped on a clean teatowel over the back of a chair.

To cook, boil in plenty of salted water for about 3 minutes. Drain well. The noodles can also be thoroughly dried and stored in airtight containers.

POPPY SEED NOODLES

Serves 4–6

A simple, colourful and wonderfully delicious way of serving noodles.

500g/1lb fresh noodles or 350g/12oz dried commercial wide noodles
50g/2oz/¼ cup butter
100g/4oz/¾ cup black poppy seeds
Salt and pepper
2 tablespoons parsley, finely chopped

Boil the noodles in plenty of salted water. Drain well. Melt the butter in a heavy bottomed pot. Add the poppy seeds and fry until the seeds start to change colour and emit a pleasant nutty smell. Add the drained noodles, mix well, season and heat through. Serve hot sprinkled with parsley.

COTTAGE CHEESE NOODLES

Serves 4–6

350g/12oz wide fresh or 250g/8oz dried commercial noodles
25g/1oz/2 tablespoons butter
150g/6oz/1½ cups fresh cottage cheese
50ml/2fl.oz/¼ cup sour cream, or more
Salt and freshly ground black pepper
2 tablespoons parsley, finely chopped
Parmesan or *katchkaval* cheese, grated (optional)

Boil noodles in plenty of salted water, drain well. Melt the butter in a heavy bottomed pot. Add the noodles and fry for a few minutes until heated through. Fold in the cheese and cream and heat for a few minutes more. The cheese should not cook as it becomes stringy and unpleasant. Add salt and pepper, sprinkle with parsley, and serve hot. Some strong, dry, grated cheese, such as parmesan or *katchkaval*, can be sprinkled on top.

KASHA VARENICHKES
Noodles with Buckwheat

Serves 6–8

This dish uses either large squares or wide- or bow-shaped (*farfelle* in Italian) noodles. The recipe is taken from Mrs Leah Leonard's *Jewish Cookery*.

250g/8oz/1 cup whole buckwheat
2 egg yolks
1 litre/2 pints/5 cups boiling water
1 teaspoon salt
4 tablespoons chicken fat or butter
250g/8oz/1 cup cooked noodles

Brown the buckwheat in a hot, dry frying pan, stirring constantly to prevent burning. When the buckwheat starts to change colour, add the beaten egg yolks and mix vigorously until the buckwheat grains are coated with egg. Add the salt and water and simmer gently until all the moisture is absorbed and the grains are tender. Add the fat and the cooked noodles. Turn into a casserole and brown evenly under a grill or in the oven. Serve hot with meat gravy or plain.

KREPLACH
Noodle Dough Turnovers

Makes approximately 60

Kreplach appear on almost every holiday table. They are normally served in soup, though sweet *kreplach* are browned in butter and served accompanied by sour cream for dessert.

1 quantity noodle dough (see *lokshen* on p. 181)

Liver filling:
500g/1lb calf or ox liver
50g/2oz/¼ cup chicken fat, shortening or oil
1 medium onion, chopped finely
Salt and freshly ground black pepper
2 tablespoons parsley, finely chopped

Heat the fat in a heavy bottomed frying pan, add the onion and fry until golden. Add the liver and continue frying until the liver is done to your liking. Mince or process. Season, add chopped parsley and mix well.

183

Roll the dough thinly. Cut the dough into circles using a glass or a 5cm (2″) pastry cutter, or cut into 5cm (2″) squares with a knife. Place about a teaspoon of the mixture in the centre of each round. Brush the edge with water, fold and pinch the edges together. Drop into plenty of boiling salted water and cook for about 10–15 minutes. Drain and serve in chicken soup. Uncooked *kreplach* freeze successfully and can be cooked from frozen.

KREPLACH WITH A CHERRY FILLING

Makes approximately 60

1 quantity of noodle dough (see recipe on p. 181)
500g/1lb cherries, stoned
1–2 tablespoons sugar
1 teaspoon powdered cinnamon
50–75g/2–3oz/¼–⅓ cup butter (preferably clarified)
Sour cream

Chop the stoned cherries roughly and add the sugar and cinnamon. Roll the dough. Cut and stuff as in previous recipe. Cook in boiling salted water and then drain well.

Either heat the butter in a heavy frying pan and fry a few at a time until well browned and crisp. Alternatively, butter a baking dish, arrange the *kreplach* and dot with butter. Sprinkle the top with some sugar and brown well in a hot oven (gas 7, 220°C, 425°F). Serve piping hot with sour cream.

EGG NOODLES FOR PESACH

Serves 4–6 as a garnish for chicken soup

In Pesach when flour is forbidden, substitute noodles were made from *matzah* meal.

3 eggs (size 3)
3 tablespoons cold water
1 tablespoon fine (cake) *matzah* meal
Pinch of salt

Beat the eggs and water, add the *matzah* meal and beat to a smooth, thin batter. Grease a frying pan and fry small quantities of batter as though you are making thin pancakes. Cook over a moderate heat until they are lightly browned on the under side. Turn out on a teatowel, bottom side up, to cool. Roll up each thin pancake and cut into thin strips or noodles. Drop into boiling chicken soup just before serving.

SOUP

KRUPNIK
Barley and Mushroom Soup

Serves 4–6

This soup is of Polish origin. When a more substantial soup was needed the amount of pearl barley was increased. Sometimes the barley was cooked in the soup, but served separately as a porridge.

2 tablespoons butter
1 onion, chopped or the white part of 2 leeks, finely chopped
100g/4oz pearl barley
1 litre//2 pints/5 cups water, vegetable stock or milk
1 large carrot, peeled and finely grated
50–75g/2–3oz dried mushrooms, washed well and soaked for ½ hour in a
    little boiling water
1 bay leaf
Salt and pepper
Sour cream, as needed for thickening and topping
Chopped parsley, for decoration

Melt the butter in a heavy bottomed pot. Sweat the onions gently until transparent. Add the barley, mushrooms and liquid. Bring to the boil, reduce the heat and simmer gently until the barley is tender (about 45 minutes). Add the rest of the ingredients, except for the cream. Continue simmering until the carrot is tender. Season. When ready to serve, thicken with sour cream and top with a little of the same. Sprinkle with chopped parsley and serve very hot.

SCHAV BORSCHT
Sorrel Soup

Serves 6

This fiercely green soup which is traditionally served on Shavouth heralded spring with its refreshing, herby sourness.

500g/1lb sorrel, picked over and washed well in several changes of cold water, chopped coarsely or left whole
750ml/1½ pints/3¾ cups cold water
1 teaspoon salt
50–75ml/2–3fl.oz/½–⅔ cup good vinegar or lemon juice to taste
1–2 tablespoons sugar or honey to taste
100ml/4fl.oz/½ cup sour cream or 4 egg yolks

Put all the above ingredients, except the cream or eggs, into a deep pot. Bring quickly to the boil, reduce the heat and simmer for 6–8 minutes, until the sorrel is tender. Chill well. Just before serving, thicken either with cream or well-beaten egg yolks. Serve cold with hot boiled potatoes.

GOLDENE YOICH
Chicken Soup

Serves 6–8

It is almost impossible to give a recipe for chicken soup. Flavourings change from family to family and from season to season. Any combination of the following vegetables could be used: onion, leek, carrots, celery leaves, parsnip, courgette and pumpkin. Sometimes whole red tomatoes were added to improve the colour of the soup. For the same reason, onions were sometimes left unpeeled to darken the colour of the soup. The most essential flavouring, which seems to have been used all over Europe, was parsley root (*petrushka*).

It is useless even to attempt this soup using a roasting chicken; the results will be insipid. An old, tough bird (boiling chicken) is needed. Include the cleaned feet as they contain gelatine.

Once the soup is ready the chicken becomes pretty much redundant. However, the thrifty Jewish cook found numerous ways of utilising it. The chicken could be basted with fat collected from the top of the soup and browned in the oven until the skin is crisp and crunchy, which makes the chicken almost edible. Or it could be made into a cold salad or served with egg and lemon sauce (lemon juice thickened over steam with egg yolks). The vegetables, although tasteless and mushy, can be served separately, as a garnish in the soup, or mashed, mixed with breadcrumbs and eggs and fried, like rissoles.

1 large old boiling fowl, washed well
Cold water to cover
750g/1½lb soup vegetables
1 medium parsley root (*petrushka*) with leaves
Bouquet garni, made with *petrushka* leaves, a few celery leaves, 2 bay leaves
  and a strip of lemon peel
A few peppercorns

Wash the chicken well in plenty of cold running water. If the feet are used, scorch them well over an open flame and rub to remove the hard skin. Put the washed chicken in a large stock pot. Cover with cold water and bring very slowly to the boil. Simmer for 10 minutes and skim the surface well. Add the vegetables with the parsley, *bouquet garni* and peppercorns and simmer, very gently, for three hours. Lift out the chicken and discard the *bouquet garni*. Skim almost all the fat from the top. It is important that a little fat should be left to achieve the customary yellow globules which add sparkle to the soup. Serve either clear or with one of the many *content* (garnishes), such as rice, baked *croûtons* (*mandlen* or soup 'almonds'), noodles (vermicelli) or dumplings (*einlauf*, *nockerals* or *kneidlach*).

TOBY'S KNEIDLACH

Makes about 20 small kneidlach

Matzah meal *kneidlach* are made for Pesach. The following recipe is for the 'light as a feather' variety. I use the same recipe to make gnocchi-like dumplings to be served with tomato sauce and grated cheese.

Some recipes recommend flavouring with powdered ginger and cinnamon while others add ground almonds or almond essence to the mix.

2 eggs (size 2), well beaten
3 tablespoons melted chicken fat or light olive or peanut oil*
4 tablespoons cold water
6 tablespoons (rounded) medium *matzah* meal
Salt and pepper

---

* To serve as gnocchi, I use a full-flavoured olive oil and a spoonful of chopped herbs (dill, parsley or basil).

Mix all ingredients together. Allow the mixture to rest in a cool place for at least two hours. Shape into small balls and cook in boiling soup or salted boiling water for 10–15 minutes or until the dumplings float to the top. Drain. Serve in chicken soup or as a side dish with stew.

SOUP MANDLEN
Soup 'Almonds'

Serves 6–8

3 eggs (size 3)
2 tablespoons oil
1 teaspoon salt
250g/8oz/2 cups sifted strong flour

Beat the eggs slightly, adding oil and salt while beating. Stir them into the flour gradually until you have made a dough stiff enough to handle. Form the dough into thin rolls on a floured board or between the palms of both hands. Slice the rolls into 1cm (½″) pieces. Either deep fry or bake on a baking sheet in a moderate oven (gas 5, 190°C, 375°F) for 5–10 minutes until nicely browned. Shake the pan or stir occasionally to brown them evenly on all sides. Switch off the oven, leaving the baking tray inside, for the *mandlen* to dry. Serve as *croûtons* in soup.

EINLAUF
'Thrown In' Egg Drops

Serves 6

1 large (size 2) egg
3 tablespoons flour
50ml/2fl.oz/¼ cup water
⅛ teaspoon salt
Pinch of black pepper

Beat the egg, add the water, flour and seasoning. Beat until smooth. Drop a spoonful of the mixture at a time from a considerable height into the simmering soup.

MEAT BORSCHT

Serves 6–8

I serve this soup with some mashed fresh garlic and homemade mustard.

500g/1lb soup beef (chuck, shin or neck)
A few marrow bones
2½ litres/5 pints/12½ cups water
1 small white cabbage, shredded
500g/1lb raw beetroot, peeled and cubed
250g/8oz sour apples, peeled, cored and cubed
100g/4oz celeriac, peeled and cubed
1 large onion, chopped, or the white part of 2 leeks, washed and shredded
Salt and pepper
2 bay leaves
Juice of 1 large lemon
Sugar (if liked)

Wash the meat and bones well. Place in a large stock pot with the water and bring to the boil. Reduce the heat and simmer very gently for 1½ hours. Skim well. Add the vegetables and seasonings. Continue to simmer for a further 1 hour. Remove the meat and slice into large chunks before returning to the pot. Serve piping hot, giving some meat and a piece of marrow bone to each diner.

POTATO AND KUMMEL SOUP
Caraway Soup

Serves 4–6

500g/1lb potatoes, peeled and cubed
50g/2oz butter
1 tablespoon caraway seeds
1 large onion, chopped
1 litre/2 pints/5 cups milk, boiling hot
Salt and pepper
Dill, chopped

Melt the butter in a heavy bottomed pan. Add the caraway seeds and fry for a few minutes. Add the onion, and continue frying until transparent. Add the potatoes and boiling milk. Cook until the potatoes are tender. Season well, and serve sprinkled with dill.

FISH

GEFILTE FISH

Serves 6–8

There are literally hundreds of ways of making this popular dish. What they all agree upon is that the mixture should contain more than one kind of fish. The most widely used proportion is ⅔ of lean white sea fish, such as cod, whiting or haddock, to ⅓ freshwater fish, such as carp or pike, etc. In Israel *gefilte fish* is made mostly with carp. Carp, especially when mixed with pike, gives a firmer texture and a more intense flavour. The colour of *gefilte fish* is also disputed. Some people tint it with onion skin to colour it brown while others use turmeric or saffron to make it yellow. The recipe given below is an amalgamation of many recipes. It can be made into round or flat dumplings or served in the traditional way — stuffed into the skin of the fish.

For the stock:
Heads, bones and skin of fish
2 large onions, sliced into rings
4 large carrots, sliced into thin rings
4 celery sticks
Water to cover
Salt and plenty of freshly ground pepper

Fish mix:
1½kg/3lb/9 cups minced fish
2 medium onions
2–3 tablespoons oil, such as mild olive or peanut oil*
2 eggs
2 tablespoons ground almonds (optional)
50g/2oz/¼ cup *matzah* meal, breadcrumbs or white bread, soaked and squeezed dry
1 medium carrot, finely grated (optional)
75ml/3fl.oz/⅓ cup very cold water
2–3 teaspoons salt (this dish takes rather a large quantity of salt)
Plenty of freshly ground black pepper

To prepare the stock: wash the fish heads, bones and skin carefully and place in a large pot. Add the vegetables and just enough water to cover.

---

* The quantity of oil depends on the oiliness of the fish. When using dry fish, a larger amount of oil is needed to keep the mixture light.

Bring to the boil, skim and reduce the heat. Simmer gently for about 30 minutes. Add salt and pepper. At this stage the fish heads and bones can be discarded, though this is not traditionally done.

To prepare the fish: the best way is to chop it in a wooden bowl with the help of a chopping blade which is known as *hachoir*, or '*hack messer*', in Yiddish. The action of chopping incorporates air into the mixture making it light and fluffy. If the preparation is done by hand, combine the fish and onions and chop them until a fine, homogenous mixture is achieved, moistening it frequently with a few drops of very cold water. Otherwise, the fish and onion can be either minced or processed. Sometimes the onions are slightly sweated in a little oil to soften their flavour before they are added to the fish mixture.

Mix the rest of the ingredients together.* If the mixture is too soft, add some more *matzah* meal. Allow the mixture to rest for at least 30 minutes in a cold place. Form the balls into either 4cm (1½″) balls or into torpedo-shaped patties.

Slide them into the boiling liquid. Reduce the heat and simmer, half covered, for one hour.† Switch off the heat and allow the fish to reach room temperature in the liquid.

Lift the fish onto a serving dish and decorate each dumpling with a slice of cooked carrot. Boil the gravy to reduce it, and chill until almost jelled. Spoon some over the decorated balls.

Chill and serve with the remaining gravy handed around in a sauce boat. Although this dish can be eaten hot, it is usually served cold, accompanied by *chrain*, a beetroot and horseradish sauce.

To stuff a whole fish:
1 large carp (about 1–1½kg/2–3lb), when boned and skinned this will yield about 500g/1lb of meat. Add other fish as before to make 1½kg/3lb and proceed to make the mixture as described above
Parsley sprigs to garnish

* If a lighter *gefilte* is preferred, the eggs should be separated. The yolks are then used in the mix while the whites are whipped into a stiff snow and added at the last stage. If this procedure is followed the mix has a very soft consistency and needs to be moulded with the help of two spoons as though making *quenelles*.

† Traditionally *gefilte fish* is simmered for a long time. Some recipes recommend simmering for up to three hours. I find, however, that the long simmering bleaches out the flavour of the fish and though the stock, when cold, is beautifully jellied and strong tasting, the fish is rather insipid. For a fresher flavour, cook for a shorter time, sometimes even ½ hour is enough. Lift out the fish and keep warm. Bring the stock to the boil and reduce the stock by half. Remove from the heat, return the fish to the pot, cover and allow the fish to reach room temperature in the liquid.

Buy the carp whole. Wash it well and rub with plenty of salt to get rid of the slimy mucous on its skin. Wash the salt away well, scale the fish and dry it with paper towels. Lay the carp on a chopping board. With a sharp, flexible boning knife make an incision along its back. Carefully separate the flesh and skin, leaving the flesh adhering to the bones. When the belly is reached, turn the fish over and proceed on the other side, until the skin is free of all meat, but the head remains attached. Wash well and dry with paper towels. Remove the intestines from the carcass, being careful not to damage the gall bladder as it is extremely bitter. Wash well and scrape all the meat from the carcass. Use the bones to make the stock.

Stuff the skin with the *gefilte* mixture, re-shape the fish and sew the opening with cotton thread. Any remaining mixture can be shaped into small dumplings which are poached and arranged around the fish for decoration. Wrap the stuffed fish in a large piece of muslin and tie the ends. Poach for 1–1½ hours in a fish kettle, covered with stock. When ready, lift out the fish, reduce the stock by half and then return the fish to the cooking liquid to cool. Lift out the fish and refrigerate for 12 hours. When cold unwrap it and remove the sewing cotton. Mask the bottom of a large serving dish with some of the jellied fish stock. Lay the fish in the centre, arrange the fish balls around, decorate with carrots and glaze with more stock. Chill to set. Serve the dish garnished with parsley sprigs and accompanied by the rest of the jellied stock and *chrain*, served separately.

CHRAIN
Horseradish and Beetroot Relish

Peeling and grating horseradish root is a painful experience for the root emits an extremely acrid smell when bruised. Peeling should therefore be done under cold, running water while grating and even processing should take place in a well-ventilated room. Pure grated horseradish, either bottled or frozen, has started to appear in supermarkets. It makes an acceptable substitute.

> 100g/4oz horseradish root, peeled and grated
> 350g/12oz beetroot raw, cooked or pickled, and grated (if pickled beetroot is used, omit vinegar)
> 1 tablespoon honey or sugar (optional)
> 100ml/4fl.oz/½ cup vinegar

Combine all ingredients. Keep the mixture in the refrigerator in a tightly sealed jar; the relish loses its hotness if kept open. It should have a well-defined and strong kick which is inexplicable to the uninitiated. It should 'clear your tubes', allowing you to appreciate the flavour of the fish.

FISH KARTOFFEL
Fish Potatoes

Serves 4–6

Although it is not strictly a fish dish, in our home the following recipe was made every time *gefilte fish* was prepared. *Fish kartoffel* was a welcomed standby on busy days of pre-holiday preparations. For me it heralded all the expected excitement of the celebration to come.

500g/1lb firm, medium-sized boiling potatoes, peeled and quartered*
Enough *gefilte fish* stock to cover the potatoes
75g/3oz/⅓ cup butter
Salt and pepper
Sour cream to accompany

Cover the sliced potatoes with stock, add the butter and season lightly. Bring to the boil and cover. Either simmer very gently on top of the stove or put into a medium oven (gas 5, 190°C, 375°F) to cook until most of the liquid is absorbed and the potatoes are beautifully brown and fragrant. Adjust seasoning and serve very hot with a dollop of sour cream.

SHARFE FISH
'Sharp' or Sour Fish

Serves 6

This recipe appeared in *Best By Taste*, a charity book published 'for the benefit of the Hebrew Infant Asylum', New York, 1914. It was compiled by Mrs Alfred Loeb.

1 large pike (1–1½kg/2–3lb) or pickerel†, carp or sea bass
1 teaspoon each of powdered ginger, salt and freshly ground pepper, mixed together

---

* The dish is also delicious made from sweet potatoes.
† 'Pickerel' is an Americanism describing young pike. It is also used as a generic name for several kinds of pike.

For the cooking liquid:
500ml/1 pint/2½ cups water
1 large onion, sliced thinly
1 small lemon, sliced thinly
50ml/2fl.oz/¼ cup wine vinegar
Salt and pepper
2 tablespoons butter
1 tablespoon flour
4 tablespoons chopped parsley
Lemon wedges and parsley sprigs to garnish

Cut the fish into serving slices, dust with the mixed spices and leave to marinate for 2 hours.

Boil the onion and lemon in water for 20 minutes. Add vinegar, salt and pepper. Bring to the boil and slide in the fish. Reduce the heat and simmer gently for 20–25 minutes. Lift the cooked fish onto a large serving dish, keeping it warm. Reduce the stock by boiling rapidly for 4–5 minutes. Make a blond *roux* from the butter and flour, add this to the liquid and boil for a few minutes to cook. At the last minute, add the chopped parsley. Pour the sauce over the cooked fish, decorate with lemon wedges and sprigs of parsley. This dish can be served either hot or cold.

SOUR FISH

Serves 4–6

This recipe comes from southern Russia and is usually made from carp heads.

1kg/2lb small carp, cleaned and sliced into serving portions, or carp heads
Juice of 2 lemons
Grated peel of 1 lemon
5–6 tablespoons chopped parsley or dill
Few celery leaves, chopped
2 bay leaves
Salt and pepper
1 or 2 small green or red chillies (optional)

Put the cleaned sliced fish into a heavy bottomed pan. Add the rest of the ingredients and just cover with water. Bring to the boil, reduce the heat and simmer for about 1 hour. Serve cold.

CARPE À LA JUIVE
Carp in the Jewish Style

Serves 4–6

This recipe is a variation on a recipe appearing in *Larousse Gastronomique* (1961).

1kg/2lb carp, sliced into serving portions
100g/4oz onions, sliced into rings
A few strips of lemon peel
2 bay leaves
12 peppercorns
Wine and water to cover
Salt
100g/4oz/½ cup raisins
100g/4oz/1 scant cup honey cake or gingersnap crumbs
50g/2fl.oz/¼ cup butter or oil
1 lemon, cut in thin slices
Parsley, chopped

Put sliced onion on the bottom of a large pan. Add the sliced carp, lemon peel, bay leaves and peppercorns. Cover with wine and water and bring to the boil. Reduce the heat and simmer for 20–25 minutes.

Drain the carp slices. Set them on a dish so they resemble the shape of a carp. Strain the cooking liquid, discarding the onion and flavourings, and reduce by half. Add the raisins, honey cake crumbs, butter or oil and lemon slices. Bring to a rapid boil. Reduce the heat and simmer for few minutes until the raisins have plumped out and the sauce is thickened. Pour the sauce over the carp and allow to cool. Sprinkle with chopped parsley and serve at room temperature.

FRIED SALT HERRING

Serves 6

6 medium salt herrings, soaked, rinsed and dried well with paper towels
Flour or *matzah* meal, flavoured with ground black pepper for dipping
75–100g/3–4oz/⅓–½ cup clarified butter or good oil for frying
Apple sauce (see *latkes*) on p. 179)

Dip the herring in *matzah* meal and fry in hot butter for about 4 minutes on each side or until they are golden. Drain well and serve hot with a tart apple sauce.

MEAT, OFFAL AND POULTRY

HELZEL AND KISHKE
Stuffed Poultry Neck and Stuffed Derma

Serves 4–6

The following recipes are Jewish versions of haggis. Although not exactly healthy or nutritious they are an ingenious way of creating a substantial dish from usable scraps. Usually the pudding is stuffed with starch and fat only. Sometimes, however, poultry hearts, gizzards and liver were minced and used in the mixture. In rich families, minced meat was incorporated; the amount of meat depended directly on the family's income. Flour or semolina were mainly used as the starchy ingredient, but potatoes, breadcrumbs and pearl barley were also sometimes included.

I usually make my pudding with soaked burgul, which makes it lighter. The stuffed puddings are either roasted or boiled in soup and browned in fat. Those puddings are also cooked in the Sabbath *chulent*.

1 chicken neck

For the stuffing:
75g/3oz/⅓ cups semolina, cooked pearl barley, grated potato or
  soaked burgul
75g/3oz/⅔ cup flour
1 small onion, finely chopped
Salt and generous amount of pepper
50g/2oz/¼ cup raw chicken fat or vegetarian suet, chopped
3–4 tablespoons dill or parsley, finely chopped

Mix all the stuffing ingredients lightly. Salt and pepper well. Sew up the small end of chicken neck and stuff loosely, allowing space for expansion. Sew up at other end. Prick in a few places with a needle. Either roast in a medium oven (gas 5, 190°C, 375°F) for 1½–2 hours, turning and moistening from time to time with water and fat until the pudding is brown, or boil the pudding for 1½–2 hours in chicken or meat stock. Lift out, transfer into a baking tin and brown in a hot oven, basting with fat and turning frequently until evenly brown. Serve sliced at the table, with a little meat gravy.

Stuffed Derma
Cleaned *derma* (small intestines or beef casing), *kishke* in Yiddish, can be bought from most good kosher butchers. Cleaning derma is a thoroughly

unpleasant job, but in case any one would like to attempt to do it at home, here is the process. Wash the casing well in plenty of water. Turn inside out and rub well with coarse salt to scrape off all loose material and fat. Wash very well in plenty of cold running water. Soak the casing in cold water, into which the juice of 1 lemon and the squeezed peel of the lemon were added (or about 100ml/4fl.oz/½ cup vinegar). Soak for few hours, rinse again and dry well. The lemon peel helps to deodorise the casing.

Stuff the casing as in the previous recipe. The quantity given above will be enough for a 30cm (12″) length. Cook as before.

GEFILTE MILTZ
Stuffed Spleen or Milt

Serves 6

Offal cooking is now a dying art. The decline started with a change of attitude towards eating organ meat. Lately this decline has accelerated because of various health scares, mainly mad cow disease, which are largely the result of the profit-motivated, careless ignorance of many meat producers. The following recipes are recorded with the hope that the situation will change and we will be able to consume offal safely again.

1 beef spleen or milt, cut for stuffing
2 tablespoons *schmaltz* or shortening
4 cloves of garlic, chopped
4 medium onions, chopped
Salt and pepper
2–3 cloves
Water

Stuffing:
150g/6oz/2 cups dry breadcrumbs
1 egg
1 large onion, chopped
50g/2oz/¼ cup chicken fat or hard beef fat, diced coarsely
½ teaspoon ginger, nutmeg or cinnamon

Trim any loose bits of skin from the spleen. Wash well and dry. Make an incision along the side of the spleen, creating a deep pocket. Mix the stuffing and stuff into the pocket. Sew the opening together or fasten with toothpicks or metal skewers. Place a heavy bottomed roasting tin on a flame. Melt the fat, add the onion, garlic and seasonings and sweat until the onions are transparent. Add the stuffed spleen and brown lightly.

Transfer to a preheated moderate oven (gas 5, 190°C, 375°F) and bake for 50–60 minutes, turning and basting frequently with a little water and pan juices until it is browned and firm to the touch. Transfer the spleen to a heated dish and keep warm. Reduce or thicken the pan juices if necessary, pour over the spleen and serve. Slice to small portions as spleen is extremely rich and savoury. Traditionally the spleen is served accompanied by mashed potatoes or noodles.

SWEET AND SOUR OFFAL

Serves 6 as a starter or 4 for main course

This stew can be made from poultry offal, such as gizzards, hearts, kidneys and wings, or other offal like lungs, livers or udders. The cooking time will be dictated by the toughness of the meat.

500g/1lb various offal or chicken wings
2 tablespoons fat
2 large onions
4 cloves of garlic (optional)
100ml/4fl.oz/½ cup water or stock
Juice of 1 lemon
1 tablespoon honey or brown sugar
1–2 bay leaves
Salt and plenty of freshly ground pepper

Melt the fat in a heavy bottomed pot. Add the onions and garlic to brown. Add the meat, then the liquid, sweetener and seasoning. Bring to the boil, reduce heat and simmer very slowly until the meat is perfectly tender. Shake the pan from time to time to prevent sticking. Check for moisture — you may need some more liquid. Serve hot with puréed potatoes or noodles.

BRAINS IN LEMON SAUCE

Serves 6–8 as a first course

Brains were eaten widely as the soft and melting texture was much loved. They were also reputed to improve one's learning powers and were thus forcefed to many children. The following recipe originated in Romania.

500g/1lb calf brains, prepared and sliced into 1.5cm (¾″) slices
Juice of 1 lemon
Matzah meal, spiced with salt, pepper and sweet paprika, for dipping
Oil for frying
4 tablespoons chopped dill
Juice of 1 large lemon mixed with water to make 150ml/¼ pint/⅔ cup
of liquid
Salt and pepper
Grated rind of ½ lemon
Pinch of sugar (if liked)
1 tablespoon capers (optional)

Soak the brains in cold salt water for 1 hour. Wash well. Blanch in water containing the juice of 1 lemon for 2 minutes. Lift out and plunge into cold water. Peel off any membranes and surface veins. Allow to cool in the refrigerator, then slice. Dip each slice in the seasoned *matzah* meal and fry for 3–4 minutes on each side until golden. Drain well on absorbent paper. Arrange the slices in one overlapping layer on the bottom of a heavy pan or pyrex dish. Mix the dill with the liquid, salt, pepper and sugar and lemon rind. Pour over the brains and simmer on top of the stove for 20–25 minutes. Sprinkle with capers, if liked, and serve at room temperature or cold.

RASEL FLEISCH OR ROSALLE
Pot Roast with Potato and Garlic

Serves 6–8

Harkavy's Yiddish dictionary describes *rasel fleisch* as pot roast. *Rasel* is also gravy or the liquid in which vegetables were pickled. This is probably the favourite way of cooking large joints of meat. The cuts used were usually chuck steak, thick flank, silverside or a special cut called *bola*. The meat must be kept in one piece.

1½kg/3lb beef
50g/2oz/¼ cup fat
8–10 fat cloves of garlic, chopped
3 large onions, chopped
Salt and pepper
Few dried wood mushrooms, crumbled
500g/1lb small potatoes, washed and scraped, or good boiling potatoes,
quartered
1–2 bay leaves and a few allspice berries, crushed
Water or stock

Melt the fat in a heavy bottomed pan. Brown the meat well. Add garlic and onion. Fry for a few minutes on a high flame until the onion starts to take colour. Add salt, pepper, crumbled mushrooms, bay leaves and allspice and cover and pot roast gently for about 2 hours. Shake the pot frequently and add a spoonful or two of liquid if needed to prevent sticking. Turn the meat from time to time. The secret of the dish is to use as little liquid as possible.

After 2 hours, when the meat starts to tenderise, add the washed potatoes and enough water or stock to half-cover them. Bring to the boil and simmer covered for a further hour or until the meat is prefectly tender and the potatoes have soaked up most of the gravy and are brown and fragrant. Lift the meat out and slice thinly. Arrange on a hot platter, surround with the potatoes and keep hot. To intensify the flavour of garlic, add 1 mashed clove of garlic to the remaining cooking liquid, bring to the boil and pour over the meat. The dish is even better the next day, when the meat is sliced cold.

ESSIG FLEICH
Sour Meat Stew

Serves 6–8

This dish probably shares ancestry with the German *saeurbraten*.

1½kg/3lb lean brisket or chuck
4 large onions, chopped
500ml/1 pint/2¼ cups water
Salt and pepper
75ml/3fl.oz/⅓ cup honey, brown sugar or syrup
75ml/3fl.oz/⅓ cup good wine vinegar or juice of 2 lemons
50g/2oz/¼ cup stale honey cake crumbs or ginger snaps
50g/2oz/¼ cup raisins (optional)

In a heavy bottomed pot brown the meat well. Add the onions and continue frying, turning from time to time until the onions are nicely browned. Add the water and seasoning. Bring to the boil, reduce the heat and simmer gently for 2 hours. Add sweetener, vinegar and crumbs and simmer for a further 20 minutes, shaking the pot frequently to prevent sticking. Sometimes 50g/2oz of raisins are added. In this case, soak the raisins in a bit of hot water for ½ hour and add at the last stage of the preparations. Serve with noodles.

SMOKED GOOSE

The following recipes for goose appear in Florence Kreisler Greenbaum's *Jewish Cookbook* which was published in New York in 1918. The first one is rather difficult to produce under domestic conditions. Try it if you have a smoker or know someone who will smoke it for you as it is extremely tasty and can be frozen or kept for up to 6 months in a cold place.

1 large fat goose, skinned (remove the skin of the neck whole and keep it; the rest of the skin is used to make cracklings or *gribens*)
Salt
15 large cloves of garlic, mashed into a paste
1 heaped tablespoon freshly ground plack pepper
1 heaped tablespoon sweet paprika

For the cure:
150g/6oz/1½ cups fine salt
50g/2oz/¼ cup brown sugar
1 teaspoon saltpetre

Sprinkle the neck skin with some salt and leave for a few hours. Then wash and dry. Remove the legs and breasts from the carcass, setting them aside. With a sharp knife remove all traces of meat and fat from the carcass and neck. Salt and pepper the scrapings lightly and stuff them into the neck skin. Close the opening by sewing with a strong thread.

Mix the garlic with the other flavourings and rub well over all the meats, including the stuffed neck. Mix the salt, sugar and saltpetre. Sprinkle a thin layer of the curing mix on the bottom of a perfectly clean earthenware pickling crock or a stainless steel container. Put a layer of meat on top, sprinkle with the curing mix, and repeat until all the meat and curing mix have been used. Weigh down with a sterilised weight. Leave for 1 week, turning the meat in the pickle each day. Cold smoke for 24 hours. Hang to dry for few days and store either in the refrigerator or in a well-ventilated cold, dry place. Serve sliced thinly.

GANZEKLINE
Fricasee of Goose Smalls

Serves 4–6

A wonderful way of utilising wings, neck and goose offal.

Wings, neck, gizzard, heart and meaty backbone of a goose, chopped into small portions, washed and dried

201

1 teaspoon ginger
1 teaspoon freshly ground black pepper
1 teaspoon sweet paprika
1 teaspoon salt
Water to cover
1 tablespoon flour
3–4 cloves of garlic, mashed with a little salt

Mix the spices and salt and dust the meat with the mixture. Leave to marinate for a few hours. Put the meat in a heavy bottomed pot and cover with water. Bring to the boil, reduce the heat and simmer for 2–2½ hours. When perfectly tender, skim off all fat, reserving 3 tablespoons. Heat this fat in a small frying pan, add the flour and cook to a brown *einbren* (*roux*). Add the *einbren* and garlic to the cooking pot and simmer for a further 20 minutes. Serve hot.

ROAST GOOSE BREAST

Serves 4–6

1 large breast of goose, with its skin
4–5 cloves of garlic, mashed with a little salt
1 teaspoon black pepper
1 teaspoon powdered ginger
2 teaspoons salt
2 teaspoons sweet paprika

Remove the skin from the breast and reserve. Mix the garlic with the seasonings to a smooth paste. Rub the spice mix on the breast and leave to marinate for a few hours, covered, in the refrigerator. Cover the breast with the reserved skin and either sew, tie or skewer it securely. Roast in a moderate oven (gas 5, 190°C, 375°F) for 25 minutes per 500g (1lb). Allow to cool and refrigerate. Use cold, sliced thinly as part of a cold meat platter or in sandwiches.

PFLAUMEN TZIMMES
Prune Tzimmes

Serves 6–8

This version also contains pumpkin which was extensively used in Southern Russia and Romania. Pumpkin was often made into *tzimmes*, cooked with rice or included in soups. It was also used for sweet jams and conserves (See *eingemacht* on p. 213).

1kg/2lb boned brisket
2 medium onions, chopped
50g/2oz/¼ cup chicken *schmaltz*, vegetable shortening or oil
Salt and pepper
500g/1lb pumpkin, peeled and sliced into large cubes
500g/1lb/2 cups prunes, washed and soaked for a few hours
100g/4oz/½ cup honey, syrup or brown sugar
1 teaspoon powdered ginger
4 cloves, crushed
Water to cover
1 tablespoon flour

Heat the fat in a large heavy bottomed pot and brown the meat well. Add the onions and brown. Sprinkle with salt and pepper. Arrange the prunes and pumpkin around the meat. Add spices and sweetener. Cover with water, bring to the boil, reduce the heat and simmer gently for 2 hours, shaking the pot from time to time. Lift out the meat and keep hot. Skim most of the fat and reserve 2 tablespoons. Put the reserved fat into a small pan, heat and add the flour. Make a pale brown *roux*. Add to the meat pot and mix well. Return the meat to the pot. Simmer gently, semi-covered, for a further 1 hour. Shake the pot from time to time and check if any added moisture is needed. Adjust the flavouring and serve very hot.

CHICKEN AND BEETROOT FRIKADELS

Serves 6 as first course

This dish originated in Besarabia, a constantly disputed area between Russia and Romania. It was traditionally made for Pesach using *rasel* (fermented beet juice) and pickled beets as a base. In the version below fresh beet is used.

500g/1lb/2 cups boneless chicken breast, minced
50g/2oz raw beetroot, finely grated
25–50g/1–2oz/2–4 tablespoons breadcrumbs or *matzah* meal
1 egg (size 2)
Grated rind of ½ lemon
Salt and freshly ground pepper
1 tablespoon chopped parsley (optional)
Oil for frying

For the pot:
25ml/1fl.oz/2 tablespoons oil
1 medium onion, sliced thinly
250g/8oz beetroot, sliced thinly
250ml/½ pint/1 cup water or semi-dry white wine
Juice of 1 lemon
1 tablespoon sugar (optional)
Salt and freshly ground pepper
2 teaspoons starch (optional)
Parsley sprigs for garnish

Mix the chicken breast with the rest of the ingredients. If mixture is too loose, add some more breadcrumbs. Form into small patties 3cm (1½″) in diameter. Heat the oil and fry the patties for a minute or two until they start to take colour. Lift and drain.

Heat the oil in a heavy bottomed pot and add the sliced onions. Sweat until they soften and become transparent. Remove from the heat. Add the slices of beetroot and place the fried patties on top. In a small pot, bring water or wine, lemon and sugar (if used) to the boil and pour over the patties. Simmer for 25–30 minutes. With a perforated spoon lift out the patties and arrange on a heated serving dish. Arrange the cooked beetroot and onions around the patties. Set aside and keep warm. Reduce the cooking liquid by rapid boiling or thicken it with 2 teaspoons starch. Pour over the patties. Sprinkle with parsley and serve hot.

DESSERTS

I found the following two recipes in Leah Leonard's *Jewish Cookery*. The first is the lightest potato *kugel* I have ever encountered. The second is called *shalet* which is probably a derivation of Charlotte. It is one of the best examples of German-Jewish middle-class cooking.

———— Halpern's Hot Pudding ————

Serves 6

100g/4oz/1 cup each, peeled raw potato, peeled raw sweet potato, unpeeled
    tart apple and raw carrots
150g/5oz/1 cup brown sugar
100g/4oz/1 cup flour
1 teaspoon baking soda
½ teaspoon each cinnamon, nutmeg
250g/8oz/1 cup chopped seeded raisins
50g/2oz/¼ cup chopped nuts
150g/6oz/¾ cup hot melted vegetable shortening

Grate and combine all the vegetables and apple. Add sugar. Sift together
the dry ingredients, adding raisins and nuts. Combine thoroughly. Melt
the shortening, fold in quickly and turn the mixture into a greased
casserole. Cover and bake for 1 hour in a moderate oven (gas mark 5,
190°C, 375°F). Remove the lid and bake for a further 15 to 20 minutes
or until browned. Serve hot.

———— Kugel ————
Four-Layer Shalet

Serves 4–6

500g/1lb of ready made filo pastry can be used instead of the strudel
dough. Use three sheets of filo, each brushed with fat, for each layer of
dough.

For the dough:
250g/8oz/2 cups flour
1 tablespoon sugar
Pinch of salt
1 egg (size 3)
3 tablespoons melted shortening or peanut oil
250ml/8fl.oz/1 cup very cold water

For the filling:
4 tablespoons melted chicken or goose *schmaltz*
250g/8oz/1 cup apples, peeled and thinly sliced
2 tablespoons sugar
Pinch of cinnamon
100g/4oz/½ cup chopped raisins
1 tablespoon flour
2 tablespoons sugar
½ teaspoon grated lemon rind
50g/2oz/½ cup chopped nuts
1 tablespoon lemon juice
2 tablespoons dry breadcrumbs

Combine all the dough ingredients and knead well until a smooth and elastic dough is achieved. Cover with a damp cloth and leave to rest for 1 hour.

Divide the dough into four equal parts. Roll out one to fit inside a greased pudding dish. Drizzle with melted fat and cover with apples. Combine sugar and cinnamon and sprinkle generously over apples. Roll out a second layer of dough and fit it over the apples. Roll the raisins in flour until coated and arrange over this layer of dough. Sprinkle evenly with sugar and grated lemon rind. Roll out a third layer of dough to cover the raisins. Drizzle a little more melted fat over the dough and sprinkle with chopped nuts, lemon juice and crumbs. Roll out a fourth layer of dough and cover.

Brush the top with the remaining melted fat. Let the dish stand for 10 to 15 minutes before baking in a preheated moderate oven (gas 5, 190°C, 375°F) for 45–50 minutes or until nicely browned. Invert onto a serving plate while warm. Sprinkle with extra chopped nuts and sugar if desired.

KUGEL YERUSHALMI
Jerusalem Lokshen Kugel

Serves 8–10

This recipe is quoted in a lovingly written collection of traditional recipes from the old Jewish, Muslim and Christian Jerusalem families.[1] The sweet *kugel* is attributed to Rivka Vinegarten, the curator of Or Chaime Museum in old Jerusalem. Her father, Rabbi Avraham Mordechy Vinegarten, was the last rabbi of the old Jewish quarter at the outbreak of the 1948 war.

500g/1lb medium width noodles
4 eggs (size 3), well beaten
250g/8oz/1 cup sugar
1 teaspoon cinnamon
1 teaspoon freshly ground black pepper

For the caramel:
50ml/2fl.oz/¼ cup peanut or sesame oil
50g/2oz/¼ cup sugar

Cook the noodles in plenty of boiling salted water for about 5 minutes until they start to get tender. Drain and rinse in cold water. Transfer into a large mixing bowl.

Heat the oil and sugar in a small frying pan, caramelise until it is dark brown but not burned. Pour the caramel over the noodles and mix well. Add the rest of the ingredients and combine thoroughly.

Pour into a well-greased round oven dish. Cover the dish tightly and bake for 1½ hours in a moderate oven (gas 5, 190°C, 375°F) or until the *kugel* crust is brown and crisp. Allow to cool for few minutes and unmould by inverting the baking dish onto a flat tray. Serve hot, warm or cold.

THE ROTHSCHILD OF KUGELS

Serves 6–8

I found the following recipe handwritten on a piece of paper in a book bought at 'Ort' charity shop. It is a delicious and wonderfully rich *kugel*.

50g/2oz/½ cup each of raisins, crystallised ginger, glacé cherries, glacé peel and dried prunes macerated for 12 hours in either rum or brandy
100g/4oz/½ cup cottage cheese
100g/4oz/½ cup melted butter or fat
1 teaspoon salt
250g/8oz wide noodles, cooked and drained
Grated rind of ½ lemon
½ teaspoon cinnamon
½ teaspoon powdered cloves
¼ teaspoon freshly ground black pepper
4 large eggs (size 2), separated
50g/2oz/¼ cup sugar

Crumble the cheese into a large mixing bowl, add all the rest of the ingredients, including the marinating brandy, except for the separated eggs and the sugar. Beat the egg yolks and sugar until thick and lemon coloured.

Fold into the mixture. Beat the egg whites to a stuff snow and fold gently into the mix. Turn into an oiled round 24cm (9½″) baking tin. Stand the tin in a pan of hot water before baking in a moderate oven (gas 4, 180°C, 350°F) for 1 hour or until set. Serve hot or cold.

HONEY CAKE

Serves 8–10

Honey cake is served at every celebration, especially on Rosh Ha'shanah. The following is my mother's recipe. The inclusion of strong, bitter black coffee adds a pleasant contrast to the sweetness of this cake. The result is fragrant, moist and light.

250g/8oz/1⅛ cups brown sugar
250g/8oz/⅔ cup good honey
4 eggs (size 3)
3 tablespoons peanut or sesame oil
300g/12oz/3 cups flour, sifted with 1½ teaspoons baking powder and a
    pinch of salt
250ml/8fl.oz/1 cup very strong coffee, cold
½ teaspoon powdered ginger
½ teaspoon powdered cloves
½ teaspoon powdered cinnamon
Grated rind of 1 lemon
Few blanched almonds for decoration

Beat the honey, sugar and eggs until they are thick and creamy. Gradually add the oil, beating constantly. Mix the flour with the flavourings and add gradually along with the coffee, beating all the time. Pour into a well-greased round 24cm (9½″) spring mould, decorate with almonds and bake in a moderate oven (gas 4, 180°C, 350°F) for 1½ hours.

AUNT SILVIA'S TEIGLACH

Serves 8–10

The name of the dish translated from Yiddish literally means pieces of dough — doughnuts. This is a confection rather than a cake. The recipe was given to me by Sylvia, the great aunt of my friend and favourite photographer, Jill Furmanovsky. The recipe originates from the border of Germany and Poland where Sylvia was born. It was carried in her memory to Zimbabwe, where Tate & Lyle Golden Syrup became an essential ingredient. The scarcity of the syrup in Israel, Sylvia maintains, is one of the reasons she does not prepare *teiglach* any more.

6 eggs (size 3) + 2 egg yolks
1 tablespoon sugar
2 tablespoons peanut or sesame oil
Enough flour to make a soft, unsticky dough (approx. 600g/18–20 oz/4½–5 cups
Soaked, stoned prunes (optional)

For the syrup:
1 tin of Tate & Lyle Golden Syrup or the same weight of honey
The weight of the syrup in sugar
Tin full of water
1 scant tablespoon powdered ginger
Sugar, crumbed almonds or coconut for dipping

Beat the eggs with the sugar and oil. Add the flour and mix to a softish, stable dough before kneading very well. Allow to rest for 30 minutes. Divide the dough into four. Roll each quarter into a long sausage 1.5cm (¾″) thick. Divide into 7.5cm (3″) strips, and shape into round doughnuts. Alternatively tear off pieces the size of a walnut and flatten each piece between the palms of your hands. Lay a small piece of soaked prune in the centre, reshape to a round ball and seal the edges well.

Put the sugar, syrup or honey and water into a large pot which must have a tightly fitting lid. Bring to a rapid boil and boil uncovered for 10 minutes. Skim well. Drop the *teiglach* in one by one. Increase the heat to bring the syrup back to the boil. Cover tightly, reduce the heat and simmer steadily for 20 minutes. The first 20 minutes are crucial; during that period do not attempt to lift the lid. Uncover and continue boiling, gently, for about 45 minutes, shaking from time to time until the *teiglach* are nicely brown. Just before removing from the stove, add the ginger and mix well. Lift the *teiglach* with a perforated spoon onto a wet surface. Allow them to cool, then dip in sugar, crumbled almonds or dessicated coconut. Store in an airtight tin or jar. *Teiglachs* can also be stored in their cooking syrup.

————————— MAMA'S CHEESE DUMPLINGS —————————

Serves 4–6

Mama was what we called our maternal grandmother, a formidable Jewish matriarch who was admired, feared and loved by all her offspring. She was a wizard in the kitchen. Although crippled for the last twenty years of her life she was the supreme ruler there, giving precise and explanatory instructions which allowed her helpers to achieve the exact results she wanted. These dumplings were usually made for Shavuot, but being so light and delicious she also used to serve them when she wanted to spoil herself or others.

The cheese used should be drained skimmed milk curds, otherwise skimmed milk curd or cottage cheese can be used. To drain curd cheese, hang it in a cheesecloth bag to drip overnight or until the cheese has a dry, crumbly texture.

> 500g/1lb/2 cups dry curd cheese
> 1 large egg
> 50g/2oz/⅓ cup semolina
> 50g/2oz/¼ cup flour
> Grated rind of ½ lemon (optional)
> Very small pinch nutmeg (optional)
> Pinch of salt (some salt is present in the cheese) and one or two grindings of
>   a pepper mill
> 75–100g/3–4oz/⅓–½ cup melted butter
> Sour cream and a good fruit jam or preserve

In a large mixing bowl crumble the cheese, adding the egg, semolina, flour, lemon peel and nutmeg. Season and mix gently to a soft, but manageable dough. Leave to rest for at least 30 minutes. Bring a large pot of slightly salted water to the boil.

With wet hands, shape the dough into 4cm (1½″) round dumplings. Slide these carefully into the boiling water, return to boiling point and simmer gently for 2–3 minutes until the dumplings have fluffed and risen to the surface. Carefully lift out the delicate dumplings onto a hot serving dish. Drizzle with melted butter and serve very hot accompanied with more melted butter, sour cream and excellent fruit preserve; *povidle*, prune jam, is best.

PICKLES

Jewish inns used to specialise in pickled vegetables and preserves. Many housewives in the *shtetl* and ghettoes also made pickles and jams to supplement the family income. Being frugal, they did not throw away the pickling juice but used it to flavour and sour many dishes, especially soups.

Toby's Sliced Cucumber Pickle

This recipe was given to me by Mrs Toby Kay; it probably originated somewhere in Russia, arriving in South Africa via London where Toby's mother was born, the daughter of Russian refugees.

2 long cucumbers, washed and sliced into 3mm (⅛″) slices
1 large clove of garlic, slivered
5 bay leaves
12 peppercorns

For the pickle:
1 litre/2 pints/4 cups water
4 tablespoons sugar
350ml/12fl.oz/1½ cups white malt vinegar
1 scant tablespoon salt

Pack the sliced cucumber into a large pickling jar, distributing garlic slivers and spices between layers.

Bring the pickle to a rapid boil. Pour the boiling pickle over the cucumbers, allow to cool and refrigerate. These are ready within 2 days.

Salt Dill Pickles

My mother, a superb pickler, maintains that the crunchiness and good green colour of pickled cucumbers are achieved by first pouring boiling water over the cucumbers, blanching them for few seconds and then refreshing them immediately with cold running water.

1kg/2lb small cucumbers, blanched and refreshed
50g/2oz dry dill stems and flower heads, bruised
5–6 fat cloves of garlic, peeled and quartered
1 teaspoon each black peppercorns, allspice and mustard seeds
4–5 bay leaves
Water
Salt
3–4 small hot chillies or to taste
Vine leaves

Wash and blanch the cucumbers. Refresh and arrange in a crock or a large glass jar in layers, interspacing them with dill, garlic and spices. Pour cold water, to cover, over the cucumbers in the crock.

Pour out the water into a measuring jug. Salt with 30g/1oz/1 tablespoon salt for each 500ml/1 pint/2 cups of water. Dissolve the salt well in the measured water and pour over the cucumbers. Place vine leaves on top, then fit a heavy plate or wooden cover inside the crock and place a weight on to hold the cucumbers submerged.

Leave in a warm place to ferment. Skim as needed during the fermentation period. When bubbles disappear, the pickles are ready to use; this can take up to 2 weeks or in a warm, sunny place it can take as little as 4–5 days. When fermentation stops, keep the pickles in a dark, cool place or refrigerate.

PICKLED FRENCH BEANS AND CARROTS

500g/1lb/3 cups fresh green beans (French beans are best), topped and tailed
500g/1lb/2½ cups carrots, peeled and sliced to thin discs
1 large head of garlic, peeled and slivered
Brine as for salt dill pickles (recipe on p. 211)

Blanch the beans and carrots separately by plunging them in boiling water. Leave in the water until boiling point is reached again. Lift out and refresh immediately in plenty of cold water. Arrange in a large crock in alternate layers, interspersed with garlic slivers. Add brine and finish as before.

BEETROOT ROSEL
Fermented Beetroot Juice

The *rosel* was made especially for Pesach when it was used for the Pesach borscht.

A quantity of beetroot, peeled and rinsed
Water to cover
Salt

A month before Pesach, scald a wooden tub or a pickling crock with boiling water. Add the peeled beets. Measure the water and salt with 50g/2oz/2 tablespoons to each 1 litre/1 pint/4 cups. Pour over the beets and weigh down to submerge. Skim well every few days. At the end of the month bottle and use as a base for meat borscht.

212

EINGEMACHT
Beetroot Preserve

The following are two more Pesach specialities. *Eingemacht* can be also made from turnips, radishes, pumpkin or carrots.

100ml/4fl.oz/½ cup water
500g/1lb/2 cups sugar
Grated peel and juice of 2 large lemons
1kg/2lb beetroot, peeled and grated
1 tablespoon ground ginger
250g/8oz/2 cups slivered blanched almonds

Put the water and sugar into a preserving pan, add the lemon juice and bring to the boil. Skim. Add the beetroot and cook for 1½ hours, mixing from time to time to prevent sticking. Add the ginger and grated lemon peel. Cook for a further ½ hour until thick. Remove from the heat and add the almonds. Bottle while hot.

INGBERLACH
Pesach Sweets

1kg/2lb carrots, scraped and washed
Water or orange juice
Sugar
150g/6oz/1 cup coarsely chopped walnuts
1 scant tablespoon ginger

Cover the cleaned carrots with water or orange juice, bring to the boil and simmer until they are soft but not mushy. Drain and allow to cool. Grate the cooked carrots on a fine grater. Squeeze out superfluous moisture and measure the pulp. Allow 250g/8oz/1 cup sugar to every 250g/8oz/1 cup carrot pulp.

Return the pulp to a clean heavy bottomed pot (a preserving pan is best), add the warmed sugar and bring to the boil. Stir all the time to prevent scorching. When the mixture comes away from the pan sides and shows signs of whitening in places, stir in the ginger and the nuts. Take off the heat and spread evenly on a wetted board or marble slab. Allow to cool and dry.

Cut into neat diamond shapes, turn over and allow to dry on the other side. Store in an airtight tin. Separate each layer of *ingberlach* with wax paper dusted with sugar.

BAKING

PURIM HALLAH

This *hallah* has a superb cake-like texture. It was traditionally served at the Purim fish dinner. The quantity is enough to make one traditionally large Purim *hallah*.

250ml/8fl.oz/1 cup milk, scalded and cooled to lukewarm
¼ teaspoon saffron
3 tablespoons honey
25g/1oz/2 tablespoons fresh yeast (or the recommended equivalent of dry yeast)
75g/3oz/⅓ cup melted butter, cooled
1 teaspoon sugar
750g/1½lb/6 cups strong unbleached bread flour
Pinch of salt
3 eggs (size 3) well beaten
A few drops of oil for the dough
50g/2oz/¼ cup seedless raisins
Egg glaze
3 tablespoons sugar, melted in a few drops of water for final glaze
Large sugar crystals or hundreds and thousands to decorate

Boil the milk together with the saffron, add the honey, and mix well. Cool to lukewarm. Dissolve the yeast in a little warm milk, add sugar, and leave to ferment for 10 minutes in a warm place.

Sift the flour and salt into a large bowl or a kneading board. Make a well in the centre. Add the yeast, milk, butter and beaten eggs. Mix to a soft, non-sticky stable dough, using more flour if necessary. Knead well until smooth and elastic (about 10 minutes). Oil the dough well to prevent the formation of dry skin, cover and leave to prove in a cool, draught-free place, preferably overnight.

Next day, knock down the dough, knead in the raisins and allow to rest, covered, for 30 minutes. Divide into four (or six) equal portions. Roll into ropes of equal thickness and plait into a large *hallah*. Transfer onto a baking tray, cover loosely and leave to rise, in a warm place for about 1 hour. Brush gently with egg glaze and bake in a hot oven (gas 7, 220°C, 425°F) for about 1 hour until the loaf is golden and sounds hollow when tapped. Remove from the oven. Brush with sugar syrup while still very hot and sprinkle with sugar crystals. Return to the oven for 3–4 minutes to dry. Cool.

KICHEL OR KICHLACH

Makes about 40

These delicate, crispy biscuits are especially made to be served with chopped herring or liver.

3 eggs (size 3)
125g/5oz/1¼ cups flour
2 tablespoons sugar
Large pinch of salt
3 tablespoons poppy seeds (optional)

Combine all the ingredients to make a smooth, thick batter. Grease a baking tray slightly. Drop a tablespoon of batter at a time onto the tray at least 2.5cm (1″) apart each way. Bake for 20 minutes in a warm oven (gas 3, 170°C, 330°F) or until lightly browned at the edges and puffed. Store in an airtight tin.

13

WESTERN FOOD

Parve Schmaltz

As far as I can tell the first commercially made vegetarian *schmaltz* was made in South Africa by Debra's. Their advertising slogan claimed that 'even the chicken can't tell the difference', which to a certain extent is true. Vegetarian *schmaltz* is a good substitute. The product can very easily be made at home. The following recipe comes from South Africa.

500g/1lb/2 cups solid vegetable fat or vegetable lard
500g/1lb onion, sliced
500g/1lb/3 cups carrots, washed and coarsely grated
750ml/1½ pints/3 cups peanut or sesame oil

Put all the ingredients in a deep pot. Heat gently and cook on a low heat until the onion is golden. Strain and keep in the refrigerator. Sometimes grated apple (about 350g/12oz) is included.

Matzah Brei

Matzah brei is a passion with some people, so much so that a *matzah brei* convention used to be held every year in New York.[1] Very orthodox Jews do not eat *matzah brei* until the last day of Pesach as there is a danger that the soaked *matzah* might ferment.

2 *matzahs* for each person
1 large egg for each person
Salt
Pepper
Oil or fat for frying

Soak the coarsely broken *matzah* in water. The shorter the soaking time, the crisper the result. Drain and squeeze out as much of the water as possible. Mix the *matzah* with the egg, salt and pepper. Fry either as small patties or as a big flat pancake until brown. Turn over and fry the other side. The colour should be golden brown. Serve very hot on its own with tomato sauce or ketchup, apple sauce, cinnamon and sugar, golden syrup, or whatever you want.

Mock Gefilte Fish

For those who don't like the taste of fish. The following recipe comes from the *Jewish Examiner Prize Kosher Recipe Book*, edited by 'Balabusta'.

Breast of a medium-sized chicken
1 slice of stale rye bread, soaked and squeezed dry
1 large onion
Salt and pepper
1 egg

For the stock:
2 onions, peeled and sliced
1 large carrot, peeled and sliced
500ml/1 pint/2 cups water
Salt and pepper

Mince the meat, bread and onion together. Add seasoning and egg. Mix well and allow to rest for 30 minutes.

Place the onions and carrots on the bottom of a pot, cover with water, season and bring to a rapid boil. Reduce the heat and simmer for 20 minutes. Shape the meat mixture into small round patties and poach in the simmering liquid for 25–30 minutes. Serve hot or cold decorated with carrot slices.

PICKLED ATLANTIC SALMON

1kg/2lb salmon, cut into thin slices
1 tablespoon salt
1 tablespoon mixed pickling spices
100g/4oz/½ cup sugar
175ml/6fl.oz/¾ cup white wine vinegar
100ml/4fl.oz/½ cup water
2 onions, sliced

Wash the salmon and marinate overnight with the rest of the ingredients except the onions. Slice the onions thinly and arrange on the bottom of a heavy pot. Add the salmon and marinade. Bring to the boil, skim well and switch off the heat. Allow the salmon to cool in the cooking liquid. Transfer into a jar and refrigerate.

MOCK CRAYFISH

Serves 6–8 as a starter

A favourite dish which looks like a seafood cocktail and does not remotely taste like crayfish. From South Africa, it makes a pleasant starter.

1kg/2lb firm white fish
Water to cover
Juice of ½ lemon
Salt and pepper

Sauce:
100ml/4fl.oz/½ cup double cream
250ml/8fl.oz/1 cup mayonnaise
50ml/2fl.oz/¼ cup tomato ketchup
1 small onion, grated
1 teaspoon mustard powder
1 teaspoon Worcestershire sauce
Tabasco and pepper to taste
Lemon wedges and shredded lettuce to garnish

Steam the fish in a little water, lemon juice, salt and pepper. It should be cooked, but still firm. Flake when cold. Combine all the sauce ingredients. Mix with the flaked fish and allow to marinate for a few hours. Serve in seafood cocktail glasses garnished with lettuce and lemon wedges.

——— LEAH LEONARD'S BOILED SALT (CORNED) BEEF ———

Serves 10–15

Serve with pickles, horseradish relish and potato salad.

2½kg/5lb salt (corned) beef
1 large onion
100ml/4fl.oz/½ cup cider vinegar
6 bay leaves
1 large clove garlic
1 tablespoon whole mixed spice (optional)
Cold water to cover

Soak the salt (corned) beef in cold water for 1 hour. Drain well. Place the beef in a deep pot, add the other ingredients and cover with cold water. Bring to a quick boil, skim, and cook over reduced heat allowing 30–40 minutes for each 500g/1lb. Test with a fork for tenderness before removing from the heat. Let the meat remain in the cooking liquid for 20 minutes before draining. Slice and serve hot or leave to cool in the liquid. When quite cold, refrigerate under a weight overnight. Slice thinly to serve.

Pressure cooker method: cook in a pressure cooker after soaking. Allow 17 minutes per 500g/15 minutes per 1lb at 15 pounds pressure, and add only 1 cup of cold water.

PICKLING SOLUTION FOR HOMEMADE SALT (CORNED) BEEF —————————— OR TONGUE ——————————

4 litres/8 pints/16 cups cold water
750g/1½lb/3 cups coarse salt
15g/½oz/2 teaspoons saltpetre
1 tablespoon brown sugar
4–5 cloves of garlic
1 tablespoon mixed whole spice
12 bay leaves

Combine the ingredients and boil for 5 minutes. This amount is sufficient to cover 2½kg(5lb) of meat or tongue.

Place the meat to be pickled in a stoneware crock fitted with a tight cover. Add the garlic and pour in the pickling solution as soon as it is cold. Weight the meat with a heavy plate or flat rock. A board that fits inside the crock may be weighted with a rock to keep the meat well under the solution. Cover with a double layer of muslin tied securely around the crock. Store the covered crock in a cool place for between 10 days and 2 weeks.

MIXED FRUIT TZIMMES

Serves 6–8

I found this unusual recipe in a book written by one of the most legendary figures of the Jewish American hotel industry. Mrs Grossinger arrived from Austria to the East Side of New York as a 7-year-old immigrant. She learned her trade in her mother's Jewish kitchen and in the kitchens of many Italian and Irish mamas who lived in the same neighbourhood. In 1914 she and her family opened a small hotel in the Catskill Mountains which became one of the best known and most luxurious American Jewish resort hotels. With the help of her mother she developed the recipes which are the foundation of the Grossinger style.[2]

250g/8oz/1½ cups dried apricots
250g/8oz/1 cup dried pears
250g/8oz/1 cup dried prunes
1½kg/3lb brisket
2 teaspoons salt
¼ teaspoon ground pepper
3 carrots, quartered
6 thin slices of lime or lemon
500ml/16fl.oz/2 cups orange juice
1 litre/2 pints/4 cups water
4 tablespoons honey or sugar

Wash the apricots, pears and prunes before soaking them in cold water for 1 hour. Drain.

Brown the meat over medium heat in a heavy bottomed pan or a Dutch oven. Sprinkle the meat with salt and pepper. Arrange the fruit, carrots and lime or lemon around it. Mix the orange juice, water and honey together and pour over all. Cover and bake in a moderate oven (gas 4, 180°C, 350°F) for 3 hours. Remove the cover and, increasing the heat to hot (gas 7, 220°C, 425°F), bake for 1 hour longer, adding a little water if necessary. Serve hot.

CHICKEN KNISHES

Makes 24 knishes

The word *knish* probably comes from the Yiddish word *knapen*, to pinch. This describes the method of shaping these delicious pastries. I came across this light and delicious *knish* in one of Toronto's kosher delis; sadly I cannot remember its name. This *knish* was shaped as a small stuffed round ball and was deep fried instead of baked. The proud owner naturally refused to give me the recipe. Yet it was so delicious that I tried to recreate it, quite successfully, in my own kitchen. My version is baked instead of fried, which makes it marginally less fattening.

Potato dough:
500g/1lb potatoes
50g/2oz/¼ cup chicken fat, vegetable shortening or peanut oil
75g/3oz/⅓ cup flour

For the filling:
150g/6oz cooked buckwheat (about 100g/4oz/½ cup raw)
350g/12oz cooked chicken meat, preferably dark meat
1 medium onion, finely chopped
2–3 tablespoons chicken fat, vegetable shortening or oil
Salt
Black pepper
Egg glaze

Cook the unpeeled potatoes in salted water. Pour off the water, return to the heat and dry the potatoes well. Mash to a smooth purée. Allow to cool. Add the melted fat and flour and knead to a smooth, softish dough. If the dough is too soft to handle, add some more flour. Cover and allow to rest for a while.

Boil the buckwheat in water until soft. Drain well. Mince or process the cooked chicken meat. Fry the chopped onion in fat until golden. Add to the chicken meat together with the buckwheat, flavour with salt and pepper, and mix well.

Divide the dough into 24 pieces, rolling each into a ball. Flatten each ball to an even circle. Place 1 heaped spoonful of stuffing in the middle and reshape. Place on a well-greased baking tray, brush with egg glaze and bake in a hot oven (gas 6, 205°C, 400°F) for 25 minutes or until the *knishes* are nicely brown.

14

ISRAELI FOOD

FIRST COURSES

Aubergine is one of the most popular vegetables eaten in Israel. The variety used there is different from the smooth, long 'Dutch' variety so familiar in Britain. The Israeli aubergine is dark, almost black-purple, and can reach gigantic proportions. It should be lighter than its size indicates; heavy aubergines contain a large proportion of seeds.

—————— AUBERGINE AND TOMATO SALAD ——————

Serves 6–8

This dish is of Romanian or Southern Russian origin where it is known as 'poor-man's caviar' or aubergine *eekra*.

1kg/2lb aubergines
250g/8oz tomatoes, peeled, deseeded and grated on a coarse grater
3–4 tablespoons good olive oil
100g/4 oz raw onion or spring onion, chopped
Lemon juice to taste*
6–8 tablespoons mint and parsley, chopped finely
Salt
2 or more green or red fresh chillies, seeds removed, chopped finely

* When using lemon juice it is always advisable to add a bit of grated lemon peel. The juice itself is rather tasteless; the 'lemony' flavour is contained in the zest.

222

For decoration:
Tomatoes, olives, mint and parsley sprigs

The best way to cook the aubergine is first to prick it in a few places and then grill it very slowly on a barbecue or directly on an open gas fire until the outside is charred and the inside is perfectly soft. The burnt skin gives the dish its characteristic smokey flavour. The aubergine can also be baked in a very hot oven (gas 9, 240°C, 465°F) for about 20–25 minutes.

When it is cool enough to handle, cut open the aubergine, scoop out the flesh and discard the charred peel. Allow the flesh to drain for 1–2 hours. Aubergine contains a large amount of liquid which must be drained, otherwise the dish will be watery and insipid. For a coarse, more interesting texture chop the aubergine by hand. For a smoother texture process in the food processor. Add the rest of the ingredients, mix well and chill. Decorate with tomatoes, olives, mint and parsley. Serve with hot pitta or toast.

CHATZILIM B'TAHINA
Aubergine Salad with Tahina

Serves 6–8

This dish is based on the Arab classic *metabbal* (*baba ghanoush*). The Ashkenazi version substitutes mayonnaise for tahina, omits the garlic and includes chopped, hard-boiled eggs, chopped raw onion and chopped gherkins.

1kg/2lb aubergine prepared as before
100g/4 fl.oz/½ cup tahina paste or 150g/6oz/¾ cup thick mayonnaise
2 cloves of garlic, crushed and mashed with a little salt
Lemon juice, to taste
Salt
2 tablespoons good olive oil
6 tablespoons chopped mint or parsley
Green and red peppers and black olives for decoration

Mix together all the ingredients, except the olive oil. Transfer to a flat serving dish. Decorate with strips of peppers and olives, dribble with oil, and serve with hot pitta bread.

223

EGG AND AUBERGINE SALAD

Serves 6–8

Dr Meyer suggested this dish for people who dislike the flavour of aubergine. It makes an interesting and easily prepared starter.

1kg/2lb aubergines, unpeeled and sliced
2 tablespoons vinegar
1 bay leaf
Salt and pepper
2 hard-boiled eggs
125g/5oz onion, chopped
50–75g/2–3oz mayonnaise
2 pickled cucumbers
Capers for decoration

Cook the sliced aubergine in boiling salted water with a few drops of vinegar and a bay leaf for 20 minutes. Drain. Mince with the hard-boiled eggs and the raw onion. Season with salt and pepper. Add mayonnaise and chopped pickled cucumber. Decorate with capers.

MOCK CHICKEN LIVER

Serves 6–8

1kg/2lb aubergines, unpeeled
50g/2oz/¼ cup olive oil
200g/8oz onion, chopped
2 tablespoons vinegar (to taste)
Salt and pepper
2 hard-boiled eggs, yolks and whites sieved separately
Oil for frying

Cut the aubergine into thin slices. Fry in hot oil until soft and golden brown. Fry the onions to a golden brown. Mince all ingredients together. Flavour with vinegar, salt and pepper and serve decorated like chicken liver with the egg yolks and whites. The dish can be done in a food processor, but the gritty texture of mincing is more suitable.

CHATZILIM MIZRACHYIM
'Oriental' Aubergine

Serves 6–8

One of the simplest and most delicious aubergine dishes. The only problem is that the dish tends to be rather oily as fried aubergine soaks up lots of oil. To prevent this, brush lightly with oil and either grill, turning once, or barbecue. Although the texture of the grilled aubergine is not as melting as the original, the smokiness of the barbecue adds an interesting flavour. Or drain the fried aubergine very well on absorbent paper towels. The dish can be served either as a starter or as part of a salad table.

1kg/2lb large aubergines, unpeeled and sliced
500g/1lb peppers of mixed colours
Hot red or green chillies, to taste
1–2 tablespoons good honey
75–100ml/3–4fl.oz/⅓–½ cup fruity olive oil
250ml/8fl.oz/1 cup vinegar, either cider, citrus or wine
Salt
10–12 cloves of garlic, sliced to thin slivers
A few hot green or red chillies

Slice the unpeeled aubergine lengthwise into thickish 1cm/⅓″ slices. Salt lightly and leave to dry in the sun for a few hours or leave for about ½ hour in a very low oven (gas 1/4, 110°C, 230°F).*

To prepare the peppers, char them on an open fire or grill. Put the charred peppers in a bowl and cover them with a tablecloth or seal for 10 minutes in a plastic bag before peeling, cleaning peppers and rinsing them well. Slice into wide strips.

Either fry, grill or barbecue the aubergines. Mix with the peppers and cover with a cloth to keep warm. Melt the honey with olive oil in a small frying pan. Add vinegar and salt and bring to a rapid boil. Then add the garlic† and sliced chillies. Boil on a very high flame for a few minutes, until the liquid looks glossy and starts to thicken. Pour over the vegetables. Adjust saltiness. Allow to marinate for a few hours.

For a less 'pickled' salad allow to stand for 30 minutes. The salad can be eaten either warm or cold.

---

* Dried aubergines soak up less oil while being fried. It is not necessary to dry the aubergine before grilling or barbecuing.

† The garlic can be added raw which makes its flavour deliciously strong. For milder results it can be lightly fried in oil before being added to the mixture.

SIMPLE AUBERGINE APPETISER

Warm, grilled or fried aubergine slices can also be served, simply, covered with grated feta (or *brindza*) and sprinkled with freshly ground black pepper and fresh, chopped mint.

CHATZILIM B'MITZ AGVANYIOT
Aubergine in Tomato Sauce

Serves 6–8

1½kg/3lb aubergine, sliced lengthwise and dried
4 eggs (size 3), well beaten
Flour for coating
Olive oil for frying
1 quantity tomato sauce (see fish in hot tomato sauce recipe on p. 242)
100g/4oz *katchkaval** or any other dry sheep's cheese

Coat the dried aubergine slices with egg and dip in flour. Fry in hot oil until golden brown. Drain well on absorbent paper.

Arrange a layer of fried aubergine on the bottom of a baking dish. Mask with a little tomato sauce, cover with another layer of aubergine, continuing the process until all the aubergine and sauce is used. The last layer should be aubergine. Sprinkle with cheese and bake in a moderate oven (gas 5, 190°C, 375°F) for 30 minutes or until the cheese has melted and is nicely browned. Serve either warm or at room temperature.

BEETROOT AND APPLE SALAD

Serves 4–6

The next two recipes are attributed to Dora Schwartz (no relation to the author). She was one of the most colourful pioneers of Israeli nutrition. In the early 1930s, inspired by the teaching of M.O. Bircher-Benner,[1] she established a successful sanatorium. An ardent and vocal advocate of vegetarianism and healthy eating, she published two cookery books and was quoted often in early Israeli cookbooks.

---

* *Katchkaval* or *katchkavali* can be bought in many Greek and Middle Eastern shops.

Lemon juice
500g/1lb beetroot
2 sweet cooking apples
50g/2oz horseradish, grated
Salt

Put the lemon juice in a deep salad bowl. Peel the beetroot and apple and grate these directly into the lemon juice. Add the grated horseradish, mix well and chill.

ISRAELI SALAD DRESSING

100ml/4fl.oz/½ cup grape or orange juice
Juice from 1 lemon
4 tablespoons yoghurt
2 tablespoons cream
Lots of mixed herbs, such as parsley, celery (leaves), dill, mint and spring
  onion, finely chopped

Mix all the ingredients together and chill. This sauce is excellent with tomatoes.

CHUMMOSE MA' A'BETINGAN
'Mussaka' with Chickpeas

Serves 8–10

This recipe was given to me by Yakira Dori, who belongs to an old Galilean family. As far as she can remember, the dish was cooked only among Sephardi families in the Galilee.

500g/1lb dry chickpeas, soaked and peeled*
Salt and pepper
500g/1lb sliced onion
1kg/2lb aubergine, sliced into 1cm/⅓″ slices, dusted with salt and drained
  for 1 hour
Olive oil for frying
250–500ml/8–16fl.oz/1–2 cups strained liquid from cooking chickpeas
Yoghurt, quartered lemons and parsley as accompaniment

* To peel chickpeas, first soak them overnight. Lay a small quantity of soaked chickpeas on a clean cloth, fold the cloth over and rub well. Although the dish is more delicate when made from peeled chickpeas, peeling is messy and time-consuming. It could be dispensed with, as the final results do not justify the bother.

Cook the chickpeas until they are soft but still retain their shape. This can take 2 hours or more according to the age of the peas. Drain and flavour lightly with salt and pepper. Reserve some of the cooking liquid. Fry the sliced onion to a deep golden brown and drain well on absorbent paper. Fry the aubergine to golden brown and drain well, too, on absorbent paper.

Arrange a single layer of fried aubergine on the bottom of a large greased baking dish. Cover with a layer of cooked chickpeas and then onion. Repeat until all the ingredients are used, finishing with a layer of fried onion. Salt and pepper the cooking liquid slightly, pour over the dish and bake uncovered in a medium oven (gas 5, 190°C, 375°F) for 1 hour or until most of the liquid has evaporated and the onion is nicely browned. Decorate with coarsely chopped parsley and quartered lemons. Serve warm accompanied with yoghurt.

CHUBEZAH
Fried Mallow

Serves 4–6 as a first course or salad

This is a Palestinian Arab dish adopted by the Jews during the Arab siege of Jewish Jerusalem in 1948. As a result *chubezah* rissoles were among the dishes suggested for the new tradition of the Independence Day celebration meal. It has a wonderfully earthy flavour. Lemon juice is essential, but should be added at the table as it changes the colour of the leaves rapidly.

1kg/2lb mallow or spinach*
1 large onion
50–75g/2–3fl.oz/¼–⅓ cup olive oil
1–2 hot green chillies
50g/2oz/¼ cup pine nuts or slivered almonds, fried in a little olive oil
Salt
Lemon quarters

Remove the tough stems from the leaves. Wash well in a few changes of cold water. Pile up the leaves and roll them into a bundle which can be sliced into thickish julienne strips.

Chop the onion coarsely. Heat two-thirds of the oil in a large heavy bottomed frying pan. Add the onion and fry gently until it is transparent,

* Mallow can be bought in season (summer) in Greek, Turkish and other Middle-Eastern shops. Spinach, sugar beet leaves or Swiss chard can also be served in this way.

but still firm. Add the chopped leaves and fry on a high flame for 4–5 minutes until the leaves are wilted. Remove the pan from the flame and lift out the leaves, draining them well. Add all the drained liquid to the frying pan, bring it rapidly to the boil and add the remaining oil. Boil rapidly until the liquid is syrupy and glossy. Adjust the saltiness, pour over the cooked leaves and toss gently.

Decorate with finely sliced chillies and pine nuts and serve with lemon quarters. This dish is served either warm (never hot) or cold as a first course or to accompany roasts.

The same mixture, with the onion sliced more finely, can be used as a stuffing for pastries and strudels. In that case, I flavour the mixture with grated orange peel which combines favourably with the earthiness of the dish.

ORIENTAL-STYLE SABRA
Prickly Pear Salad

Serves 8–10

Prickly pear has recently begun to appear in UK shops and supermarkets. Served raw and chilled, it is juicy and sweet with a delicate characteristic aroma. The following recipe is from Chaim Cohen, head chef and consultant for the kibbutz movement catering school.

8 prickly pears, peeled
250g/8oz onion, sliced into thin rings
250g/8oz apple, sliced into julienne strips
150g/6oz gherkin, sliced into fine julienne strips
150g/6oz pickled sweet red pepper (*gamba*)
Lemon and olive oil vinaigrette

Slice the prickly pear into thick slices. Add sliced onion, apple, gherkin and red pepper. Dress with vinaigrette and toss gently. Serve well chilled.

FALAFEL

Makes about 150 balls

Falafel was originally flavoured with a mixture of powdered cumin and coriander. I prefer to use whole cumin and caraway seeds. Falafel can be served as an appetiser, accompanied with a tahina sauce, or stuffed into a pitta bread and topped with various fresh salads and pickles as a substantial meal, the way it is served in Israel.

The quantity given here is enough to make around 150 × 2.5cm (1″) balls. This may sound like a large quantity, but they disappear very quickly. The falafel mixture freezes successfully, although it is better to add the raw onion to the mixture after defrosting as its flavour deteriorates when it is frozen.

500g/1lb/2 cups chickpeas, soaked overnight
150g/6oz onion
1 large bunch of flat-leaved parsley or a mixture of parsley and coriander
2 or more green chillies
150g/6oz/1½ cups flour
150ml/5fl.oz/⅔ cup water
1½–2 scant tablespoon whole caraway seeds or mixture of caraway and cumin
1 scant tablespoon salt
25g/1oz/1 tablespoon fresh yeast, dissolved in a little water
Oil for deep frying (sesame or ground nut)

Mince (through a coarse blade) the soaked chickpeas, onion, parsley and chillies. Some people mince the mixture twice for a smoother result. It can also be successfully processed in a food processor but processing must be done with care to maintain a coarse texture.

Add the rest of the ingredients and mix to a soft mass which will hold its shape when squeezed together. Add some more flour if necessary. Leave covered in a warm place for about 2 hours.

Shape into round, flattish, 2.5cm (1″) patties. The shaping is made easy with a special falafel maker. These can sometimes be bought in Middle Eastern and Israeli shops.

Fry the patties in hot oil until they are rich, deep, golden brown. Drain well and serve hot.

STEWED BAMIA
Stewed Okra or Lady's Fingers

Serves 6

The following recipe is a blueprint for the Palestinian way of cooking vegetables. The same recipe is suitable for courgettes, aubergines, green beans, spinach, etc. It is simple and delicious. Care should be taken not to overcook the vegetables.

500g/1lb *bamia* (okra, lady's fingers), prepared
25–50ml/1–2fl.oz/about ¼ cup strong olive oil
250g/8oz onion, coarsely chopped
5–8 fat garlic cloves, sliced into big chunks
1–2 green or red chillies, sliced
Za'atar (see page 118 — optional)
Salt
Chopped parsley and lemon wedges for decoration

To prepare the *bamia* remove the hard stem, taking care not to damage the main part of the vegetable. Wash well and leave to dry in the sun (or in a very low oven).

Heat a heavy bottomed pan, add some oil and fry the dry bamia over a high heat, turning frequently until they start to colour. Lift out and drain on absorbent paper.

Add the rest of the oil and fry the onion and garlic over a high heat until they start to brown but remain crunchy. Add the *bamia* and chillies, moisten with a small amount of water, season with *za'atar* (if using) and salt, cover with a lid and cook until the *bamia* is tender but still firm.

Serve at room temperature decorated with chopped parsley and lemon wedges. The lemon is essential. It is added at the table because it changes the colour of the green vegetable if added during cooking.

The same technique is used for vegetables in tomato sauce. In this case the tomatoes (250g/8oz, peeled, deseeded and chopped) are added to the frying onion. The onion and tomato mix is fried on a high flame until most of the tomato liquid has evaporated, after which the pre-fried *bamia* (or any other vegetable) is added and the cooking is finished as described above.

Tahina Sauce

Juice of 2 or more lemons
250g/8oz/1 cup raw tahina paste
About 175ml/6fl.oz/¾ cup water
Salt
Garlic to taste
4 tablespoons finely chopped parsley

Add the lemon juice to the tahina paste and mix well. In the beginning, the tahina paste seems to separate and turns into a lumpy, grainy mass. Keep mixing, adding small quantities of water, until the sauce reaches the right consistency.

When eaten as a dip, tahina should be the consistency of a thick double cream. For cooking, however, it needs to be thinner — like single cream. Dilute to the right consistency with lemon juice, water or milk. Add salt, garlic and parsley.

HUMMUS
Chickpeas Dip

Hummus is always served with fresh and pickled vegetables and hot pitta bread. A good combination is sliced raw onion, spring onion, young cos lettuce, crunchy sweet peppers, olives, pickled turnip, pickled aubergines and sprigs of fresh mint. The vegetables as well as the pitta are used to scoop the hummus.

The quantity below makes about 2kg/4lb hummus which is enough for a starter for about 20 people. It is a good idea to make a large quantity as hummus freezes very well. Normally hummus is not flavoured with spices although I have found a few recipes which use cumin powder in the preparation.

> 500g/1lb/2 cups chickpeas, soaked overnight
> 250g/8oz raw tahina paste
> Juice of 4–5 lemons, or to taste
> 4–5 or more cloves of garlic, mashed with a little salt
> Salt
> 50g/2oz/¼ cup olive oil
> Olive oil, finely chopped parsley, sweet paprika and black olives for
>   decoration

Cook the chickpeas in unsalted water until they are very soft. This may take up to 2 hours or longer if the peas are old. Some people add bicarbonate of soda to the water to reduce the cooking time. However, the soda affects some of the minerals and vitamins present and also leaves an unmistakable aftertaste. The quickest way to cook chickpeas is in a pressure cooker: they take about 45–50 minutes and unsoaked will cook in about 1½ hours.

When the chickpeas are perfectly soft, drain and reserve some of the cooking liquid and a few whole peas for decoration. Mash the rest to a smooth paste. Traditionally this is done either by pounding or passing the peas through a fine sieve. The advantage of sieving is that some of the tough skin is removed. The paste can also be made successfully in a food processor. In this case lemon juice or some of the cooking water should be added for easy processing.

Add the tahina, lemon juice, mashed garlic, salt and olive oil.* Mix until smooth, adjusting the consistency with lemon juice or cooking liquid. The mixture has to be slightly runny as it thickens after resting for a while. Hummus also absorbs more lemon juice than expected.

To serve: arrange a border of hummus on individual plates or a large platter, placing a few of the reserved chickpeas in the centre of the dish. Sprinkle all over with olive oil, making sure it covers the bottom of the dish. Sprinkle with paprika and parsley and decorate with olives. Serve with hot pitta and vegetables.

ISRAELI SALAD

Serves 6–8

Although this dish is always referred to as Israeli it is of pure Arab origin, but eaten widely by Jews and Arabs alike. What makes this salad extraordinary is the meticulous way the vegetables are sliced into small (1cm/½″) almost geometrically perfect cubes. The flavouring used varies. Some people include powdered cumin, coriander or pepper while others use *za'atar*.

2 beef tomatoes or 4 small ones, washed and cubed
4 small cucumbers,† unpeeled, washed and cubed
1 medium onion, peeled and chopped finely
1 each red and green sweet peppers, de-seeded, washed and cubed
1 clove garlic, finely chopped (optional)
½ large radish,‡ chopped
6 tablespoons chopped fresh mint, parsley or dill, or a combination of all three
1 teaspoon *za'atar* (optional)
4–6 tablespoons good, fruity olive oil
Juice of 1 lemon or more, to taste
Salt

* The addition of olive oil is important, especially when the hummus has to stand for a while as it prevents the formation of a skin. Hummus containing oil also sours less quickly.
† The cucumbers used all over the Middle East are different from those in Britain. They are smaller (the size of courgettes), and have a firmer, crunchier texture. They can be bought in Greek and Indian shops and recently have begun to appear in some supermarkets.
‡ Large radishes can be bought in Greek, Chinese and Indian shops. They come in different sizes and shapes. Any variety can be used. In Israel, they normally have a red skin and a pungent, hot flavour.

Mix all the cubed ingredients together. Add the garlic, radish, herbs and *za'atar* (if used). Dribble with olive oil and lemon, add salt, and mix the salad very carefully so as not to damage the vegetables. Leave to marinate in a cool place for about an hour. Adjust saltiness and serve.

BUREKAS

Makes 24 large or 60–80 cocktail size

Burekas belong to a large and delicious family of savoury pastries served all over the Middle East and the coast of the Mediterranean. Each country has developed a different dough for those pastries. In Lebanon, they use a short pastry (based on olive oil) or yeast dough for their pastries which are called *sanbusak (sambusak)*. In Greece, Turkey and Bulgaria, they use the wonderfully thin filo *(fila)*. A close relative of the *burekas* are the North African *cigarellos* and *briks* which are traditionally made from *warkha* (similar to filo) and are fried rather than baked. Made very small (cocktail size) they are ideal to serve with drinks.

500g/1lb filo pastry
Melted butter or oil
beaten egg yolk for glazing
Sesame seeds

Mallow stuffing:
Mix together 1 quantity of cold fried mallow (see recipe on p. 228) and
100g/4oz crumbled *brindza* or feta cheese. Flavour with a few scrapings of
nutmeg and finely grated orange peel.

Aubergine stuffing:[2]
3 tablespoons olive oil
1 large onion, peeled and grated
1kg/2lb aubergine, unpeeled and grated
3 peeled, deseeded and finely chopped tomatoes or 1 tablespoon tomato
concentrate
Freshly ground pepper
Salt
4–6 tablespoons finely chopped parsley or fresh coriander (optional)

Heat the oil in a large frying pan. Add the grated onion and aubergine and fry for few minutes. Add the salt and tomato together with a small amount of water to prevent sticking. Continue frying, shaking the pan constantly until most of the liquid has evaporated. Allow to cool, adjust the saltiness and season with pepper and herbs.

To assemble large burekas: slice leaves of filo pastry lengthwise to 10cm (4") wide rectangular strips. Take one at a time and brush with oil or melted butter. Place a rounded tablespoon of mixture about 2.5cm (1") from the short edge. Fold one corner over the filling, making a triangle. Fold the triangle over and over again until the whole strip is folded. Brush any loose edge with oil or melted butter and tuck in neatly. Place on a baking sheet. Brush with melted butter, oil or well beaten egg yolk and sprinkle with sesame seeds. Bake in a moderate oven (gas 5, 190°C, 375°F) for 25 minutes or until crisp and golden. Serve hot.

To make the cocktail size version: slice the filo widthwise into 6cm (2½") rectangular strips. Brush each strip as before and place a scant teaspoon of filling near the end. Either fold as before or roll twice to make a small cigar shape. Fold in the two open edges, brush the folded edges with a little butter and keep rolling until all the strip is used. Brush edge with butter and tuck neatly. Glaze as before and bake for about 15 minutes.

They can also be deep fried in boiling oil, in which case ready made *samosa* or Chinese spring roll pastry is more suitable than filo. Serve hot.

COOKED ARTICHOKE SALAD

Serves 6–8

This recipe is one of my mother's specialities. It makes a refreshing, pleasantly sour salad with a most unusual delicate, pale green colour.

6 globe artichokes
Water to cover, and juice of 1 lemon*
1 bunch spring onions, cleaned and trimmed but with some green leaves
    retained, and cut in halves lengthwise
Juice of 2 lemons, or to taste
About 250ml/8fl.oz/1 cup water
3–4 tablespoons olive oil
Salt
½ tablespoon flour or corn starch for thickening (optional)
Lemon wedges, for decoration

* The moment an artichoke is sliced the exposed flesh turns black with amazing speed. To prevent, rub the exposed flesh in lemon juice and keep the peeled artichokes in acidulated water until they can be cooked.

If the artichokes are young and the stems are not woody, peel the stem and leave them attached. Otherwise remove the stems to within 2.5cm (1″) of the heart. Rub the cut surfaces with lemon. Pull away all the leaves.

With a small sharp knife remove all the hard green end of leaves, leaving only the white part. Rub with lemon. With a teaspoon, remove the inedible choke, leaving just the edible heart. Rub with lemon. Quarter the clean artichoke and plunge immediately into the acidulated water.

Arrange the artichokes and onions on the bottom of a heavy pan, add lemon juice, water, olive oil and salt. Bring to the boil and simmer gently for about 20 minutes or until the artichokes are just soft. Lift them and the onions to a serving dish.

Thicken the sauce with either a few teaspoons of flour or corn starch or reduce it by rapid boiling until it is glossy and starts to thicken. Adjust salt and acidity before pouring it over the artichokes.

This dish may be used as a first course, decorated with lemon wedges, or as a salad accompanying a main course. Serve either warm or cold.

RAW ARTICHOKE AND CARDOON SALAD

Serves 8–10

Cardoon is a thistle-like vegetable related to the globe artichoke. It is much loved in North Africa. It can sometimes be bought from Greek grocers. This recipe is of Algerian origin.[3]

Juice of 1½ medium lemons
7 cardoon stems
7 large artichokes, prepared as in previous recipe
5–6 tablespoons olive oil
1 teaspoon *harissa* (see recipe on page 261)
1 teaspoon salt
Freshly ground black pepper
10–15 cloves of garlic, chopped (or less to taste)

Put the lemon juice in a deep salad bowl. With a small sharp knife remove the outer skin and stringy parts of the cardoons. Rub immediately with lemon. Rinse and slice to 3cm (1½″) lengths. Add to the lemon juice and coat thoroughly to prevent blackening.

Slice the cleaned artichokes into bite-sized slices and add to the lemon juice. Add the rest of the ingredients and mix well. Serve chilled.

Ekra

Serves 4–6

This recipe is of Romanian origin and is a version of the Adriatic *tarama*.

Roes from 2 salt herrings (about 150g/6oz)*
Water or milk for soaking
75g/3oz/2 thick slices white bread
Small onion, peeled
100ml/4fl.oz/½ cup peanut or mild olive oil
2 tablespoons citrus or white wine vinegar

Soak the roes for a few hours in water or milk to get rid of any excess salt. Peel off the fine membrane covering them. Soak the white bread in water and squeeze dry. Process the roes, onion and bread in a food processor for few seconds. Add the oil in a thin, steady stream while processing. Add the vinegar. Serve stuffed into tomatoes or like *tarama*, with plenty of hot pitta or toast.

Pickled Cucumbers Stuffed with Herring

Makes 12

I include this recipe by Dr Meyer as it is a delicious combination of traditional ingredients.

6 small pickled cucumbers†
100g/4oz Bismark herring fillets (soaked in milk or water to get rid of the excess salt)
2 hard-boiled eggs, chopped
1 onion, chopped
2 tablespoons dill, chopped, plus some whole leaves for decoration

Cut the cucumbers lengthwise and scoop out the centres, creating boat shapes. Chop the centres and add chopped herring, egg and raw onion. Mix in the dill. Fill the cucumbers and decorate with dill. Serve on toasted bread fingers.

---

* Hard herring roes can be bought anywhere whole herring is sold. Unfortunately they cannot be bought separately. Ask the shopkeeper to select female herrings with roes.
† Israeli pickled cucumbers in brine are usually the right size.

HERRING AND POTATO PIE

Serves 6–8 as first course or 4–5 as a main course

The following recipe appeared in 1947 in a collection of recipes by Wizo. It is easy to make and rather delicious.

1kg/2lb firm boiling potatoes, washed and scrubbed
4 soaked, salted (*schmaltz*) herrings
150ml/5fl.oz/⅔ cup plain yoghurt
4 (size 3) egg yolks
50g/2oz/¼ cup butter or margarine

Boil the potatoes until just soft. Allow to cool. Either peel them or not, then slice them into thin slices. Skin and bone the herring. Slice to bite-sized pieces.

Arrange layers of sliced potato and herring in a baking dish. This should preferably be glazed or glass because exposed metal will affect the flavour of the herring. Mix the yoghurt with the egg yolks and pour over the potatoes. Dot with butter.

Bake in a moderate oven (gas 4, 180°C, 350°F) for 25 minutes or until the potatoes are nicely browned. Serve hot or warm.

SOUPS

GRAPE SOUP

Serves 4–6

This makes a deliciously different cold soup which can be served as a starter or as a refreshing non-alcoholic drink for summer.

250g/8oz 'blue' or red grapes
1 litre/2 pints/5 cups cold milk
50g/2oz/¼ cup sugar or to taste
Rind of 1 lemon
Vanilla sugar (optional)
Seedless green grapes for decoration

Sieve the grapes into the cold milk. Flavour with sugar and lemon peel and decorate with seedless green grapes. Serve immediately.

SOUR TOMATO SOUP

Serves 6

This soup is one of the many summer soups which are normally served cold. In some households cold soups are kept in the refrigerator and drunk instead of water or fruit juice. They are extremely refreshing on a hot summer's day. Soup can be made in the same way from the following ingredients: spinach, chard, beetroot, courgettes and pumpkin.

1kg/2lb ripe tomatoes
Bouquet garni: few stalks of celery, some parsley, few strips of lemon peel, 1 bay leaf
700ml/25fl.oz/3 cups water
Juice of 1 lemon
Sugar (optional)
1–2 egg yolks, beaten, or sour cream
Salt

Slice the tomatoes into chunks, cover with water, add the *bouquet garni* and simmer for about 15 minutes until they are perfectly soft.

Discard the *bouquet* and pass the tomatoes through a sieve.

Transfer the purée to a clean pot and add the cooking liquid. Add the lemon juice and sugar, if used, and boil once. Remove from the heat, adjust the flavour and beat in the egg yolks.

Serve very cold. Sour cream can be used instead of egg in which case it is not mixed in when the soup is hot, but served separately at the table.

FISH

JELLIED CARP

Serves 6–8

This recipe was a part of a menu designed to represent an Israeli cooking style which appeared in *Food and Kitchen*. This magazine was, until its closure in 1990, the only means of communication available to the Israeli food industry. The menu was designed and cooked at the Tel Aviv Hilton Hotel. I like this recipe as it is a modern adaptation of an old Ashkenazi dish given an Israeli sting. It is an elegant and delicate first course.

1.5kg/3lb carp, filleted and boned with the skin left on
350ml/12fl.oz/1½ cups Sauvignon Blanc
500ml/16fl.oz/2 cups fish stock, made of the carp head and bones, and flavoured with onion, carrots, celery, parsley, bay leaf and 2 long pieces of lemon peel
50g/2oz/2 tablespoons gelatine powder
Grated peel of 1 lemon
1 carrot, sliced into a fine julienne strips and blanched
Salt and white pepper
5 tablespoons onion, finely chopped, blanched and chilled
1 tablespoon pickled green peppercorns
For decoration: fresh tomato, peeled, finely chopped and flavoured with olive oil, salt, pepper and chopped dill.
Thinly sliced cucumbers, endive or baby lettuce leaves

Slice the fish into wide slices. Poach in wine and stock for 8–10 minutes or until cooked. Lift carefully and leave to cool on a tray. Boil the poaching liquid for 5–6 minutes to intensify the flavour. Strain and add the gelatine, which was softened first in a little wine or water. Leave to cool, until the gelatine begins to set. Fold in the grated lemon peel.

Mask a long loaf tin or hinged mould with a thin layer of the gelatine. Arrange alternate layers of fish and vegetables, dot with green peppercorns and pour gelatine between each layer. Top up with the rest of the gelatine and refrigerate for at least 12 hours. Slice and serve with the fresh tomato *concasse*, cucumber and endive.

SANIYA OF FISH

Serves 6–8

This dish is one of my mother's creations and reflects a clever use of the traditional Ashkenazi *gefilte fish* mixture cooked in an Arab technique (*saniya*) with available local ingredients. A truly original Israeli dish.

½ quantity *gefilte fish* mix (see recipe on page 190)
Small bunch of flat-leaved parsley, chopped
Oil for frying
2 large apples, peeled and sliced
2 large beef tomatoes, peeled and sliced
1 each red and green peppers, sliced into thin rounds
4 sticks of celery, sliced
2 large onions, sliced into thin rounds
2 green chillies, sliced
250ml/½ pint/1¼ cups fish stock or water
Juice of 2 lemons
Salt
2 teaspoons sugar (optional)

Combine the *gefilte fish* mixture with the parsley. Shape into small 2.5cm/1″ round patties. Fry in oil for about 2 minutes on each side until slightly brown and firm. Drain on absorbent paper.

Line a deep baking dish with alternate layers of half the sliced vegetables. Add a layer of fish and cover with the rest of the vegetables.

Mix the fish stock with lemon, salt and the sugar if used. Pour over the fish and bake covered in a medium oven (gas 5, 190°C, 375°F) for ½ hour. Uncover, increase the heat to gas 7, 220°C, 425°F and bake for further 15–20 minutes or until most of the liquid has evaporated. Serve cold.

FISH IN TAHINA SAUCE

Serves 6

Any fish suitable for frying can be used, though I found trout a bit too delicate for this treatment.

6 clean and gutted fish
Spiced but not salted flour for dipping

For the sauce:
100g/4oz/½ cup tahina paste
Juice of 2 or more lemons
About 150–175ml/5–6fl.oz/⅔–¾ cup milk*
3–4 tablespoons parsley, chopped
3–4 tablespoons dill or fennel leaves, chopped
1 clove of garlic, crushed and mashed with a little salt (optional)
Salt
Chopped parsley, pine nuts and lemon wedges for garnish

* Milk softens the slightly bitter aftertaste of the tahina.

Make the sauce by mixing the tahina paste with lemon and milk until it has the consistency of single cream. Add the chopped herbs and garlic and mix well.

Coat the fish with flour. Either grill or fry until it is almost done. Transfer to a baking dish and cover with tahina sauce. Bake in a hot (gas 7, 220°C, 425°F) oven for 15 minutes or until the sauce bubbles and begins to brown. Serve hot or at room temperature garnished with chopped parsley, fried pine nuts and lemon wedges.

LEMON AND GARLIC SAUCE FOR FRIED FISH

For 6 fish

This sauce works very well with most fatty fish. It is especially good with fresh grilled mackerel.

Juice of 2–3 lemons
150ml/¼ pint/⅔ cup good fruity olive oil
2–3 cloves of garlic, crushed and mashed with a little salt
4 tablespoons parsley, chopped
4 tablespoons dill, chopped
2 or more green or red chillies or some chilli powder (optional)
A little water
1 teaspoon sugar (optional)
Salt

Mix all the ingredients. Either serve in a separate sauceboat or pour over hot grilled or fried fish, leaving it to marinate for 5 minutes.

DAGIM B'MITZ AGVANYUTE
Fish in Hot Tomato Sauce

Serves 6

This is one of the most popular ways of preparing fish in Israel. After the declaration of the State of Israel food was rationed. One of the cheapest fish around at that time was imported fish 'fillet': frozen white fish, mostly cod, from Scandinavian countries. Often of poor quality, it had a pronounced 'fishy' flavour. The best way to conceal the flavour was to cook it in a well-spiced, hot tomato sauce. The same technique is also suitable for fresh firm fish, especially grey mullet.

1kg/2lb cleaned fish, cut into serving slices (about 5cm/2")
50–75ml/2–3fl.oz/¼–⅓ cup olive oil
250g/8oz finely chopped onion
8 cloves of garlic, finely chopped
4 celery sticks,* finely chopped
Red or green chillies, chopped, to taste or chilli powder
2 tablespoons powdered cumin (optional)
500g/1lb peeled, de-seeded, chopped, fresh or tinned tomatoes
2 tablespoons tomato concentrate
100ml/4fl.oz/½ cup water, tomato juice or white wine
Bouquet garni consisting of 2–3 strips of orange and lemon peel and a bay leaf
   or two
Salt
Lemon wedges and dill for garnish

Heat the oil in a heavy bottomed pot or a deep frying pan. Add onion, garlic, celery, chillies and the cumin if used. Fry for a few minutes until the onion is translucent and begins to colour. Add the tomatoes, tomato paste, liquid, *bouquet garni* and salt. Bring to the boil, reduce the heat and simmer gently for about 30 minutes until the sauce has thickened.

Add the fish and simmer gently for 15 minutes until cooked. Serve either hot or cold strewn with chopped dill and decorated with lemon wedges.

MEAT

LEG OF LAMB YOSKA

Serves 6–8

This recipe is a reconstruction of a dish which was cooked by the first amateur male cook I ever met. He was a widower friend of my parents who learned to cook during his wife's long illness and later turned cooking into a hobby. Sadly I never had the chance to get his exact recipe for this. The following is a modern interpretation of childhood memories.

Israeli lamb is fattier than those raised in the UK and the States. It is also slaughtered when it is more mature and therefore needs a longer

---

* The celery used in Israel is the highly fragrant leaf celery, which can be bought at Greek grocers. American (stick) celery is a good replacement but does not have the intensity of flavour.

marinating time. Spring lamb needs only 24 hours. Decorate the roast with rosemary sprigs and pomegranate seeds. Served accompanied by *pilav* made from either rice or burgul.

1 × 2kg/4lb leg of lamb
1 litre/2 pints/9 cups fresh pomegranate juice* or 500ml/1 pint/2 cups juice
    and 500ml/1 pint/2 cups fruity red wine
100ml/4fl.oz/½ cup good olive oil
20 pickling onions
250g/8oz carrots, sliced into large chunks
250g/8oz/1 cup prunes
Bouquet garni of 2 bay leaves, 1 teaspoon black peppercorns, 1–2 small sprigs
    of rosemary, 1–2 strips of lemon or orange peel
Salt and pepper

Mix together all the ingredients and marinate the lamb for at least 24 hours.

Transfer everything into a deep roasting tin and bake in a moderate oven (gas 4, 180°C, 350°F) for 18–25 minutes per lb.† Turn and baste the joint frequently; 15 minutes before the meat is done, increase the temperature to very hot (gas 9, 240°C, 465°F) and brown the joint, turning it once.

Lift the joint onto a heated serving plate. Discard the *bouquet garni*. Drain the cooked vegetables and arrange around the joint. Cover loosely with foil and keep warm. Strain the cooking juice into a clean saucepan, skimming most of the fat. Bring to a rapid boil and reduce to a shiny and syrupy gravy. Flavour with salt and freshly ground pepper. Glaze the joint with some gravy and serve the balance in a sauceboat.

* Pomegranates are easily obtainable from Greek and Indian grocers. Around the Jewish New Year they are also sold by some supermarket chains, especially in Jewish areas. To obtain their juice: slice and squeeze on a juicer as you would a lemon. If fresh pomegranates are not available, a concentrated juice can be obtained in Greek and Middle Eastern shops. The concentrate should be diluted with 2 measures of water to each measure of juice. It is a good substitute though it lacks the subtle fragrance of the fresh juice.
† Lamb, like all other meats, is preferred well done in Israel. It is considered ready when it is very soft and almost falling off the bone. This can take up to 35–40 minutes per lb.

LAMB SANIA

Serves 4–6

This dish takes its name from the flat round tray in which it is baked.

750g/1½lb/3 cups finely minced lamb
250g/8oz onion, chopped very finely or minced
4 tablespoons olive oil (optional)
75g/3oz/2–3 cups coarse burgul,* soaked in cold water for 1 hour
4 tablespoons parsley or mint, finely chopped
1–2 teaspoons cinnamon and allspice or a mixture of cinnamon and
    cardamom
Salt and pepper
Olive oil for brushing
250ml/8fl.oz prepared tahina sauce (see recipe on page 231)
Lemon juice or water to dilute tahina sauce
50g/2oz pine nuts, slightly browned in oil

Mix the onion, burgul, herbs, spices and seasoning with the minced lamb. Sometimes the onions are first sweated in oil to soften their flavour. Knead the mixture well. Leave to rest in a cool place for about 1 hour.

Oil a large baking tray and spread the meat mixture into a even flat 2.5cm/1″ layer. Brush with oil and bake in a moderate oven (gas 4, 180°C, 350°F) for about 40–45 minutes until the surface is nicely browned.

Cover with tahina sauce diluted with either lemon juice or water to the consistency of thin cream. Increase the oven heat to maximum (gas 9, 240°C, 465°F) and bake for approximately 10 minutes until the sauce bubbles and starts to brown. Sprinkle with pine nuts and serve very hot, accompanied with rice or a green salad.

HUMMUS IM BASHAR
Hummus with Meat

Serves 6–8

I must confess that this dish is one of my absolute favourites; when well made it is a glorious combination of flavours and textures. I have not managed to pinpoint the origin of the dish, but I suspect that it originated in Syria or Lebanon.

---

* Traditionally fine burgul is used, which makes the texture of the cooked dish rather dense.

It is extremely well-balanced and nutritious, containing all three vital sources of protein — meat, legume in the hummus and wheat in the pitta. It is a complete meal in one dish. I serve it sprinkled with pine nuts and parsley, decorated with a few whole parsley leaves and a sprinkling of sweet paprika together with hot pitta and salads. In the pomegranate season I decorate the dish with pomegranate seeds which add a jewel-like brilliancy to this wonderful recipe.

750g/1½lb leg of lamb, boned, with all the fat and sinews removed
1 tablespoon olive oil
2 heaped tablespoons freshly ground coriander seeds
Juice and grated peel of one lemon
1 large bunch of flat leaf parsley, stems removed,* chopped coarsely
1kg/2lb hummus (see p. 232)
75–100ml/3–4fl.oz/⅛–½ cup olive oil for frying
75g/3oz pine nuts, slightly fried in a little oil or roasted in the oven

Slice the lamb meat into julienne strips measuring 5cm × 1cm (2″ × ⅓″). This is easily done after the meat has been made firmer by freezing for an hour or two. Sprinkle the sliced meat with 1 tablespoon of olive oil, powdered coriander and the grated peel of the lemon. Mix well. Leave to marinate for 2 hours.

Keep some of the chopped parsley for decoration. Mix the rest of the parsley with the hummus and adjust flavouring.

Arrange a crown of hummus on a large serving platter or individual plates, dribble over a little olive oil to prevent drying, cover and leave until needed. The last stage has to be done immediately before the dish is served.

Heat the olive oil in a large frying pan until it is just smoky. Add the meat and fry quickly for a minute or two to brown. Reduce the heat and add the lemon juice. Toss the meat well in the pan juices and lift with a perforated spoon to a heated bowl. Cover and keep hot.

Increase the heat and boil the pan juice until it is shiny and thickened. Return the meat to the pan and coat in the thickening sauce. Pour the meat, which should be still pink in the middle, and the sauce into the centre of the hummus crown. Serve with fresh salad, pickles and plenty of hot pitta.

---

* Do not throw away the stems. They have a strong fresh flavour and are ideal for flavouring stocks and stews.

EL-HAMAM DIL'ARUSA
Stuffed Pigeon

Serves 2

Pigeons have been eaten in Israel since Biblical times. Although there have been some experiments in raising pigeons commercially, they are sadly rare now. They were served stewed, roasted or stuffed on all special occasions, especially at weddings when white doves were served to the newly weds.

The wedding recipe below, of Moroccan origin, is an adaptation of a recipe which appeared in Rivka Levi-Mellul's *Moroccan Cooking*. The dish can be made with small *poussins*, but their rather mild flavour may be overwhelmed by the rich flavour of the stuffing. Although usually made just for the bride and groom, this recipe gives ample for 4. Serve with rice or burgul *pilav*.

2 large pigeons or small *poussins*

Stuffing:
250g/8oz/1 cup rice or burgul
100g/4oz minced meat either lean lamb, veal or a combination of the two
2 small onions or 1 large bunch of spring onions (trimmed with some of the green removed), chopped and sweated in olive oil
50g/2oz/¼ cup large seedless raisins, chopped
4–5 prunes, soaked and chopped
5–6 dried apricots, soaked and chopped
50g/2oz/¼ cup roasted and chopped nuts (almonds, pecan or walnuts)
1 egg
4 tablespoons olive oil
6 tablespoons chopped parsley
1½ teaspoons mace
¼ teaspoon nutmeg
¼ teaspoon ginger
½ teaspoon cinnamon
Few grindings of pepper
Salt

For the sauce:
50ml/2fl.oz/¼ cup oil
2 small onions, chopped
Flat tablespoon good honey
100g/4oz/½ cup dark raisins
250ml/8fl.oz/1 cup water
Juice of 1 small lemon
Freshly ground pepper
Few strands of saffron
Salt

Blanch the rice for 5 minutes in boiling salted water. If burgul is used, soak for ½ hour in hot water and then drain. Mix all the stuffing ingredients well. Stuff the cavity of the cleaned pigeons and sew the opening. If some stuffing is left, use it to fill small greased dariole moulds. Cover and steam them for 1 hour. Unmould and serve with the pigeon.

Heat the oil in a heavy bottomed pan in which the pigeons will fit snugly. Brown the pigeons on all sides in the hot oil, lift out and keep warm. Add the onion and sweat gently until it starts to take colour. Add the honey, salt, pepper, saffron, raisins, and water, bring to the boil and simmer for a few minutes. Add the pigeons.

Cover and transfer the pot to a preheated oven (gas 6, 205°C, 400°F). Bake covered for 25 minutes, basting constantly. Remove the pigeons and keep hot. Skim some of the fat, add the lemon juice, and boil rapidly until the sauce is glossy and slightly thickened.

Transfer the pigeons onto a serving dish and pour over the sauce.

CHICKEN A LA SABRA
Chicken in Orange Sauce

Serves 4–5

Although its name is slightly pretentious, this dish is a classic which found its way onto the menus of five-star hotel restaurants after winning a cooking competition. It is served on a bed of rice or burgul *pilav*.

1kg/2lb chicken, cut into 8 serving pieces
125ml/4fl.oz/½ cup fresh orange juice
125ml/4fl.oz/½ cup dry white wine
Peel of ½ orange, grated or cut into fine julienne strips
Scant teaspoon each of salt, paprika and freshly ground black pepper
50ml/2fl.oz/¼ cup good olive oil
1 onion, finely chopped
8 stoned green 'broken' olives, blanched for a few seconds in boiling water to
    remove excess salt
Mint or dill to garnish

Mix the chicken pieces with the orange juice, wine, peel and seasoning. Leave to marinate for 2 hours.

Heat the oil in a heavy pan which will be large enough to hold the chicken. Lift the chicken pieces out of the marinade and dry well. Brown the chicken pieces in the hot oil. Lift and drain, keeping them warm.

Add the onion and sweat until it starts to change colour. Add the marinade and simmer for ten minutes. Return chicken to the pan, and continue to simmer, on a very low heat until it is cooked; about 35–40 minutes. Lift out the chicken, cover and keep hot.

Add the olives to the remaining liquid and boil rapidly until glossy and starting to thicken. Pour over the chicken. Sprinkle with chopped mint or dill and serve hot.

STUFFED VEGETABLES

Serves 8

Stuffed vegetables cross all ethnic barriers because they make good economic sense. They use little meat and are light and refreshing. Traditions about stuffing vegetables exist both in Ashkenazi and Sephardi kitchens.

The base for the stuffing is similar — rice or rice and meat but the flavouring is different. The Ashkenazi *holishkes* (*galuptzi, paarkes*) tend to be milder and sweeter, spiced mainly with black pepper, but occasionally with a little cinnamon and powdered ginger, as well. Cabbage is mainly used for the shell although onions* and potatoes are also used. The Sephardi *machshi* (the word means stuffed in Arabic; also known as *mefrum* in North Africa and *dolma* in Greece and Iraq) is differently spiced with extremely fragrant mixtures of allspice, cinnamon,

---

* Large onions are boiled in water until they are almost soft. The layers are then carefully separated, creating perfect shells for stuffing.

cumin, coriander, mace and black pepper. Sometimes cardamom is used, giving an exceptionally delicate refreshing flavour.

These spices are used either separately or ground together to create a basic flavouring powder similar to the Indian *masala*. Lemon peel is sometimes grated into the stuffing.

Nowadays the meat used is mainly beef, though traditionally lamb was used because it is lighter and more delicate than beef.

The list of vegetables used for stuffing is endless. Small purple aubergines, red tomatoes, delicate young artichoke hearts, vine leaves, chard, beet leaves, mallow leaves, cabbage, courgettes, and even fruit such as sour apples, prunes and dried apricots.

Below are two stuffings which come from the Sephardi kitchen. One is vegetarian and the other uses meat. Both could be stuffed into any vegetable. The quantities are enough for 8 largish vegetables.

Vegetarian:
300g/10oz/1¼ cups rice, blanched for a few seconds in boiling water
1 large onion, finely chopped
2 large tomatoes, peeled, deseeded and chopped
2–3 cloves of garlic, chopped
1 egg
4 tablespoons chopped parsley or mint
Grated peel of 1 lemon
½ teaspoon powdered cumin
½ teaspoon powdered allspice
Salt and plenty of freshly ground pepper
Chopped flesh left after hollowing the vegetables
3 tablespoons olive oil
50g/2oz/¼ cup of raisins or other dried fruit (optional)

Meat:
500g/1lb/2 cups lamb or beef, minced twice
100g/4oz/¾ cup burgul soaked in water for ½ hour, drained
1 onion, finely chopped
6 tablespoons chopped parsley or mint
1 small egg
3 tablespoons olive oil
2–3 tablespoons water
2 teaspoons mixed spices (cumin, coriander, allspice, mace, cardamom, etc., to taste)
Freshly ground pepper
Salt
50g/2oz/¼ cup raisins
Grated rind of 1 lemon

For the sauce:
3 tablespoons olive oil
1 large onion
2–3 tablespoons tomato paste
500ml/1 pint/2 cups water
Juice of 1½ lemons
Few strips of lemon peel
Salt
1 cinnamon quill

Mix the stuffing ingredients thoroughly. Stuff into the hollowed-out vegetables or leaves.

To prepare the sauce: heat the oil in a heavy bottomed pot large enough to contain all the vegetables tightly packed in one layer. Add the onion and fry until golden.

Remove the pot from the heat and pack the stuffed vegetables tightly into it. Mix the tomato paste with water, lemon juice, peel and salt. Pour over the vegetables and add the cinnamon quill.

Return the pot to the heat, bring to the boil, cover and simmer for 45 minutes until the vegetables are done and most of the cooking liquid is absorbed. Shake the pot frequently to prevent sticking. Serve warm or cold, either as a first or main course.

DESSERTS

Sweets and cakes are much loved by Israelis. Sabbath would not be complete without sweetmeats and cakes. Even today's women who would not cook during the week will cook and bake for the Sabbath. However, many now buy ready-made sweets and cakes. These are supplied by a large number of relatively cheap bakeries dotted around the country, some of which produce excellent ranges of traditionally made delicacies.

Another striking aspect of the Israeli sweet kitchen is the use of the vast array of fresh and dried fruit which is constantly available. Fresh fruit is consumed in amazing quantities, served either raw or in a salad, or cooked into many kinds of *liftanim*, a generic name for fruit soups, compôtes and thin fruit purées.

The following recipes include only two cake recipes, both of which are tasty examples of the resourcefulness which characterised the early Israeli kitchen. Both appeared in Dr Meyer's *How to Cook in Palestine.*

PLAIN CAKE

Serves 6–8

The inclusion of haricot beans in a cake sounds strange, but the results are excellent. It produces a moist cake with a delicate, chestnut-like flavour.

> 4 small eggs (size 4), separated
> 250g/8oz/1 cup sugar
> Juice and grated rind of 1 lemon
> 1 tablespoons rum
> 300g/10oz haricot beans, cooked, strained and sieved
> Blanched almonds for decoration

Beat the egg yolks with the sugar until creamy. Mix in the rest of ingredients except the egg whites. Beat the egg whites to a stiff snow and fold into the mixture. Pour into a well-greased 22cm (8in) tin.

Bake in a moderate oven (gas 4, 180°C, 350°F) for 1 hour. Leave to rest in the baking tin for at least 12 hours. Unmould, slice and fill with good quality jam. Melt some jam and brush over the cake. Decorate with blanched almonds.

BREAD CAKE

Serves 6–8

> 6 small eggs (size 4), separated
> 100g/4oz/½ cup sugar
> 100g/4oz/⅔ cup ground nuts (peanuts, pecan, almonds)
> 100g/4oz/½ cup stale brown bread, ground to fine crumbs
> Grated rind of 1 lemon
> Pinch of cinnamon
> 1 tablespoon vanilla sugar or a few drops of vanilla essence
> Orange or citron marmalade for filling
> Sifted icing sugar

Beat the yolks with sugar until the mixture is thick and creamy and reaches the 'ribbon' stage. Mix in the rest of ingredients except the egg whites. Beat the egg whites to a stiff snow and fold them in gently. Grease a 22cm (8½″) tin very well and sprinkle with dry crumbs. Pour in the cake mixture and bake for 40 minutes in a pre-heated oven (gas 5, 190°C, 375°F).

Cool and leave overnight. Next day, slice through and fill with orange or citron marmalade. Dredge with icing sugar.

BAKED QUINCE 'OLYMPUS' STYLE

Serves 10

Olympus is an old and famous Tel-Aviv restaurant where the food is of Balkan origin. The original restaurant is based in the centre of the textile district of Tel-Aviv.

5 ripe quinces
750g/1½lb/3 cups sugar
400ml/14fl.oz/1¾ cups freshly squeezed lemon juice
75g/3oz cinnamon sticks
Water
Cream as accompaniment

Make a syrup from the water, the lemon juice, 500g/1lb/2 cups sugar and the cinnamon. Boil for ten minutes and skim.

Wash the quinces well, slice in two, remove the hard core and peel. Plunge them into acidulated water to prevent browning. Then add the quinces to the boiling syrup, reduce the heat and simmer for about 15–25 minutes until they are soft.

Arrange the cooked quinces in a baking dish, cored side down. Pour over enough of the syrup to come three-quarters of the way over the fruit. Dredge with the rest of the sugar.

Preheat the oven until it is very hot (gas 9, 240°C, 465°F) and bake the quinces until golden brown (10–15 minutes). Reduce the heat to minimum (gas 1/4, 110°C, 230°F) and leave for 1½ hours. Serve at room temperature with cream; it is especially delicious with clotted cream.

FRESH FRUIT SALAD

Serves 15–20

It is almost impossible to make this salad in small quantities for its uniqueness is the large variety of contrasting fruit which go into it. It is full of colour and has a bold, refreshing flavour.

Marinating liquid:
Juice of 1 lemon and 1 orange
1 tablespoon orange blossom water
2 tablespoons fragrant honey (orange blossom if available)
Few drops bitters (preferably orange bitters), to taste
50ml/2fl.oz/¼ cup Sabra or any other orange-flavoured liqueur

Fruit:

250g/8oz/1 cup Galia or Ananas melon, either shaped into balls or peeled and
  cubed
250g/8oz/1 cup Sharon fruit (persimmon or *kaki* fruit), washed and cubed
250g/8oz/1 cup mango, peeled and cubed
250g/8oz/1 cup white seedless grapes
250g/8oz/1 cup black grapes, seeded
250g/8oz/1 cup dates, seeded and peeled
250g/8oz/1 cup strawberries, washed and quartered
3 tablespoons mint, shredded by rolling the leaves and slicing them into very
  thin strips
Sprigs of mint and a few perfect strawberries with their green stems attached
  for decoration

Mix all the marinade ingredients. Prepare all the fruit except the dates, strawberries and mint. Add the prepared fruits to the marinade as soon as they are sliced, folding them carefully but thoroughly into the liquid. The mixing should be done with great care so as not to damage the fruit. Leave to marinate in the refrigerator for a few hours or overnight.

Just before serving, add the dates, strawberries and mint. Combine very carefully. Decorate with whole strawberries and sprigs of mint.

LIFTAN ME'PEROTE ME'UBASHIM
Dried Fruit Compôte

Serves 10–12

This compôte is traditionally served by some Ashkenazi communities at the end of the Seder.

100g/4oz/½ cup dried cherries
100g/4oz/½ cup dried apple rings
100g/4oz/½ cup dried pears
100g/4oz/½ cup seedless raisins
100g/4oz/½ cup prunes
100g/4oz/½ cup dried apricots
Juice of 1 large lemon
2 tablespoons honey (optional)
500ml/15fl.oz/2 cups white demi-sec wine, water or orange juice
2 cinnamon quills
6–8 cloves
4–5 cardamom pods
1 small lemon, washed well and sliced, un-peeled, into fine rings

Wash the dried fruit in a few changes of clean cold water. Transfer to a large bowl and add just enough water to cover the fruit. Soak for 12 hours.

Transfer into a glazed or stainless steel pot, adding the flavourings. Bring to the boil and simmer gently for about 30 minutes. Add the sliced lemon and simmer for a few minutes more. Chill and serve.

LIFTAN
Stewed Fresh Fruit

Serves 4–6

This recipe uses fresh mulberries to make a wonderfully vivid purple compôte which looks very striking when a spoonful of double cream is dribbled over the top. The same method can be used for many other fruit. Especially good are compôtes made from guavas, apricots, Sharon fruit or mango.

500g/1lb/3 cups fresh black mulberries
Juice of 1 lemon
Honey or sugar to taste (50–100g/2–4oz/¼–½ cup)*
Water to cover
1–2 tablespoons cornflour, arrowroot or other thickeners (optional)

Pick over the mulberries and wash them. Transfer into a heavy, glazed or stainless steel pot. Add lemon juice and honey and just cover with cold water. Bring to the boil and simmer gently until the fruit is soft. Then either pass through a sieve to purée or leave the fruit whole. If a thicker *liftan* is preferred, return the puréed fruit to the cooking pot, bring to the boil and thicken with slaked starch. Chill well and serve on its own or with sour or double cream.

MANGO MOUSSE

Serves 6

2 large green, slightly unripe mangos (about 1kg/2lb), washed
About 50ml/2fl.oz/¼ cup water or sweet white wine
1 tablespoon honey or sugar
250ml/8fl.oz/1 cup whipping cream
1 tablespoon icing sugar
Few drops of orange blossom water
Whipped cream, fresh mango and mint for decoration

---

* The quantity of sugar depends on personal taste and the sweetness of the fruit. Some need very little added sweetness.

Put the mango, unpeeled, in a pot, adding the water and honey. Cover tightly. Cook for 20–25 minutes or until the mango is perfectly soft. Allow to cool.

Scoop the cooked flesh and pass it through a sieve.

Reduce the cooking liquid to a thick syrup, add to the fruit purée and allow to cool. Chill.

Whip the cream until it holds its shape but is still soft, adding the icing sugar and a few drops of orange blossom water. Fold the cream gently into the mango purée. Pour into a serving dish and chill thoroughly. Decorate with whipped cream, fresh mango and sprigs of mint.

PICKLES

PICKLED STUFFED AUBERGINES

Makes about 3 × 500g/1lb jars

I always thought pickled stuffed aubergine was a pure Middle-Eastern dish. To my surprise on a visit to New York I saw it in a Jewish-Russian deli displayed with a wide range or other pickled vegetables, all stuffed with the same combination of celery, carrots and garlic. The recipe below is my mother's; her pickled aubergines are the best I have ever tasted.

1kg/2lb small aubergines*
Salt (25g per 500ml/1oz/2 tablespoons per 1 pint/16fl.oz/2 cups of water)
6 fat cloves of garlic
3–4 stalks of leaf celery
2–3 large carrots, peeled and either sliced into fine julienne strips or grated on a coarse grater
1–2 red chillies, sliced
Water
2–3 teaspons vinegar

Wash the aubergines in cold water. Trim their crowns but leave the stems on. Create a pocket by slitting the aubergines lengthwise, leaving both ends still attached.

Bring a large pot of water to the boil, add salt or a quarter of a cup of

* Small aubergines are sold in most Indian and Greek greengrocers.

vinegar and plunge the aubergines into the boiling water. Reduce the heat and simmer for about 5 minutes. The aubergines should be only half cooked, softish but still firm.

Lay the cooked aubergines in a colander, cover with a board or plate and weigh down overnight to drain any excess moisture.

The aubergines may also be steamed which seems to improve the colour of the finished product.

To prepare the stuffing: first roughly pound or chop the garlic and celery, add the carrot and chillies to taste (2 chillies will make it medium hot). Add about 2 teaspoons of salt. Stuff each aubergine with a teaspoonful of mixture and put it snugly into a wide-mouthed pickling jar.

The easiest way to judge the quantity of water needed to make the brine is to fill the jar with cold water when it is full of aubergines. Once full, the water can be emptied into a measuring jug and the appropriate amount of salt added.

Dissolve the salt in cold water and add the vinegar to make the brine.

Place a few whole cloves of garlic, a few celery leaves, some vine leaves (if available) and a few small, fresh or dried, red chillies on top of the aubergines. Add the brine.

Cover with a clean stone or a small plate, lightly weighted to keep the aubergines from floating. Cover the jar loosely and place in a sunny, warm place to ferment. This takes 3–4 days in a hot climate.* After fermentation stops, the pickles should be kept tightly sealed in the refrigerator where they will last for up to six months.

* In cold climates the jar could be placed in a warm spot in the kitchen. One word of warning: the aubergines when fermenting omit delicious garlicky fumes. Although delicious, the smell is overpowering and persistent and can become a nuisance after a while. It is advisable to keep the jar out of the kitchen.

SPICED PRICKLY PEAR JELLY

Makes about 4 × 500g/1lb jars

Red prickly pears are especially suitable for this jelly.

1.5kg/3lb prickly pears, peeled and mashed
500ml/1 pint/2 cups water
A muslin spice bag containing: 1 teaspoon lightly crushed allspice berries and
    4–6 dried red chillies, including the hot seeds, crushed to fine powder
100ml/8fl.oz/½ cup lemon juice, freshly squeezed and strained
500g/1lb/2 cups of warmed dry white sugar for each 500ml/1pint/2 cups of
    fruit juice
500ml/1 pint/2 cups citrus or cider vinegar
4–6 fresh bay leaves
Salt to taste (about 1 teaspoon)
1 tablespoon arak*

Mash the prickly pear. Place in a glazed or stainless steel preserving pan, add the water, mix thoroughly and bring to the boil. Add the muslin bag, reduce the heat and simmer for 20 minutes.

Transfer to a jelly bag and drain overnight without squeezing.

Next day, measure the resulting liquid together with the lemon juice, and weigh the sugar accordingly. Return the liquid to a clean preserving pan, adding the vinegar. Bring to the boil and add the sugar and salt. Boil rapidly, mixing frequently to prevent burning, until a soft set is achieved (about 30 minutes).

Add the arak, off the heat. Cool and bottle. This is recommended for serving with cold meats, steamed vegetables or as a piquant addition to various spreads.

* Arak is the Israeli *eau-de-vie*. The alcohol is produced from a variety of ingredients, including fermented dates. During distillation, it is flavoured with aniseed. Some of the domestically produced araks were sometimes made weaker and sweetened for women. Arak is reputed to be the overall folk remedy of the Middle East. It is good for coughs and, used in small quantities, for mild tummy pains. The jelly can be made with any anise-flavoured *eau-de-vie*, like Greek ouzo or Turkish raki.

PICKLED TOMATOES

Makes about 2 × 500g/1lb jars

Use either green or very hard red tomatoes. Best of all are the hard, small tomatoes which usually arrive in the UK at the end of the winter. They are sweet-sour with meaty hard flesh and a thick skin.

1kg/2lb hard tomatoes
A few sprigs of leaf celery or celery sticks
4–6 fat cloves of garlic, unpeeled, squashed
2–4 fresh hot red chillies
Few vine leaves (optional)
Enough water to cover the tomatoes
Salt
A few sprigs of dill flowers and stems

Pierce the tomatoes in a few places with a needle. Arrange them in one or more glass jars, distributing the celery and garlic between them.

To measure the amount of water needed, top up the tomato jar with water. Empty this water into a measuring jug and add the salt (25g per 500ml/1oz per 1 pint/2 tablespoons per 2½ cups. The liquid must be nice and salty. Pour over the tomatoes.

Put the vine leaves on top and weigh down with a heavy stone or a saucer full of water. Place in the sun for about a week, until fermentation stops. When ready, cover tightly and store in the refrigerator.

PICKLED RADISH OR TURNIP

Makes about 2 × 500g/1lb jars

The radish used is the large red or white variety. *Mooli*, the long white radish available from Indian and Chinese shops, is suitable, so is turnip.

750g/1½lb large radish, sliced into 1cm (⅓″) rounds
250g/8oz raw beetroot, sliced into 1cm (⅓″) rounds
Water
Salt (see previous recipe)

Pack the washed and sliced vegetables into a glass jar.

Measure the water as for tomatoes in the previous recipe. Add salt as for the tomatoes. Cover the sliced vegetables with brine, weigh down with a clean stone, cover loosely and leave in a warm place or in the sun, until fermentation stops. This takes about 7–10 days. When ready, seal tightly and keep in a cool place or in the refrigerator.

PICKLED COURGETTES

Makes about 8 × 500g/1lb jars

Young small courgettes can be pickled in exactly the same way as the tomatoes. The resulting pickle is a delicate and interesting version of pickled gherkins. The only problem is that pickled courgettes tend to go soft rather quickly. Therefore the pickle should be consumed within three months of making.

GRAPE JAM

Although this jam can be made purely from grapes the result is very soft. The inclusion of apples makes a more stable, firmer jam.

2kg/4lb seedless grapes
500g/1lb cooking apples, peeled and cored (core and peel should be reserved, tied in a piece of muslin and added to the jam while it cooks as they contain pectin)
Juice of 1 large lemon
1½kg/3lb/6 cups sugar, warmed in a cool oven

Remove the grapes from their stalks and place in a preserving pan. Add the muslin bag and a few tablespoons of water. Cook until the grapes exude liquid and are soft. Add the apple, cover the pot and cook until the apple has disintegrated. Add the warmed sugar and boil until setting point is reached. Bottle while hot and seal.

SWEET ORANGE AND DATE JAM[4]

Makes about 4 × 500g/1lb jars

6–7 large sweet oranges, peeled and sliced
250g/8oz/1 cup dates, stoned
Grated rind of 3 oranges
100ml/4fl.oz/½ cup water
Juice from 1 large lemon
500g/1lb/2 cups warmed sugar

Mince together the oranges and dates. Transfer to a preserving pot, adding the grated rind and water. Boil rapidly for ½ hour. Add the lemon juice and sugar and boil until the jam is thick, stirring frequently to prevent sticking. Bottle while still hot and seal.

HARRIEF
Hot Sauce

Makes about 1 × 500g/1lb jar

This hot and piquant sauce or paste is used to flavour many dishes. It is also known as *schug* (Yemenite), *harissa* or *sachka* (North Africa). All these sauces are more or less the same though each community naturally uses some different flavourings. The version below is my own.

500g/1lb fresh or dried hot red chillies*
10 large cloves of garlic, peeled
100ml/4fl.oz/½ cup vinegar
100ml/4fl.oz/½ cup olive oil
1–2 heaped tablespoons ground cumin
2 teaspoons salt

If dried chillies are used, soak them in water for 2 hours. Drain and dry with a kitchen towel. Remove the hard stems and de-seed. If fresh chillies are used, remove the hard stems and de-seed. Mince or process the garlic and chillies while adding the vinegar, oil and flavouring.

Bottle in a glass jar and cover with a thin layer of oil to prevent drying. The paste can be stored in the refrigerator for up to 3 months.

YEMENITE GREEN SCHUG

Makes about 1 × 500g/1lb jar

250g/8oz/1 cup hot green chillies, stemmed and de-seeded
350g/12oz/1½ cups fresh coriander leaves, washed well
150g/6oz/⅔ cup fresh mint, washed well, tough stems removed
15 large cloves of garlic
100ml/4fl.oz/½ cup peanut or sesame oil
10 pods of cardamom, powdered, or 1 teaspoon powdered cardamom
1 teaspoon powdered cloves
A large amount (2–3 teaspoons) freshly ground black pepper
2 teaspoons salt

---

* Chillies vary greatly in their hotness. I use fresh ones as they tend to be a bit milder. Great care should be taken when dealing with them. Either use rubber gloves or wash your hands constantly as chillies can burn sensitive skin and cause great pain if they come in contact with the eyes.

Either mince or process all the above ingredients. Transfer into clean jars. Cover with a thin layer of oil to prevent drying and mould. The paste can be stored in the refrigerator for up to three months. It can also be divided into 100g/4oz bags and put into the freezer where it can be kept for up to 12 months.

BEVERAGES

MRS LILIAN CORNFELD'S MELONADE

Serves 6–8

An original, refreshing and fragrant non-alcoholic punch.

1 large, very ripe fragrant melon (Galia or Ananas)
250ml/8fl.oz/1 cup water
150–200g/6–8oz/¾–1 cup sugar or less, to taste
Juice of 1 large lemon
Soda water to taste
Ice cubes
Mint sprigs for decoration

Make a syrup from the sugar and water. Cool. Sieve the melon. Mix with the cold syrup and lemon juice. Dilute with soda water to taste and serve on ice decorated with a sprig of mint.

Mango can be used instead of melon.

ORANGE LIQUEUR

Makes about 2 × 1 litre/2 pint bottles

Oranges with thin peel and an intensive aroma yield better liqueurs. Homemade liqueurs are an important way of utilising surplus oranges. This recipe is simple and excellent.

350g/14oz/1¾ cups sugar
750ml/1½ pints/3 cups water
25 sugar cubes, rubbed on all sides with orange peel
750ml/1½ pints/3 cups orange juice, strained through muslin
500ml/1 pint/2 cups alcohol (96%)*

* Can be sometimes bought at off-licenses; 100% proof vodka or *eau de vie* can also be used.

Boil the sugar and water. Skim and strain through muslin. Put the rubbed sugar cubes into the hot but not boiling syrup. Mix until melted. Allow to get cold.

Add the strained orange juice and the alcohol. Bottle and leave undisturbed for 4–5 weeks. Syphon into clean bottles, discarding the accumulated sediment, and cork tightly. The liqueur is then ready for use, but would be improved by a few months or years maturing.

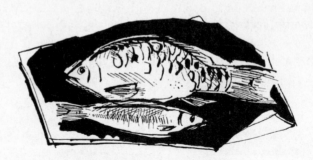

BIBLIOGRAPHY

A MAJOR PART of my research into ancient Jewish food involved re-reading the Bible and attempting to delve into the vast and fascinating writing of the Talmud.

Two translations of the Bible were used for the research: the King James Bible and the *Good News Bible* (Collins, Today's English Version). Although the language of the King James version is sometimes obscure, it gives the epic scale of Biblical Hebrew. Sadly, neither can portray the colourful and essentially Middle Eastern flavour of the original.

The research for the last chapter presented a problem. Not much work has been done on the ethnological and folklore aspects of food, both as a result of a shortage of resources and an inherently snobbish attitude amongst academicians about cultural food research. A large amount of material exists both as personal letters and documents in the vast collections of manuscripts belonging to various institutes and archives. Unfortunately time did not permit the exploration of this potential treasury of food lore. The chapter is based on personal observation and conversations with Israeli cooks, chefs and members of the food industry.

I am especially grateful to Ya'akov Lishansky, one of the most revered and liked 'fathers' of the Israeli kitchen. With love and fundamental knowledge he has captured, in writing and in, sadly, as yet unpublished research, a vast treasure of both Palestinian Arab and original Israeli recipes.

I am also grateful to all the writers who lovingly recorded a vast amount of material on general and Jewish history, folklore, anthropology, cooking and Bible studies. Without them my research would have been very dull.

Following is a list of books which I found particularly useful.

264

Jewish History

Avi-Yonah, M. (ed.) *A History of the Holy Land*, Steimatzky, Jerusalem, 1969. Written in English. In co-operation with Weidenfeld & Nicolson.

Gilbert, Martin, *Jewish History Atlas*, Weidenfeld & Nicolson, London, 3rd edn, 1988.

Halevi, Ilan, *A History of the Jews, Ancient and Modern*, Zed Books Ltd, London, 1987. Originally published as *Question Juive, La Tribu, La Loi, L'Espace*, Editions de Minuit, Paris, 1981.

Filixe, Yehuda, *Olam H'zomeach H'mikraey*, ain 63, Tel Aviv, 1946.

Johnson, P., *A History of the Jews*, Weidenfeld & Nicolson, London, 1987.

Katz, Jacob, *Tradition and Crisis. Jewish Society at the End of the Middle Ages*, Bialik Institute, Jerusalem, 1975. Written in Hebrew.

Koestler, Arthur, *The Thirteenth Tribe*, Hutchinson & Co., London, 1976.

Roth, Cecil, *A History of the Jews*, Schocken Books, New York, 1961.

Safrai, S., *The End of the Second Temple and the Mishnahic Time*, Ministry of Education, Jerusalem, 1970. Written in Hebrew.

Vallentine's Jewish Encyclopaedia, Shapiro, Vallentine & Co, London, 1938.

Biblical Cooking

Cutler, Daniel S., *The Bible Cookbook*, William Morrow, New York, 1985.

Gaden, Eileen, *Biblical Garden Cookery*, Chappaqua, N.Y., Christian Herald Books, c. 1976.

O'Brien, Marian Maeve, *Herbs & Spices of the Bible*, CBP Press, St Louis, 1984.

O'Brien, Marian Maeve, *The Bible Cookbook*, Bethony Press, New York, 1985.

General Reference

Brothwell, D. & P., *Food in Antiquity*, Frederick A. Praeger, New York, 1969.

Barer-Stein, Thelma, *You Eat What You Are. A Study of Ethnic Food Traditions*, McClelland & Stewart, Toronto, 1979.

David, Elizabeth, *Italian Food*, Penguin, London, 1954.

Davidson, Alan, *Mediterranean Seafood*, Penguin, London, 1981.

Der Haroutunian, Arto, *A Turkish Cookbook*, Ebury, London, 1987.

Drummond, J.C. & Wilbraham, A., *The Englishman's Food*, Jonathan Cape, London, 1936.

Flower, B. & Rosenbaum, E., *Apicius, Roman Cookery*, Harrap, London, 1958.

Lamb, Venice, *The Home Book of Turkish Cookery*, Faber & Faber, London, 1973.

Montagne, P., *Larousse Gastronomique*, Hamlyn, London, 1973.

Revel, Jean-François, *Culture and Cuisine. A Journey Through the History of Food*, A Da Capo Paperback, New York, 1982.

Renner, H.D., *The Origin of Food Habits*, Faber & Faber, London, 1954.

Root, W., *Food*, Simon & Schuster, New York, 1980.

Stobart, T., *Herbs, Spices and Flavourings*, Penguin, London, 1970.

Tannahill, R., *Food in History*, Stein & Day, New York, 1973.

Vehlim, J.B., (ed), *Apicius, Cooking and Dining in Imperial Rome*, Dover Publications, London, 1977.

Visser, M., *Much Depends on Dinner*, McClelland & Stewart, Toronto, 1986.

Jewish Folklore

Bergman, Dr Y., *Jewish Folklore*, (?) Israel, 1973. Written in Hebrew.

The Religious Tract Society, *The Manners and Customs of The Jews and Other Nations Mentioned in the Bible*, The Religious Society, London, 1838.

Kosher

Cohen, Rabbi, J., *The Royal Table*, New York, 1973.

Dresner, Samuel H., *The Jewish Dietary Laws*, The Rabbinical Assembly, New York, 1982.

Forster, Robert & Ranum, Orest, *Food and Drink in History*, The Johns Hopkins University Press, Baltimore, 1979.

Freedman, Symor E., *The Book of Kashruth*, Bloch, New York, 1970.

Kashruth Consumer's Guide (monthly), Published by Rabbi Max Felshin. First published 1950.

Kosher Food Guide: Organized Kashruth (OK) (monthly), published by Kosher Food Guide. First published in 1935.

Lazarus, Harris M., *The Ways of Her Household. A Practical Handbook for Jewish Women on Traditional Customs and Observance*, Jewish Memorial Council, London, 1966.

Farb, P. & Armelagos, G., *Consuming Passions*, Houghton Mifflin Co., Boston, 1980.

Levinger, I.M., *Kosher Meat (Mazon Kasher min Hachai)*, The Institute for Agricultural Research according to the Torah, Jerusalem, 1980. Published in Hebrew.

Lipman, Yom Tov, *The Koshering of Meat. A Short Guide in English, Hebrew & Yiddish for the Jewish Housewife*, Hamakrik Book Binding Co., London, 1959.

Simoons, F., *Eat Not This Flesh*, Greenwood Press, Connecticut, 1961.

Holidays

Goldman, Rabbi Solomon, *A Guide to the Sabbath*, Jewish Chronical Publications, London, 1961.

Halevi Donin, Hayim (ed.), *Sukkot*, Keter Books, Jerusalem, 1974.

Schauss, Hayyim, *The Jewish Festivals*, Schocken Books, New York, 1962.

Wahrmann, d'r Nchum, *Chgy Ysral umuaedyu (mnhgyhm us'mlyhm)*, Achyas'p bae'm, Tel Aviv, 1975.

Sephardi

Alchech Miner, Vivian, with Linda Krinn, *My Grandmother's Kitchen; a Jewish Cookbook, An Exotic Collection of Sephardic Recipes, combining Turkish, Greek, Bulgarian, Romanian & Spanish Cuisines*, Comet Books, 1986.

David, Suzy, *Sephardic Kitchen (Kosher) Ha'mitbach Ha'sfaradi*, Jerusalem Publishing House, Jerusalem, 1980. Written in Hebrew.

Day, Irene F., *Kitchen in the Kasbah*, André Deutsch, London, 1976.

Der Haroutunian, Arto, *Middle Eastern Cookery*, Pan Books, London, 1984.

Howe, Robin, *The Mediterranean Diet*, Weidenfeld & Nicolson, London, 1985.

Levy-Mallul, Rivka, *Moroccan Cooking*, Jerusalem Publishing House, Jerusalem, 1982. Written in Hebrew.

Menasce, Elsie, *The Sephardi Culinary Tradition*, The Sephardic Cookbook Co., Cape Town, 1984.

Perez, Pascal, *North African Cooking*, Bayit Va-Gan Publishing Co. Ltd, 1983. Written in Hebrew.

Roden, Claudia, *A Book of Middle Eastern Food*, Penguin, London, 1970.

Servi-Malchin, Adda, *Classic Cuisine of Italian Jews*, Giro Press, New York, 1981. Also published in Hebrew by Keter, Jerusalem, 1986.

Shilo, Varda, *Kurdistani Cooking*, Kaneh, Jerusalem, 1986. Written in Hebrew.

Tzabar, Naomi & Shimon, *Yemenite and Oriental Food*, Sadan Publishing Co., Tel Aviv, 1962. The first 'ethnic' cookery book in Hebrew.

Zadoc, Moshe, *History and Customs of the Jews in the Yemen (Yehudy Thymn; Tuldutyhm vorchot chayihem)*, Am Oved, Tel Aviv, 1983. Written in Hebrew.

Ashkenazi

Avnon, Naf, *So Eat My Darling*, Stematzky, Tel Aviv, 1977.

Bialik, Ch. N., *Collected Writings*, Berlin, 1923. Written in Hebrew.

Bruin, H., *Das familiaen kach boch*, with English addition, Hebrew Publishing Co., New York, 1914. Written in Yiddish.

Chimrenski, Hayym, *My Shtatel Moteli*, Dvir, Tel Aviv, 1951. Written in Hebrew.

Harkavy, Alexander, *Yiddish-English-Hebrew Dictionary*, Schocken Books, New York, 1988.

Greenboum Kreisler, Florence, *Jewish Cook Book*, Bloch, New York, 1918.

Ha'Galil, Hayym (Fikel), *The Shtetl that was (Ha'ayara sh'haita)*, Moreshet, Tel Aviv, 1955. Written in Hebrew.

Herbest-Krausz, Zorica, *Old Jewish Dishes*. Introduction by Dr Jzsef Schweitzer, Director of the Institute of the National Rabbinical Studies. Consultants to the British edition: Ellision, J.A. & Bacon, Josephine. Corvina, Budapest, 1989.

Lapid, Joseph & Sirkis, Ruth, *Paprika*, R. Sirkis Publishers Ltd, Israel, 1986. Written in Hebrew.

Shalom, Aleichem, (Translated by I.D. Berkovitz) *Collected Writings*, Dvir, Tel Aviv, 1939. Written in Hebrew.

Zborowski, Mark & Herzog, Elizabeth, *Life Is With People. The Culture of the Shtetl*, Schocken Books, New York, 1962.

British

A Lady (Lady Montefiore), *The Jewish Manual or Practical Information in Jewish & Modern Cookery with a Collection of Valuable Recipes & Hints relating to the Toilette*, A facsimile of the first Jewish cookbook in English. With an introduction by Chaim Raphael, Sidgwick & Jackson, London, 1985. First published in London by T & W Boone, 1846.

Atrutel, Mrs Estella, *An Easy & Economical Book of Jewish Cookery upon Strictly Orthodox . . .* Dedicated to Baroness Lionel de Rothschild, Alabaster & Passmore, London, 1874.

Brook, S., *The Club*, Pan Books, London, 1989.

Emden, P.H., *Jews of Britain*, Sampson Low, Marston & Co., Allen & Co., London, 1943.

Greenberg, Florence, *Florence Greenberg's Cookery Book*, Jewish Chronicle Publications, London, 1947.

Greenberg, Florence, *Jewish Cookery*, Penguin, London, 1971.

Henry, May, *Dainty Dishes . . . For Jewish Families*, Williams Lea & Co Ltd, London, 1916.

Kaye, Ann & Rance, Hatty, *So This Is Kosher – Modern Cooking, A new approach to Jewish cookery*, Ward Lock Ltd, London, 1986.

Mayhew, Henry, *Mayhew's London*, Bracken Books, London, new edition, 1984.

Romain, J.A., *The Jews of England*, Michael Goulston Educational Foundation, London, 1988.

Rose, Evelyn, *The Complete International Jewish Cookbook*, Pan Books, London, 1978. First published by Robson Books Ltd, London, 1976.

Roth, Cecil, *A History of the Jews in England*, John Trotter Publishers, London, 1989.

Tattersall, Miss M.A.S., *Jewish Cookery Book* (Compiled for use in the cookery centres under the School Board for London), Williams, Lea & Co. Ltd, London, 1895.

The Friday Night Book (a Jewish miscellany), Soncino Press, London, 1933.

Wald, Ann, *Cooking the Jewish Way*, Spring Books, London, 1961.

Zeff, Linda, *Jewish London,* Piatkus Ltd, London, 1986.

American

Alperson, Myra & Clifford, Mark, *The Food Lover's Guide to the Real New York*, Prentice Hall Press, New York, 1987.

Autumn, Violeta, *A Russian Jew Cooking in Peru*, 101 Productions, San Francisco, 1973.

The Auxiliary Cook Book, Published by the Auxiliary Society of the Hebrew Guardian Society of New York Orphan Asylum, New York, 1909.

'Balabusta' (ed.), *Prize Kosher Recipe Book, Jewish Examiner*, Brooklyn, 1937.

Beard, James, *James Beard's American Cookery*, Little, Brown & Co., Boston, 1972.

Beilenson, Edna (ed.), *Simple Jewish Cookery*, Peter Pauper Press, New York, 1962.

Best By Taste. Non-Kosher, Compiled by Mrs Alfred Loeb for the benefit of the Hebrew Infant Asylum, New York, 1914.

Gethers, Judith & Lefft, Elizabeth, *The world famous RATNER'S meatless cookbook*, Bantam Books, New York, 1975.

Greenberg, Mrs Betty (Davis), *The Jewish Home Beautiful*, The League of the United Synagogue of America, New York, 1941.

Greenstein, Gabrielle, *We remember, Bubba*, Brooklyn, Flare Inc., New York, 1976.

Jones, Evan, *American Food*, Vintage Books, New York, 1981.

Grossinger, Jennie, *The Art of Jewish Cooking*, with an introduction by Paul Grossinger, Random House, New York, 1958.

Kinnereth Cook Book, Hadassah Wizo Canada, Toronto, 1979.

The Naomi Cook Book, Hadassah Wizo Canada, 4th ed., 1960.

Jewish Food Merchant (monthly), Published in Yiddish and English, New York. First published 1934.

Kasdan, Sara, *Love & Knishes*, New York, Vanguard Press, 1956. Published in the UK by Arco Publications, 1957.

Kaufer Green, Gloria, *The Jewish Festival Cookbook, An International Collection of Recipes & Customs*, Robert Hall, London, 1988. First published in the US as *The Jewish Holiday Cookbook*.

Leonard, Leah W., *Jewish Cookery. In Accordance with the Jewish Dietary Laws*, André Deutsch, London, 1968 (revised ed). First published in the US as *Jewish Cooking in Accordance with the Jewish Dietary Laws*, Crown Publishers, New York, 1949.

Leonard, Leah W., *Jewish Holiday Cook Book*, Crown Publishers, New York, 1955.

Levi, Shoshana (Biegelson), *Across the Threshold; A Guide for the Jewish Homemaker*, Farrar, Strauss & Cudaby, New York, 1959. Also Schocken Books, 1976.

Levy, Esther (Mrs, née Esther Jacobs), *Cookery Book. On Principles of Economy, adapted for Jewish Housekeepers, with the Addition of Many Useful Medicinal Recipes and Other Valuable Information Relative to Housekeeping and Domestic Management*, W.S. Turner, Philadelphia, 1871. Facsimile edition published by Pholiota Press Inc., California, 1982.

Nathan, J., *The Jewish Holiday Kitchen*, Schocken Books, New York, 1979.

Schapiro, Mary L., 'Jewish Dietary Problems', from the *Journal of Home Economy*, New York, 1919.

Shenker, I., *Noshing is Sacred*, The Bobbs-Merrill Co. Inc., New York, 1979.

Shosteck, Patti, *A Lexicon of Jewish Cooking*, Contemporary Books, Chicago, 1979.

Temes, Ruben Sandra, *Welcome to my Kitchen. International and Jewish specialities*, Sandra Temes Cooking School, Toronto, 1979.

The Great Hadassah Wizo Cookbook, Hurtig, Edmonton, 1982.

Vineberg, Trina, *Family Heirlooms*, McClelland & Stewart Ltd, Toronto, 1965.

Jewish South African Cookbooks

Brodie, Selma, *The Singing Kettle*, Port Elizabeth Branch of the Union of Jewish Women, 1968.

Witter, Violet & Cohen, Gertrude Harvey (eds), assisted by Deborah Malkin, *International Goodwill Recipe Book*, Johannesburg Women's Zionist League, Johannesburg, 4th ed., Nov 1963. First published, 1950.

Rootshtain, Gloria, *Cooking with a Connoisseur*, Jonathan Ball, Johannesburg, 1981.

Shaban, Sara, *Bread and Peacocks*, Grosvenor Publishing Co., London, 1969.

Wolf, Paddy & Kangisser, Marion (eds), *Cookery Capers*, Society of the Jewish Handicapped, Johannesburg.

Israeli Cookbooks

Bar David, Malckha, *Sefer bishol folklorysty; mataemym l'chagy ysrael*, Tel Aviv, 1963. Written in Hebrew.

Bar-David Lyons, Molly, *The Israeli Cook Book. What's Cooking in Israel's Melting Pot*, Crown Publishers, New York, 1964.

Bar-David Lyons, Molly, *Jewish Cooking for Pleasure*, Paul Hamlyn, London, 1965.

Cohen, Tamar (ed.), *Ethnic Shavuot Food (Machly aidot l'chag H'shvout*, Ministry of Agriculture, Tel Aviv, 1973. Written in Hebrew.

Cornfeld, Lilian, *Israeli Cookery*, Avi Publication Co., Connecticut, 1962.

Cornfeld, Lilian, *What Should I Cook?*, Machbarot, Tel Aviv, 1953.

Danin, Odetta, I., *Way Out*, Domino, Jerusalem, 1990.

Jerusalem, Hamidrasha Le'thzuna, *Usimachth levav aurchic*, Midrasha Le't-zuna, 1953.

Kaufman, Sybil, *The Wonders of a Wonder Pot*, JNIV, Tel Aviv, 1973.

Meyer, Dr Erna, *How to Cook in Palestine* (The title is also in Hebrew *Eich Avashel B'eretz Israel* and in German *Wie Kocht man in Erez-Israel*, H.N.Z. Palestine Federation of Wizo, 1935.

Perez, Pascal, *North African Cooking*, Bayit Va-Gan Publishing Co. Ltd, Tel Aviv, 1983.

Perez-Rubin, P., *Israeli Flavour*, R. Sirkis, Israel, 1987. Written in Hebrew.

Valero, Rina, *Delights of Jerusalem (Yrusalaym shel Matamim)*, Nahar Publishing Steimatzky, Jerusalem, 1984.

Wizo, *Cook Book*, Mesada, Tel Aviv, 1947.

Zukerman, Lyaurh, *Cook Book*, Amichay, Tel Aviv, 1963.

Israeli Background

Avizor S., *Collected Articles. Ariel.* In co-operation with the Society for the Preservation of Nature, Jerusalem, 1988. Written in Hebrew.

Bialik Institute, *Dictionary of Kitchen Terms (Milon le'monachy ha'mitbach)*, Milony va'ad ha'lason ha'evrit, Mus'd byalyk sae'y hs'cnuth hyhudyth lerz ysral, yruslym thrzch, Jerusalem, 1937. Hebrew-English-German.

Dganyah Way, compiled by the members of kibbutz Dganyah, published by Davar Publications, 1962.

Peres, Y., *Ethnic Relations in Israel*, Tel Aviv University, 1976. Written in Hebrew.

Vilbush, N. (S. Avizur, ed.), *Haroshet Hama'ase*, Milo, Tel Aviv, 1974. Written in Hebrew.

NOTES AND SOURCES

Introduction

1 Cecil Roth, *A History of the Jews*, p.137.

1 Food in the Bible

1 Cookery instruction manuscripts exist both in Chinese and Indian cultures.

2 Kashruth

1 Rabbi J. Cohen, *The Royal Table*.
2 In Hebrew the word for a meal comes from the same root as guest (*oreach* and *arocha*).
3 H.D. Renner, *The Origin of Food Habits*, p.203.
4 *Trabor* is a Yiddish word which is probably of Czech origin. *Prog.* comes from the latin root 'purge'. Both mean to dig out, to remove.
5 I.M. Levinger, *Kosher Meat (Mazon Kasher min Hachai)*.
6 I feel I should add a postscript to the question of ritual slaughter. Admittedly care is taken not to distress the animal unduly and the law stipulates that the slaughtering should be done with a perfectly sharp knife, and that the animal should be fit and rested before death. Nevertheless, the law is at least 2000 years old and our understanding and attitudes toward animals have changed. The idea of animals being slaughtered and bled to death without being previously made unconscious goes against the grain of the Jewish compassionate attitude to animals reflected elsewhere.
7 M. Visser, *Much Depends on Dinner*.
8 The Bible mistakenly identified the cony and the rabbits; although purely herbivorous, they do not ruminate.
9 F.J. Simoons, *Eat Not the Flesh*.

272

10 Numbers 11:5
11 Rabbi Moshe Ben-Maimon, 1135–1204.

3 Food of the Patriarchs

1 S. Avizor, 'Clay Churns', in *Collected Articles*, Jerusalem, 1988. Written in Hebrew.
2 R. Tannahill, *Food in History*,
3 T. Stobart, *Herbs, Spices and Flavourings*,
4 W. Root, *Food*,
5 *Ibid.*
6 Aronson was famous also for organising 'Nily', a spy network which informed the British of the position and movement of the Turkish army during the First World War.
7 R. Tannahill, *Food in History*, p.56.
8 The following is based on S. Avizor, Announcers of bread (Mevasrei Halechem) in *Collected Articles*, Jerusalem, 1988. Written in Hebrew.
9 A clue to this technique is given in Samuel 2 17:19. The women from Bahurim, in an attempt to hide King David, 'spread a covering over the well's mouth, and spread ground corn thoron' (the word *riffot* was translated as ground corn or groats), describing the method of drying *riffot* on cloth which was laid on an elevated surface (well or roof) for protection against vermin.
10 R. Tannahill, *Food in History*, pp.66–9.
11 Farb & Armelagos, *Consuming Passions*, p.166.
12 The dabbing of blood is the origin of the Mezuza, a scroll which carries Biblical verses nailed to the doorpost of every Jewish household, still identifying the origin of the household.
13 H. Schauss, *The Jewish Festivals*, p.296.
14 Jean Soler, 'The Semiotics of Food in the Bible', in *Food & Drink in History*, p.130.
15 H. Schauss, *The Jewish Festivals*, p.79.
16 The prohibition is against eating leaven which is not allowed throughout the duration of the Pesach. *Matzah* is compulsory only at the Seder table.

4 Food of the Kingdom

1 S. Safrai, *The End of the Second Temple & the Mishnahic Time*, p.64.
2 B. Flower & E. Rosenbaum (eds), *Apicius, Roman Cookery*, p.49.
3 S. Avizor, 'Ground Vessels' in *Collected Articles*, Jerusalem, 1988. Written in Hebrew.
4 Sabbath 16:2.
5 Figs were rarely used, probably due to the purgative properties of their juice.

5 By the Rivers of Babylon

1 The Talmud, of which two versions exist (Jerusalem & Babylon), was concluded between 400–500AD. The following chapter is mainly based on the Mishnah.
2 Nedarim 6:1.

3 The following information was taken from S. Safrai, *The End of the Second Temple & the Mishnahic Time* (B'shalhay Ha'bayte Ha'shni Ub'tkifath Ha'Mishnah). Written in Hebrew.

4 Ktuvote 5:8.

5 Demay 1:1.

6 Kelim 5:3.

7 Kelim 5:2.

8 Kelim 21:1.

9 Kelim 2:7.

10 Kelim 13:

11 Kelim 25:3.

12 Kelim 25:3 and others.

13 Kelim 3:3.

14 Only once, Isaiah 1:8.

15 Articles by G. Stetman in *Halamish*, no. 6., Israel, 1988. Written in Hebrew.

16 Okatzim 3:4, Me'asroth 4:6, Me'asroth 4:5 and many others.

17 Okatzim 3:7.

18 Me'asroth 4:6.

19 Me'asroth 1:4.

20 *Apicius*, translated by J.D. Vehling. New York, 1977.

21 S. Tulkovsky, *Citrus*.

22 H. Mayhew, *Mayhew's London*, new edition.

23 *Apicius, Roman Cookery*.

24 Cooked wine is a term used now to describe wine made kosher by heating.

25 Shvy'it 7:7.

26 Sabbath 20:2.

27 Minchoth 8:6.

28 Psachim 7:1.

29 Psachim 7:2.

30 Psachim 3:2.

31 The origin of the name shallot is probably from Ashkelon, a Philistine coastal town.

32 Nedarim 3:10.

33 Sabbath 1:10.

34 The same word is also used for water kept hot for the Sabbath.

35 Sabbath 4:1.

36 Sabbath 3:4.

37 Henrich Hiene (1797–1856), German poet of Jewish origin, quoted in Leah Leonard, *Jewish Cookery*.

38 Pascal Perez-Rubin, *Israeli Flavour*. Written in Hebrew.

39 This is not strictly true, as chickpeas are also used in the Ashkenezi *hamins* of South Russia and Romania.

40 F.J. Simoons, *Eat Not This Flesh*, p.113.

41 S. Safrai, *The End of the Second Temple and the Mishnahic Time*. Written in Hebrew.

42 Z. Vilnaie, *Legends of the Sacred Land,* new edition, Jerusalem, 1981. The book was also published in English by The Jewish Publication Society of America, Philadelphia, 1978. It is the most extensive collection of folk tales about the Land of Israel.

43 Machshirin 6:3.

44 Sabbath 22:2.

45 Yom Tov Beitza 4:5.

46 B. Flower, *Apicius, Roman Cookery.*

47 Edoyoth 7:2.

48 Yom Tov Betzha 2:6.

49 The following are based mostly on M. Avi-Yona's article published in *The Oil Pot Collection* for the celebration of twenty years of the establishment of *Shemen,* The Israeli Oil Industry, Haifa, 1945. Written in Hebrew.

50 D. and P. Brothwell, *Food in Antiquity,* p.155.

51 The Mishnah gives a list of oils which are acceptable for lighting on the Sabbath. It includes sesame, nut, reddish seed and fish, which were used also for cooking.

52 Hallah 1:4.

53 Kelim 5:1.

54 Jeremiah 17:11 and Samuel 1, 26:20.

55 Holin 8:1.

56 Nedarim 6:2.

57 Sabbath 3:3.

58 Sabbath 8:5 and Sabbath 9:5.

59 Machshirin 6:3.

6 Almonds, Spice and Sunshine

1 Channel 4. 'Sense of Belonging', 1991.

2 C. Roth, *A History of the Jews,* p.151.

3 See Havdalah in Ashkenazi food on p.80.

4 P. Johnson, *A History of the Jews,* p.171.

5 Hafeez Noorani, *The Roti and the Naan,* Air India's In Flight Magazine, 1981.

6 I suspect that some digging into thousands of exciting unexplored manuscripts will one day reveal such documents.

7 See 'Oranges and Lemons', p.100–2.

7 Ashkenazi Food

1 For more information about the Khazars and their effect on the European Jewish community see Arthur Koestler, *The Thirteenth Tribe,* London, 1976.

2 M. Zborowski and E. Herzog, *Life Is With People,* pp.72–3.

3 One must stress that the *shtetl* way of life was not, by any means, the only way of life of the European Jewry. Yet it represents the most common shared experience of all European Jews and as such it was used to illustrate the development of the Ashkenazi kitchen.

4 Chaim Nachman Bialik, b. 1873 in Russia, d. Vienna, 1934.

5 H.N. Bialik, 'That Which Grows of Itself' in Vol. 2, *Collected Writings*, Berlin, 1922. Written in Hebrew. My translation.

6 M. Zborowski and E. Herzog, *Life Is With People*, p.373.

7 J.C. Drummond & A. Wilbraham, *The Englishman's Food*, pp.408–9.

8 M. Zborowski and E. Herzog, *Life Is With People*, p.372.

9 Proverbs 31:10–31.

10 Judges 11:29–40.

11 Book of Maccabees 7.

12 Elizabeth David, *Italian Food*, p.94.

13 J. Nathan, *The Jewish Holiday Kitchen*, p.97.

14 The word *loksh* (singular for *lokshen*), means in Yiddish a strip. It entered the popular vernacular, meaning a tall person (*lange loksh* — long *loksh*) which is understandable. Yet to tell a *loksh* means to fib.

15 An old custom of unknown origin.

16 M. Zborowski and E. Herzog, *Life Is With People*, p.257.

17 *Ba'al guff* can mean corpulent but also means *nouveau riche*.

18 Although the repertoire does include a few *tzimmes* which do not contain meat, such as carrot *tzimmes*, traditionally served for Rosh Ha'shanah.

19 In some communities even women were permitted to slaughter poultry. Certificates qualifying Elvira Finzi, of Cento, Italy, 1689, and Bella Dona Gallichi, of Siena, 1684, as slaughterers are on display at the Israel Museum in Jerusalem. The permission was granted only to slaughter poultry. Women slaughterers also practised in Yemen.

20 As fodder became scarcer, the beginning of winter was the traditional time for animal slaughter.

21 H. Schauss, *The Jewish Festivals*, p.224 and notes 261 and 262 on p.308.

22 Achad Ha'am (Asher Ginzberg), Hebrew writer and thinker, b. Russia 1856, d. 1927 in Tel Aviv.

23 H. Schauss, *The Jewish Festivals*, p.34.

24 Sabbath 2:6.

25 H. Schauss, *The Jewish Festivals*, Footnote 25, p.288.

26 Mrs Esther Levy, *Jewish Cookery Book*.

27 Lady Montefiore, *The Jewish Manual*.

28 Although *kugel* is a purely Ashkenazi dish, the Yemenite Jews developed independently a similar dish called *kubana*, which is yeasted dough cooked overnight with a large amount of fat and served on the Sabbath. There is an unleavened version of the dish called *jichnon*.

29 Leah Leonard, *Jewish Cookery*, p.43.

30 *Chassid* means pious, a name of a Jewish sect which originated in the 18th century among the Jews of Eastern Europe. The success of the sect amongst the masses was mainly due to their new approach to worship. They maintained that God can also be worshipped in joy and ecstasy in contrast to the dry intellectual worship of their opponents, the *Mitnaggdim* (opposed).

31 Nehemiah. Instruction for Sabbath food. 8:10.

32 Dr Y. Bergman, *Jewish Folkore*, p.000. Written in Hebrew.
33 The Pentateuch, the first five books of the Bible, is traditionally divided into three parts. The other two are Prophets and Writings.
34 J. Nathan, *The Jewish Holiday Kitchen*.
35 For a detailed explanation of the origin of *Purim* see H. Schauss, *The Jewish Festivals*.
36 Shalom Aleichem, Mishloach-monos, in Holidays, a collection of short stories. My translation from Hebrew.
37 Pentecost comes from the Greek for fifty as the holiday is celebrated on the fiftieth day after the beginning of the barley harvest.

8 Oranges and Lemons

1 J.A. Romain, *The Jews of England*, p.11.
2 P. Johnson, *A History of The Jews*, p.208.
3 The Marranos are forcefully baptised Spanish and Portuguese Jews.
4 P.H. Emden, *Jews of Britain*, p.52.
5 Eliza Acton, *Modern Cookery for Private Families*, p.346.
6 Quoted in Emden, *Jews of Britain*, p.96.
7 *Ibid*, p.90.
8 *The Jewish Manual or Practical Information in Jewish & Modern Cookery With a Collection of Valuable Recipes & Hints Relating to Toilette*, edited by a Lady, was published by T. Goodelman and W. Boon, London, 1846. A facsimile of the book was published by Sidgwick & Jackson, London, 1985. For a full discussion of the book and its historical implication see: Barbara Kirshenblatt-Gimblett, 'The Kosher Gourmet in the Nineteen-Century' in the *Journal of Gastronomy*, Vol 2, no 4, winter 1986/87. Also in the Introduction to the facsimile edition of the manual, by Chaim Raphael.
9 Barbara Kirschenblatt-Gimblett, 'The Kosher Gourmet'.
10 Waverley Root, *Food*.
11 Henry Mayhew, *London Labour and London Poor*, London, 1851. An edited and abridged edition was published by Bracken Books, 1987.
12 Quoted in S. Brook, *The Club*, p.34.

9 The New Jerusalem

1 Cecil Roth, *A History of the Jews*, p.356.
2 *Ibid*, p.358.
3 P. Johnson, *A History of The Jews*, p.373.
4 Mary Schapiro, Jewish Dietary Problems, New York, 1919.
5 Traditional joke quoted in the *Jewish Merchant* which started publication in January 1934.
6 James Beard, *American Cookery*, p.805.
7 Evan Jones, *American Food*, p.164.
8 Richard Yaffe, *Kosher Food Guide: Organized Kashruth*, 1964.
9 I. Shenker, *Noshing is Sacred*, p.30.

10 J. Beard, *American Cookery*, p.143.

11 A Yiddish word describing a good housekeeper.

12 *The Kashruth Consumer's Guide* under the supervision of Rabbi Max Felshin was first published in 1950.

10 The Recurring Cycle

1 *Sabra* (prickly pear) is the name given to Israelis who were born in Israel. The prickly pear which is tough and prickly on the outside but soft, juicy and fragrant on the inside is supposed to symbolise an Israeli's characteristics.

2 *Sahleb* is the Arabic word for orchid. Now the sweet is mostly made with rice starch as orchid starch is very expensive.

3 One should point out that by Palestinian the good doctor means Jewish citizens of Palestine.

4 Wizo advertisement in the foreword to Dr E. Meyer, *How to Cook in Palestine*.

5 As far as I know there has been no research done on the effects of dietary propaganda on health and national palate. The above is based on personal observations.

6 The vinegar available then came mainly in the form of concentrated acetic acid sold in small, clear glass bottles which had to be diluted with water, creating a harsh, tasteless sourness. Much better was crystallised citric acid known as lemon salt. Recently, with the impact of Sephardi cooking, *sumac* is having a modest comeback appearing in salads, especially a raw onion salad which is served with falafel.

7 Although Hebrew was the natural selection, there was some suggestion of using Yiddish as the official language.

8 The modernising of Hebrew became established through the monumental work of Eliezer Ben-Yehuda (1858–1922), known as the father of modern Hebrew. He immigrated to Israel from Lithuania in 1881 and was the first teacher to instruct in Hebrew and speak Hebrew as an everyday language. He also wrote the first Modern Hebrew dictionary and was one of the founding members of Va'ad Ha'lashon (the committee for the development of Hebrew language).

9 The first committee was established at the request of the owners of the first Jewish passenger liner *Tel Aviv* who wanted their menu to be written in Hebrew. Sadly, the shipping venture was shortlived. The work of this committee was combined with that of the second committee which was created by the Haddasa organisation who needed a standardised vocabulary for their cooking training programmes.

10 Milon L'monachy H'Mitbach (Dictionary of Kitchen Terms), Jerusalem, 1937, published by Va'ad Ha'lashon Ha'evrit (the committee for the advance of the Hebrew language) in association with the Bialik Institute affiliated to the Jewish Agency in Eretz, Israel. It also contains indexes in English and German.

11 *Mitbach ha'poalim* was established as a workers' co-operative in Haifa (1928). It entered the *Histadruth* (trade union) statuary book in 1930.

12 'Hebrew' was a term used to identify Israeli before the creation of the state. The campaign to use 'Hebrew' products was an important political issue. The 'Hebrew' products had to compete with the cheaper 'Arab' products. 'Hebrew' labour was much more expensive; Jewish workers were used to higher living standards, refusing

to work for the exploitive salaries their Arab counterparts managed to survive on.

13 The competition was mainly from restaurants called *tnuva* which sprang up in all urban and semi-urban settlements. *Tnuva* described small, privately owned, mainly dairy eating houses, which supplied homemade cheap breakfasts and lunches. The food, like that in *mitbach ha'poalim*, was based on vegetarian dishes, soups and salads; sometimes fish, especially boiled carp or *gefilte* fish were also served. *Tnuva* is also the name of the central distribution system of the kibbutz movement.

14 The labour movement, like the ibbutz, saw work in the kitchen as un-productive. Kitchen workers were usually elderly women who could not be placed anywhere else.

15 Quoted in Y. Peres, *Ethnic Relations in Israel*, Tel Aviv University, 1976. Written in Hebrew.

16 The situation was the same with all institutional feeding. Institutional feeding is very important in Israel, most Israelis encounter it during their life. Subsidised food is an essential fringe benefit for a large number of workers. Lunch is the main meal of the day and is usually eaten at the work place.

17 One can encounter it in Tel Aviv where it started and then spread to most urban centres. A different style evolved in Jerusalem whereby the falafel and salad are wrapped in a flat thin pitta called *esh tanur* (oven's fire).

18 Preference for very hot food is widespread throughout Israel. Eating very hot food is also associated with a macho image; the more the man the hotter the food he can tolerate.

19 The reference to *fricassee* comes from Pascal Perez, *North African Cooking*. The *fricassee* is probably derived from *pan bagna*, the favourite sandwich of the French Riviera.

20 *Dganyah Way* (Darka Shel Dganyah). Written by the members of Dgania Davar Publication, 1962. Written in Hebrew.

21 *Guardian*, 21 August 1982.

22 As I mention above, food was traditionally prepared by the old women helped by other female members of the family, especially amongst the Sephardi community.

23 In Israel preservatives are a necessary evil. Although manufacturing is done hygienically, the standard of retail outlets varies greatly. Until those standards are drastically improved, the industry policy of being safe rather than sorry seems generally justified.

24 Recently conditions have changed. As a result of the Gulf War many West Bank Arabs have stopped working in Israel and a large proportion of the Filipinos have returned home. Their place is being slowly taken by the new Russian immigrants who are desperate for work.

11 Biblical and Historic Recipes
1 Yom Tov Betzha 4:5.

12 Ashkenazi Food
1 Rina Valero, *Delights of Jerusalem*, Nahar, Jerusalem, 1984.

13 Western Food

1 I. Shenker, *Noshing is Sacred.*

2 J. Grossinger, *The Art of Jewish Cooking.*

14 Israeli Food

1 Dr Bircher-Benner (1867–1939), a Swiss doctor who developed a method of treating diseases, especially of the digestive system with a balanced diet of raw vegetarian foods.

2 This version is based on a recipe by Pascale Perez-Rubin in *Israeli Flavour.*

3 *Ibid.*

4 This is an adaptation of Mrs Cornfield's recipe in Ha'mitbach Ha'meshubach.

INDEX

INDEX OF RECIPES

288